Ted Willi~~ams and the~~
1969 Washington Senators

ALSO BY TED LEAVENGOOD

The 2005 Washington Nationals:
Major League Baseball Returns
to the Capital (McFarland, 2006)

Ted Williams and the 1969 Washington Senators

The Last Winning Season

Ted Leavengood

McFarland & Company, Inc., Publishers
Jefferson, North Carolina, and London

LIBRARY OF CONGRESS CATALOGUING-IN-PUBLICATION DATA

Leavengood, Ted.
 Ted Williams and the 1969 Washington Senators : the last
winning season / Ted Leavengood.
   p.   cm.
 Includes bibliographical references and index.

 ISBN 978-0-7864-4136-5
 softcover : 50# alkaline paper ∞

 1. Washington Senators (Baseball team : 1961–1971) — History.
2. Williams, Ted, 1918–2002.   I. Title.
GV875.W3L43 2009
796.357'6409753 — dc22
                                        2009001124

British Library cataloguing data are available

On the cover: Manager Ted Williams (National Baseball
Hall of Fame Library, Cooperstown, NY)

Manufactured in the United States of America

*McFarland & Company, Inc., Publishers
 Box 611, Jefferson, North Carolina 28640
 www.mcfarlandpub.com*

Table of Contents

Your baseball team is like your children —
you don't love them because they are good,
you love them because they are yours.
        —*Anonymous Fan*

Introduction

Looking backward across over four decades of history, it is difficult to see in baseball or in the cities in which it is played many lingering effects of the crisis that gripped America in the late 1960s. American cities have wiped away much of the old blight from that era, and baseball is resurgent. But in 1969 baseball was in a war for the hearts and minds of the sports public, and it was losing badly. The National Pastime, as it has been known, was losing its preeminent status while professional football gained in popularity. Despite remarkable affluence at the time, baseball was not attracting the crowds or the money it once had. In 1968, in particular, crowds in some cities on a given night could be as sparse as a thousand fans scattered across the stands. Total attendance for many teams was less than a million patrons for the year.

The 1969 season was the first effort by organized baseball to come to grips with its problems and that year ushered in changes that began what was ultimately a remarkable new era for the game. Baseball at the end of World War II and for the next decade was in its heyday, but the game that Babe Ruth had turned into a cultural icon was in crisis during the late sixties. At the beginning of the sixties there were two All-Star Games each season, and soon there were two nationally broadcast games each weekend. Fans were as loyal to the baseball *Game of the Week* as they were to *Gunsmoke* or *The Ed Sullivan Show*.

Baseball's ownership, however, was concerned that the game's popularity on television was drawing fans away from the stadiums, where they made their money. Television revenue was a new issue for the game in the sixties, and over the course of the decade attendance figures suggested that Americans were enjoying watching games at home as much as at the ballpark.

The love affair with the game seemed to melt at the end of the decade, and it took years to bring it back. The 1968 season marked the nadir of baseball in general and Washington, D.C., in particular. After that season the

1

best minds in baseball — the Official Playing Rules Committee — were convened by the Executive Council of Baseball to tinker with time-honored rules that governed the way the game was played. The rules committee lowered the pitching mound and restricted the strike zone to give the batter a better chance. No one knew why pitchers had gotten better and why batters were less able to contend with them in what is the central drama of baseball.

Regaining baseball's popularity in the late sixties was a more complicated equation than the best minds of baseball could construct. The nation was at war in Vietnam, the first conflict to spark such widespread turmoil and protest. The civil rights movement had turned violent. Ugly riots killed scores of persons in numerous cities across the country and left large swaths of many large cities across the nation smoldering in ruins. Drawing crowds back into the urban core to watch baseball games was a challenge greater than simply tinkering with the rules. Americans were focused intently on the war and concerned about the backdrop of social unrest. Baseball seemed to be little more than a distraction.

No team was more affected by the social disorder of the times than the Washington Senators. The city was the focal point for civil rights and anti-war protests throughout the sixties; one of the most violent riots occurred in Washington in 1968 following the assassination of Dr. Martin Luther King, Jr.

When baseball returned to the city in 2005, I was a novice regarding the history of the Senators. I also experienced the angst of the sixties away from Washington, D.C. It was inexplicable to me that baseball had left the nation's capital in the first place, and I was drawn to the story. When Dick Bosman — the last Senators ace — handed the game ball to Livan Hernandez for opening night at RFK Stadium on April 14, 2005, I knew Bosman only as a baseball card, a collection of statistics from my youth. I knew little about his rich history with the Washington Senators or that of other Senator players on the field that night.

For me the death throes of the old Senators were just another part of the maelstrom of social change in the late sixties and early seventies. Yet when all of the Senators players stood on the field alongside the new Nationals taking their place that April evening in 2005, I knew my home team had landed. I did not know who was passing the torch from those many years before, but I wanted to find out.

As a result, I started to research the history of baseball in Washington. I discovered books about the 1924 team, Walter Johnson and his Hall of Fame teammates, and the rich history of the first three decades of baseball in D.C. What I could not understand is what happened to that winning tradition. I could find nothing to explain the downward spiral of the team after the glory years in the twenties and early thirties.

How did a city as important to the country as Washington lose the game that in 1960 was still an unrivaled cultural icon? How could the Griffiths have been allowed to steal baseball from the fans of Washington? Brad Snyder's book, *Playing in the Shadows of the Senators*, provided convincing evidence that race played a role in the first Senators team leaving town. It is a complex issue, but one that nonetheless had a major part in the Griffiths' decision and their vocal contention that Washington, D.C., could not support baseball.

Then in 2006 I ran into Fred Valentine, one of a handful of African Americans who played for the Senators. Fred has lived in the area since playing for Washington from 1964 to 1968. He was speaking to a Kiwanis group in Northern Virginia, and after the meeting I chatted with him about the old Senators, asking him some of the questions I had about why the team left town. Much of this story came from that initial spark, from his stories about the 1968 season and what went wrong for the team in the ensuing years.

Fred was not part of the Bob Short era, not part of the remaking of the Senators under the tutelage of Ted Williams. But after talking to Fred, I knew there was a story worth hearing, and I set out to talk to some of Fred's teammates. Fred sent me to Jim Hannan, who told me the first stories about Ted Williams and the Senators.

Ted Williams is one of the great stories of baseball in the twentieth century and much has been written about him. Yet there was little in the books about his history as the manager of the Senators. It was not a success for Teddy Ballgame in the end, but how did he come to support owner Bob Short's efforts to relocate the team? How could someone of such rock-ribbed integrity be part of baseball's demise in Washington?

During the first two years of the new Nationals' return, many of the old concerns about Washington and whether it could support baseball reappeared. It appeared as though the drama from 1971 would be replayed, as if no one had been watching all those years before. I was reading the old history in the evenings and watching as it threatened to unfold again the next morning in the newspapers.

With part of the history of 1969 gone now that RFK Stadium has been replaced with a wonderful new ballpark, it is more important than ever to preserve what happened and understand it as well as possible. I was there for the last Washington Nationals game at RFK in September of 2007. There were many old Senators fans in attendance that day, carrying banners decrying the crimes of Bob Short. The evidence that the sense of betrayal from long ago remains fresh was everywhere.

The story of the 1969 season is a compelling one and I hope it provides a good point of entry for new fans with limited knowledge of the Senators. For others it is an important thread in the larger story of Washington baseball, one worth understanding in all its complexity. For a brief moment, for one last season, the old Senators shrugged off the prognostications of their demise and breathed with new life and energy. Ted Williams strode onto the field at RFK, and legends were alive for the Senators again.

Baseball is like no other sport in its deep appreciation of its history. Greater knowledge of our baseball history here in D.C. can help sink the new roots further into the soil. The rebirth of baseball in Washington is important not only to area fans, but to the sport as a whole. We as baseball fans in Washington are against the idea — started by Commissioner Bud Selig at the start of the twenty-first century — that baseball can survive by limiting the number of cities in which it is played.

Commissioner Selig broached the issue of contraction, reducing the number of cities in which fans can go out to the ballpark and sit under the stars and watch the National Pastime. Commissioner Selig at the time believed that baseball could not survive in Minneapolis or Montreal, and was skeptical that it could succeed here. Washington baseball fans made believers of the cynics and proved that the game should be expanded, that there are millions of Americans still hungry for major league baseball.

I would like to thank all of the 1969 Senators who took the time to speak with me about their experiences in that season. Jim Hannan, Mike Epstein, Fred Valentine, Dick Bosman and Frank Howard were all kind enough to take time away from their lives to talk to me about a season long ago. They were gracious enough to answer questions from one largely ignorant of their playing years in Washington. Their insights into the era and the game were the spark that gave meaning to this project.

Bill Nowlin, Rounder Books' well-regarded Ted Williams expert, was kind enough to read the manuscript and offer his insights, although all errors are my own. His help is much appreciated. I want to thank my very good friends Ken Voytek and Joel Cohen, who encouraged me from the moment I mentioned this idea and helped me think through some of what I heard from the players and others. Reverend Ed Winkler and Bill Seedyke provided edits of the earliest drafts, and their knowledge of the game was a great help as well. I want to thank my oldest friends, Rob Clayman and his wife, Carol Miller, who read the proofs of my last book and have continued their good-humored support again.

Scott Shagin, Kim Ringler, Jon Witty and his wife Merrill are part of the Oberlin support network, but the greatest Oberlin alum for my money is my wife, Donna Boxer. She is a great editor and an even better friend. I can only hope at the end of each season that she renews my contract.

My daughters, Julia and Claire, continue to be a source of inspiration and my companions at an occasional game. I hope they, like others, will come to appreciate the long history of baseball in this town and will bring new fans to the game over the years. I hope we will all live to see baseball return to glory in Washington, D.C., to watch over a rebirth of the legacy of Washington baseball, one that will send new favorites to the Hall of Fame and raise new pennants to fly over Nationals Stadium to mark our great victories.

1

War, Race and Baseball

It was the last spring training game of 1968 for the perennial cellar-dwellers, the Washington Senators. The spring had been good for the Senators, surprisingly good. The writers and fans were taking note of the slow, steady climb in the standings over the preceding three seasons, and there was a hint of optimism about the team and the coming year. That spring of '68 the Senators sat atop the Grapefruit League with the best record of any team. Manager Gil Hodges and George Selkirk, the general manager, had masterminded the Senators' rise in the American League in 1967, and though Hodges had moved on to the New York Mets, hope was running high that the Senators in 1968 would finally clear the second division.

The game that day was in Fort Lauderdale against the Yankees. The great Yankee teams of the 1950s and early '60s were a fading memory by 1968. An aged-looking Mickey Mantle, playing in his last season, sat in the dugout across the field from the Senators as they jogged to their positions to start the fourth inning. Fred Valentine, the Senators' starting center fielder, remembers distinctly where he was standing when the announcer's voice interrupted play with a startling but somber statement. Martin Luther King, Jr., had been shot in Memphis, Tennessee. Play continued, but some of the fielders were clearly shaken while others seemed preoccupied by the news. An inning later the announcement was made that Dr. King was dead.

Valentine was one of a handful of African American players on the Senators who remembers that spring day with clarity. He was shaken to his core, though he played out the game that was won by New York. The usual events marking the end of spring training continued much as planned. The Senators made their final roster moves, rookies were sent packing, and the best twenty-five players got their families ready for the trip north. The first stop was Louisville, Kentucky, for two exhibition games against the Boston Red Sox.

Only one of the two exhibition games planned for Louisville was actually played. On Thursday evening following the assassination of Dr. King, rioting began to spread across many areas of the country. The BBC in London, viewing the carnage from afar, cataloged rioting in 100 American cities. Back in Washington, D.C., large and angry mobs spread out along 14th Street and parts of Georgia and Florida avenues as well. As the darkness deepened on Thursday night, the rioters grew bolder, taunting police and breaking windows as they roamed down commercial strips. A fire started in a liquor store that would be the first of many to fill the city's skies with thick, dark smoke.

The riots grew in intensity on Friday, and mobs overran the ability of local police until four thousand armed troops were deployed across the city. The anger boiling from the Washington streets did not abate. Rioting continued late into Friday night, and another eight thousand troops were brought in on Saturday. Four people were dead by Sunday morning and three thousand were sent to jail.

The Senators watched the action from Louisville and waited. The news was dominated by film footage of fiery nights in Washington. The Sunday game in Louisville was cancelled, and Washington Opening Day — known then as Presidential Opening Day — was moved back a day, from Monday to Tuesday of the next week. Team officials said the games were cancelled out of respect for Dr. King. While respect may have played a part, of equal concern was the ability to restore order in the city where riots were taking a visible toll.

Martin Luther King, Jr., had been in Washington just days before his death. Speaking inside the towering sanctuary arches of the National Cathedral on April 1— just four days before his assassination — he announced an ambitious expansion of his poor people's campaign. He spoke of ominous anger in the black ghettoes of America, stating, "I don't like to predict violence, but if nothing is done between now and June to raise people's hopes, I feel this summer will not only be as bad, but worse than last year." An overflow crowd of 4,000 onlookers at the cathedral heard the words not realizing, sadly, how soon his words of prophecy would play out.

As the Senators flew into National Airport from Louisville, the dense smoke rising from Washington could be seen as the plane circled the city. The players were glued to the windows as they drew closer to the scenes of chaos and destruction lying just beneath them. Long stretches of 14th Street and other major arteries between the airport and RFK Stadium were closed off because of the violence.

Fred Valentine remembers the concern of the team members as everyone boarded the bus for the trip across town to the stadium. The white players insisted that the African American players sit in clear view in the front seats of the Greyhound bus. "Now you want us in the front of the bus, after all those years in the back," the black players said with wry smiles, savoring the irony. The team joked about the violence, but the concern was very real.

The 14th Street corridor cooled, but left a crater in the collective soul of the city. The Senator baseball team in 1968 seemed to lose its way as well. The club never lived up to the early hopes in Florida, and by May they were in a tailspin, on their way to losing nearly 100 games — 96 to be exact. The '68 season returned Washington fans to an all-too-familiar despair, their Senators once again last in the American League. Attendance at RFK was only 546,000, down by more than 200,000 from the previous season. Many attributed the decline to the fears of suburban whites uncertain what they would find in the city and at the Senators' stadium near its core. Ironically, other riot-torn cities had banner years. The Detroit Tigers went on to beat the St. Louis Cardinals in the World Series, with Mickey Lolich surprising the almost invincible Bob Gibson to win a memorable Game Seven, and drew more than two million fans during the campaign.

Baseball often intertwines language with politics, culture, and life itself, providing non-threatening metaphors of familiarity for weightier topics. But in 1968, sides were being chosen, and sport was being cast aside as too trivial for a generation caught up in the maelstrom of events that seemed to spin more chaotic and out of control as the seasons turned. Yet even those most alienated by events would sneak a peek at the standings in the morning paper to see where their beloved team sat. Even as American history seemed about to burst asunder, baseball could still freeze time for a moment, stop the headlong descent, and provide bearings for those undone by it all.

Washington was the center of the political drama in 1968, but its baseball team offered its citizens little respite from events that season. By June of 1968, there was no need to check the standings because the Senators were dead last, which is where they would stay. Washington fans took some solace from a meager set of positive developments for the Senators. Camilo Pascual, who had starred for the original Senators before they left for Minnesota prior to the 1961 season, returned to Washington to anchor the rotation, and a new young pitcher, Joe Coleman, emerged to complement Pascual. The pitching was still horribly thin, and the team could not hit a lick. Rookie Del Unser led off, but hit only .230 and had an on-base percentage below .300. The starting catcher, Paul Casanova, failed to hit .200, as did Ron Hansen, the shortstop brought over from the White Sox to replace Eddie Brinkman, who had proved in 1967 that he could not hit his weight.

Frank Howard had a career year with 44 home runs, but the rest of the lineup, other than Ken McMullen, seemed completely hapless. Fred Valentine slumped after a career year in 1967, and was traded to Baltimore to replace an injured Paul Blair. The team just up the road in Baltimore provided a sharp contrast. There the Orioles featured a powerful lineup of sluggers and young pitchers coming into their own. They were on the rise, finishing second to the great Detroit team.

Yet at the end of the '68 season, fans could not help believing a curse had been resurrected, as though the devil from the Broadway musical, *Damn Yankees,* was still waiting for a deal to be struck, upping the ante each season, teasing the fans up to the bar, just close enough for the aroma of a winner to tickle their taste buds, but always ending as a sad joke. There was no one in D.C. to sell their soul for a long-ball hitter or any small morsel of baseball success. The writers and fans began to worry about baseball as an ongoing enterprise in D.C.

When the original Senators were relocated by Calvin Griffith in 1960 to Minneapolis, he left saying Washington was a bad baseball town, "just a sleepy little southern town," as many local journalists called it. Some were beginning to believe Griffith — maybe Washington, D.C., was just not meant to have a baseball team.

Dour as the future looked, baseball was not foremost in the collective mind of Washington, D.C., as 1968 wore on. Before the riots, President Lyndon Johnson had announced at the end of March, "I shall not seek, and I will not accept the nomination of my party for another term as your President." The war in Vietnam was Johnson's, and leaving it as a legacy was just another unfathomable enigma for a country without explanation for so much of what the news was bringing each day.

His surprise withdrawal gave sudden hope to the presidential aspirations of other candidates. One in particular began to step forward. Former vice president Richard Nixon was running for president for a second time, and President Johnson's surrender gave his candidacy a huge boost. Nixon began calling for an end to the bombing of North Vietnam, and a nation sick of the war took notice, took heart.

In 1968 the war in Vietnam was a somber mask drawn over the ascendant prosperity of America. As Tom Wicker, *New York Times* editor, said, "Nineteen sixty-eight was a year of repeated shocks to what remained of American certainty, of brutal blows to Americans' perceptions of themselves and their country, of devastating challenges to old ideas of authority and values. The long, bloody struggle in Vietnam seemed more and more senseless; worse, it appeared endless."

The conflict that shaped the culture and history of the era saw casualties reach their highest point in 1968, with 14,589 Americans dying in combat. Their funerals and the horrors from which they sprang dominated the news each evening. American invincibility was called into question as the Tet Offensive of '68 — by combined Viet Cong and North Vietnamese troops — overran much of South Vietnam, the fighting reaching even into the American Embassy compound in Saigon. War-weary Americans saw Richard Nixon's campaign, his promise of a "secret plan" to end the war, as a hope that peace and normalcy were possible.

War and race are two forces that have shaped the city of Washington, D.C., since its beginnings. The Civil War was the first to effect dramatic changes in the city. That war made Washington a powerful magnet for free blacks emerging from the southern states, one of the closest safe harbors where opportunities were relatively abundant. The proportion of blacks living in D.C. quadrupled from 1860 to 1880, rising to almost 50 percent of the city's total population. As the city and its government grew, the proportion of African American citizens diminished. But at the beginning of the twentieth century, when the American League was founded, Washington alone had a significant percentage of African American citizens, almost twice the percentage of any other city on the junior circuit.

The city's minority population and reliance on government rather than industrial wealth kept alive the perception of Washington as a "sleepy southern town." The civil rights era brought race to the surface as a sharp divisive issue for every American city, but for Washington the issue had always been there. For Washington's baseball fortunes, it would prove fatal with time.

When the original Washington Senators joined the American League in 1901, the team exhibited the same ineptitude that would mark much of its history. But in 1911, a watershed event occurred when Clark Griffith came to the team as a successful manager. As a pitcher in the late nineteenth century, Griffith had been a six-time twenty-game winner who as a player-manager ingratiated himself to Ban Johnson and the other colorful, determined men who founded the American League.

As a manager of the Senators, Griffith achieved success immediately by guiding his first Washington team in 1912 to a second-place finish. But it was not until he purchased the club outright in 1920 that he was able to acquire the last pieces of the puzzle and take the team to the pinnacle of success, the World Series. In 1924 the Senators were crowned world champs by beating John McGraw's New York Giants. Fans filled Pennsylvania Avenue for a long and happy victory celebration, the likes of which have not been seen since in the city.

The Senators won the American League pennant again in '25 and were competitive for much of the first two decades Griffith was affiliated with the team. From 1912 until their last American League pennant, in 1933, the Senators never finished last and were in the bottom half of the eight-team league only six times in twenty-one years.

Clark Griffith was a small yet burly man, and he had the sharp competitive edge that some small men develop. He had never been willing to accept second best at any point in his long and colorful life. But in 1934, at sixty-four years of age, the "Old Fox" was facing his toughest challenges. His Senators were 1933 American League champions with a team whose roster was studded with players who would go on to the Hall of Fame. The '33 Senators still featured Sam Rice and Goose Goslin, whose heyday in the mid–1920s had brought the team two pennants and a World Series win. Sure-handed Ossie Bluege remained at third base from the '24 team, but the weight for the '33 Senators was carried by two remarkable hitters, Heinie Manush and Joe Cronin. Neither of these Hall of Fame players were sluggers in the modern mold, but both hit higher than .300 for their long careers and manned the middle of the Senators' batting order in '33 — Manush, batting third, and Cronin, cleanup.

Joe Cronin was the leader of that team, the same way that Clark Griffith had been the leader of Chicago White Sox in 1901, managing and pitching his team to a pennant in the first year of the American League. Now, Cronin was taking on that same role for Griffith, leading not just on the field, but in the dugout as player-manager. Griffith had taken Cronin to the owners' meetings at the end of the '32 season, and moves Cronin initiated at the off-season winter meetings created the last great Senators team in '33. But it was a late-season run largely attributed to Cronin's bat that brought the American League pennant to Washington for one last time.

Joe Cronin was engaged to marry Griffith's adopted daughter, but the aging Clark Griffith had neither money nor at sixty-four much time to make more of it. As a result, he sold Joe Cronin to wealthy Red Sox owner Tom Yawkey for $250,000. Babe Ruth fetched far less, only $100,000 in 1919, but the two Depression-era seasons of 1932 and '33 are the only years that baseball as a sport lost money. Clark Griffith was a man whose fortune depended on baseball. Yawkey had a family fortune, and spending money on baseball was a sporting venture. For men like Connie Mack and Clark Griffith, the game was life itself and their wealth depended on the fortunes of the teams they owned. As the Depression deepened, they lost much of that wealth.

The Senators in 1934 plummeted to the bottom, where they stayed for two decades of financial struggle and loss for Clark Griffith. He sold his baseball soul to keep his family business afloat. Clark Griffith died in 1956, turning the team over *not* to one of the most respected names in the game,

Joe Cronin, but to his son Calvin, who had none of his father's baseball acumen.

From the moment he assumed control, Calvin Griffith was looking to extricate himself from what he saw as an untenable situation. Old Griffith Stadium — located near Howard University — was the cash cow of the Griffith family. They kept the turnstiles spinning at a feverish pace. During the baseball season, the stadium hosted the Senators, as well as the Negro League's great Homestead Gray teams. Stadium rentals, especially to the Grays, pushed the Griffith's ledger books into the black each year. The Grays drew larger crowds than the Senators when the white team was playing on the road, away from D.C. The crowds were not surprising. With Hall of Fame players like Josh Gibson and Buck Leonard, the Grays brought a level of baseball talent to Washington in the years after 1934 that the Senators could not match.

On off-season Sundays, Griffith Stadium was home to the Redskins. On weekend nights loud raucous wrestling events brought in large crowds to help pay the bills. For all of the efforts by the Griffith family to stretch the money-making capacity of their patch of real estate, it was located in the heart of an African American neighborhood, becoming poorer with each passing year. Clark Griffith's attempts to wring every nickel from the old cow were making it obvious she wasn't what she used to be.

Like the Senators baseball team itself, Griffith Stadium suffered from economic neglect. Never a showpiece, the stadium had its share of eccentricities similar to other older ballparks. The outfield wall jutted in sharply in dead center field, a necessity to accommodate five owners who refused to move when property was aggregated for the building of the ballpark in 1911. There were rare fly balls that would force the outfielder to watch anxiously to see which way the ball would carom depending upon the face of the protruding wall it struck.

A huge tree loomed just beyond the wall, its limbs extending almost to the field of play. By 1954, in the waning years of Clark Griffith's life, crowds at the stadium had dwindled by an alarming proportion, with fewer than 500 customers at one game that year. The seating capacity was less than thirty thousand, and the Griffiths' inability to retool, replace, or move the ballpark was more at issue than the neighbors.

Baseball teams were on the move in the late 1950s. Baltimore received the Orioles in 1954 from St. Louis and the hapless Browns. Walter O'Malley took one of the oldest franchises in history, the Brooklyn Dodgers, to California in 1957. They, along with the Giants who left the Polo Grounds in New York City, began a general westward march for major league baseball.

It quickly became easier for Calvin Griffith to solve his economic dilemma in Minneapolis, Minnesota, than in Washington, D.C. Minnesotans were offering cash, and the Griffiths had a history of needing infusions of that commodity to run their baseball team. Calvin Griffith was convinced that he could *not* make the Senators into a paying enterprise in Washington.

Griffith's concern was that Griffith Stadium was "getting to be all colored." In remarks years later he gave an even greater depth of understanding to his troubling motivations for the Senators' move. "You only have 15,000 blacks here," he said to Minnesota businessmen in a speech in the 1970s. In the same speech he continued by emphasizing the Minneapolis fan base's "good hard working white people."

Relocating the Senators to Minneapolis fixed the problems that beset old Griffith Stadium, but more importantly fixed the bottom line problems of a family that had nothing other than baseball to support it. Yet baseball's ownership club supported moving a team from the nation's capital, supported abandoning one of the ten largest metropolitan areas in the country. Baseball was still king and fans were easy to come by. That situation would change during the next decade.

When the Senators left town in 1960, there were questions asked, but no one broached the subject of race. Few questioned why the nation's capital, one of the ten largest metropolitan areas in the country and considerably larger than Minneapolis-St. Paul, could pass as a "sleepy southern town." Sportswriters lined up to agree that Washington was not a good baseball town, but few questioned what that meant.

The Senators did not go gently. There were many influential fans that fought the move. Senators and congressman introduced legislation pressuring baseball's anti-trust exemption. But like a team of horses pulling an old stump from the ground, the forces working against Washington's baseball Senators were just too much. The owner's club was stronger than the representatives of the fans. Finally, President Eisenhower intervened to extract the promise of a new team for D.C. The concept of expansion was born from Ike's demands. It was a new phenomenon in 1961, but adding teams to the core of eight National League and eight American League teams would become a staple as the national pastime grew along with the country in the coming decades.

In November of 1960, a group of investors led by Eisenhower's director of the Federal Aviation Administration, Elwood "Pete" Quesada, bought the rights to the old name, the "Senators," and an expansion team to go with it. Neither Quesada nor any other individual in the investment group had the depth of financial resources to support the team, and they continued the bargain basement approach that had prevailed during the previous 25-year history with the Griffith family.

To balance the additional franchise, baseball created another team in Los Angeles that was purchased by Gene Autry, the singer and actor whose large fortune was in stark contrast to that of his counterparts in Washington. The franchise was named the Los Angeles Angels and became the second team in the Los Angeles area, in recognition of the exploding population in Southern California. An additional expansion team maintained symmetry for the league, and procedures for drafting new teams from the rosters of the existing clubs were set in place for the first time.

Washington hired Mickey Vernon as its manager. Vernon had starred on the Senators' only post-war team with a winning record, in 1952. The '52 team had featured a solid lineup of hitters — Vernon, Eddie Yost, and Pete Runnels — but few who could pitch well. The expansion draft in 1960 brought to the fore colorfully named players like Coot Veal, Joe Hicks, and Dutch Dotterer, but few of great talent. Bobby Shantz, Gene Woodling, Dale Long and other respected names in the game were included, but most of these players were well beyond their primes as players.

For all the fading stars now playing in a new stadium, Washington sports fans felt betrayed. The final moment of that betrayal came when the Minnesota Twins clinched the 1965 American League championship in a double-header in late September in Washington. Many of the players from that Twins team had left Washington with Calvin Griffith, had once been the hope of the Washington Senators. The Twins were champions while Washington fans were asked to settle for a team most believed was little better than amateurs. The newly-minted Griffith family team winning the pennant in Minneapolis was a particularly rude slap in the face for Washington fans.

The other expansion team, the Los Angeles Angels, was able to field a contender within the decade of the 1960s, showing baseball acumen and the backing of a wealthy owner in Gene Autry. Washington had only the devil standing by the door — no brain trust, no money, and no winners. Washington's new team continued to finish dead last year after year as baseball moved deeper into the sixties.

2

Can't You Hear That Rooster Crowing?

The new year dawned in 1969 with signs of change as far as the eye could see. A new commissioner, Bowie Kuhn, ruled the roost in baseball and would guide the game through its first seasons of player dissent. Kuhn had tended the scoreboard at old Griffith Stadium as a boy and might have been looked to as a friend of the expansion team in Washington. In Kuhn's first year, baseball expanded for the first time beyond the borders of the United States as Montreal fielded an expansion team, the Expos. Divisional play was introduced in both the American and National leagues, with each circuit having an East and West division of six teams. Expansion of both leagues brought four new teams into play, pushing the total number of clubs to 24.

A second round of expansion had been proposed initially in 1967, and along with divisional play, was scheduled to be rolled out in 1971. Charlie Finley's move of the A's to Oakland had led Missouri Senator Stuart Symington to once again threaten baseball's anti-trust exemption loud enough that, as in 1960, the owners hastened to add teams to smooth the troubled waters. Expansion and divisional play were moved up and put in place for the 1969 season.

The American League expansion teams included the Seattle Pilots and the Kansas City Royals, adding one each to the new East and West divisions. In the National League, the San Diego Padres joined Montreal to even the numbers. For the first time, schedules would concentrate games divisionally, with teams playing eighteen games against divisional rivals and only twelve against teams in the other division. Spring training in '69 would feature a new experiment, allowing a designated hitter to hit throughout games for the pitcher — an attempt to add offensive punch after increasing domination by great pitchers.

Baseball perceived itself at a crossroads. Baseball writers were saying in 1968 that "baseball was dull and lacking much of the old excitement." Twenty percent of all games involved one team being shut out. Bob Gibson shattered all prior records with an earned run average of 1.12. Denny McLain became the first pitcher in three decades to reach thirty victories by winning thirty-one. Home runs diminished by 300, and batting average in the American League had fallen steadily during the sixties, losing seventeen points over the previous four seasons. Almost every offensive indicator was down precipitously by the end of 1968, and those who loved the game most were worried.

Historical analysts said the previous year had been the worst offensively during the modern era, worse than the deadball era early in the twentieth century. Red Barber, the famed broadcaster, wondered aloud what changes could be initiated to "even the competition between pitcher and batter." In the article "Can Baseball Be Saved?" he suggested that the mound be moved back twenty-four inches to help the offense. He further recommended the season be shortened to 142 games so that it ended in September and reduced the conflict with baseball's once-poor cousin, professional football.

Ralph Kiner, the great home run hitter, broadcasting for the New York Mets, recommended that the fences be moved in, saying, "There used to be quite a few ballparks that had a short fence in either right or left field. But these new parks are symmetrical — and they're all bigger." Not only was the excitement of each game diminished by the lack of offensive fireworks, but competition seemed to disappear as the Cardinals ran away from everyone in the senior circuit, deciding the National League championship in August. Attendance was down in both leagues.

It was hoped that adding four teams was one solution that would increase overall attendance and bring new fans in different parts of the country — and a new part of the continent — into the action. Breaking the two leagues into two divisions would generate additional competition and keep the public eye on baseball further into the early fall. Now there would be four pennant races rather than two, meaning more fans could be caught up cheering their teams down the wire. Attendance would swell in those parks, it was hoped, and television audiences would grow as well, along with increasingly important broadcast revenues.

In response to the hue and cry regarding the crisis of the game, two rule changes were decided by baseball officials during the off-season. They were announced quietly in December of 1968 after the meeting of the Official Playing Rules Committee in San Francisco. This select brain trust of the game made two alterations intended to shift the advantage to the hitter. The first was to lower the pitching mound, from fifteen inches to ten. The second would be to restrict the top part of the strike zone from the top of the shoulders of the crouching batter to the bottom of the armpits — across the uniform letters. Red Barber decried the action of the committee, saying the changes were not bold enough. Most, however, were willing to wait and determine what effect the new rules might have.

As critical as were the changes set in motion for the baseball world in 1969, they were lost except in the eyes of the most myopic fan. American society was in its greatest moment of upheaval since the end of Second World War. The inauguration of Richard Milhous Nixon on January 21 brought an outspoken sports fan to town whose interest in the Senators would focus new attention on a team that badly needed the spotlight. Although Richard Nixon's aching desire to possess the athletic ease and social grace of his sports heroes might have shed light on his intriguing personality and the political chaos to follow, the average American in the spring of 1969 knew only that Nixon was their best hope to end what *New York Times* and *Washington Post* writer Myra McPherson called "the most divisive time of battle in our country since the Civil War" — the war in Vietnam.

Much like the country at large, revolutionary winds of change were sweeping the Washington Senators. On December 4, 1968, the *Washington Post* announced the sale of the Senators baseball team to Robert E. Short, a trucking magnate with ties to the recently defeated Democratic presidential nominee, Hubert Humphrey. Bob Short was the treasurer of the Democratic Party and had run unsuccessfully several times for elected office in Minnesota, most recently for Lieutenant Governor in 1966. He had lived briefly in Washington in the late 1940s. Short attended Georgetown Law School after World War II and served as an assistant U.S. Attorney in Washington for a few years before returning to the Twin Cities.

Short acquired majority ownership in the Senators for $9.4 million from James H. Lemon. The sum was thought to be more than the struggling franchise was worth. The conventional wisdom in baseball circles was that Short "got took." Bob Hope, the well-known and wealthy entertainer, had expressed some interest, and may have driven up the price. Short, though, was the more persistent suitor for Lemon's interest in the team. As part of the deal, Short retained the same minority ownership group that had participated with Lemon in trying to steer the expansion team toward success. The move to retain ties to the local business community did nothing to smooth the waters in a town that distrusted him from the start.

The *Washington Post* reported that the minority owners had sought a stipulation to the sale that would require Short not to move the team for "a long period of years." The article was indicative of the immediate concern that the sale of the team could lead to another relocation of the team less than a decade after the loss of the original Senators. Lemon and the ownership group, many of whom had been on board since the original expansion in 1961, were clearly concerned about the motivation of the new owner. The tone of the article was another indication that many believed "Senators were on their way out of town again."

Short described himself as a friend of Calvin Griffith, the owner of the Minnesota Twins, who had moved the Senators just eight years earlier. He declared himself a loyal Twins fan in early newspaper accounts and had in fact been a minority owner in the Minnesota team. The divided loyalties did little to impress a town with no love for Griffith nor the Twins. Yet it was the uncertainty of his affiliations that raised eyebrows. The core of concern for Washington fans and sportswriters arose from the manner in which he had dealt with his last sports team.

Short's first venture into the world of sport came when he purchased his hometown basketball team, the Minneapolis Lakers, in 1957. The team was one of the NBA's founding franchises in 1947, and the first great center in the game, George Mikan, would lead the team to five championships in the 1950s. But Short took all of this local history and, with regard only for the money it could bring him, moved the team to Los Angeles. After establishing the team there, he sold it for a handsome profit a few years later.

As he had done in Minnesota, Short immediately began to make significant changes to the Washington Senators. In Minnesota he fired a much-respected coach who brought five NBA championships to the team in seven years. Short hired new staff with loyalty only to himself. He repeated the same process in Washington. He fired Jim Lemon, whose first year as manager during the 1968 season had been a disappointing one. But he did not stop there. He fired highly respected baseball man George Selkirk, who had served as general manager since 1962. Short surprisingly told critics he would be his own general manager. A former player, Selkirk had overseen steady improvements to the organization and rising hopes.

Short went on to fire the radio and television announcers as well as anyone who might be construed as part of the old regime. Dan Daniels, one of the departing announcers, speculated that Short did so not because of concern for the loyalty of the group or their performance, but because he did not have the money to meet payroll. "His purchase of the team was highly leveraged and he had cash flow problems. He had done the same thing with the team he bought in Minnesota," Daniels said.

Shelby Whitfield, hired by Short as an announcer, said in a tell-all book several years later that Short spent only $1,000 of his own money and borrowed everything else he paid for the team — and at interest rates well over prime. He put up only $2 million in business equity to secure the loans, and

Ted Williams at bat. Only Joe DiMaggio matched the magic Ted Williams brought to the game of baseball. National Baseball Hall of Fame Library, Cooperstown, N.Y.

the resulting interest rates kept his baseball operations on the economic edge from the start.

Short's actions provided fertile soil for growing suspicion about his motives and where he was taking the team when he made no moves to replace either Selkirk or Lemon. It was the off-season, though, and the furor quieted. Short controlled the baseball side of the Senators himself during the winter months. What articles there were about the Senators in the *Washington Post* or the *Washington Star* idly speculated whether Nellie Fox would be elevated from coach to manager. But Short was an energetic man who had bigger plans, plans for transforming the team as a box-office success, for keeping his new venture financially viable while he figured out what to do with it.

On February 21, with the attention of the sports world slowly awakening to a baseball season still more than a month away, Short convulsed the landscape of D.C. baseball with a remarkable announcement. Ending two weeks of intensifying speculation, he issued a press release with the news that Hall of Fame Red Sox great Ted Williams would manage the 1969 Senators. Not since the departure of Joe Cronin in 1933 had there been a moment of greater drama in the history of baseball in the nation's capital. An American legend was coming to town.

It was as if Babe and the Blue Ox or Paul Bunyan had walked off the page, and the newspapermen with their notepads flew with pencil in hand to grab the nearest phone to call in the news. Up and down the eastern seaboard the lines were buzzing about baseball in the nation's capital. Bob Short was smiling from ear to ear.

Only Joe DiMaggio matched the magic Williams brought to the game of baseball. A nation heading into war in 1941 had been kept on the edge of its seats watching as Ted Williams kept his batting average above the .400 threshold during the entire summer and ended with a dramatic flourish to establish the still unfathomable standard of .406.

Ted Williams' reputation as a brash, outspoken and controversial ballplayer began as soon as he stepped onto a major league playing field. When he reported to big league camp for the first time as a Red Sox player, Bobby Doerr is purported to have said to the rookie, "Wait'll you see Jimmy Foxx hit." Foxx was one of the greatest hitters playing at the time, but the upstart newbie is said to have replied, "Wait'll Foxx sees me hit." Teddy Ballgame won six batting titles and two Most Valuable Player awards.

Among the remarkable Ted Williams statistics buried among the home runs and batting average is the remarkable dearth of strikeouts measured against the number of base on balls. Williams struck out 64 times in his first campaign, in 1939, but after that rarely struck out fifty times in a season. By contrast he led the league in walks many years with well over 100 each season, reaching his high mark of 162 in both '47 and '48. His batting eye was so sharp that umpires were thought to defer to it. It was said that he could read the label on a phonograph record even as it was spinning, but Williams said it was the intense concentration more than the eyesight. The concentration and control of the strike zone were remarkable attributes that would be part of his success as a manager.

The man with super-human eyesight was part of the legend, part of the persona created by a press hungry for heroes, but feasting on their foibles. Williams had his obvious weaknesses and he paraded them with few inhibitions. Williams became an epic story at a time in history when Americans needed heroes, and a time when baseball was the king of American sport with no rival on the horizon.

The story of Ted Williams took on even larger proportions when he was twice summoned to serve as a fighter pilot, first during World War II, but even more notably when called upon a second time by serving in Korea. As a jet fighter pilot in Korea, he survived a crash landing of his plane after it was shot on one of his first missions. Forced to land at the nearest friendly airstrip, Williams recounted how the commanding officer of the air field drove his jeep pell-mell to meet the smoking plane as it came to rest on its belly. Williams quickly jumped from the cockpit, fearing an explosion. As he ran from the plane, he was met by the colonel, who was running to meet him with pencil and paper outstretched to get Williams' autograph.

Williams flew thirty-nine combat missions and served with John Glenn, whose status as another American hero was just beginning. Williams was a war hero, but when he returned to the game, his unmatched ability to swing a bat made him the beloved figure of a grateful nation.

Williams had turned down opportunities to manage in both Boston and Detroit over the years. He had said, "Never," when others had offered the job. In his autobiography (written with John Underwood) *My Turn at Bat*, Williams said, "Managing is essentially a loser's job. They are the most expendable pieces of furniture on earth." At the end of his career, many assumed that Williams had no taste for managing, and that his love of the game had ended when he hung up his spikes in 1960. The Boston press, which Williams so loathed, wrote of his prospect of managing, "Manage twenty-five men, heck, he can't even manage himself."

Now at fifty-one he claimed he was more grown up, more ready. He had learned that the traits many felt made him unfit to manage might be assets. Asked whether his reputation as a loner would hurt, he said, "I think that's where my strength lies, they'll respect me."

As a manager Williams had great role models to draw upon. Ted started out in 1939 as a player tutoring with one of the great managers, Joe Cronin of the Red Sox. Cronin led the Red Sox for thirteen years, and in 1946 he led the team and Teddy Ballgame to the American League pennant with an amazing 104 wins. Williams had great admiration for Cronin, but the Boston manager could be just as hot-headed as Williams at times, and the two had their dustups.

Ted considered Cronin a great hitter's manager because he was always willing to talk hitting with Williams. Cronin, as an offensive player himself, always gave his hitters plenty of time in the batting cage. But Williams reserved his superlatives for Joe McCarthy, the great Yankee manager who came over to the Red Sox in 1948 and 1949 for two of Williams' greatest seasons. McCarthy said of Williams, "I would play for nothing if I could hit like Ted Williams." McCarthy was late in his career when he managed Williams. He was an aging icon and father figure, and Williams clearly revered him. Ted was also a seasoned veteran by 1948 and could appreciate the discipline McCarthy brought to the Red Sox clubhouse.

It was the measured professionalism of McCarthy that Ted Williams knew he could bring to the Senators. McCarthy had never sought to be close to his players, wanting only to make them better players. McCarthy relied on strict rules of discipline, and one of the first pronouncements from Williams in the Washington press was a list of McCarthy's ten commandments. Williams believed he could emulate McCarthy and set about doing so with the Senators.

Bob Short probably cared little whether or not Ted Williams could manage a ball club. He saw only the baseball icon and was clearly a bit starstruck in the early days. For Short, Ted Williams the manager was the answer to his very immediate needs to pump up the value of a franchise for which he had just paid $9 million. Short knew the situation called for someone or something exciting and new to bring baseball alive in Washington, D.C. Drawing on a lawyer's courtroom presence and a salesman's braggadocio, Short sought out the reclusive Williams at his home in the Florida Keys and convinced him with wit and charm to consider the unthinkable. It was hard work and took all of Short's seemingly endless supply of energy to sell Williams on managing a team few might have considered.

Short devised a unique sales campaign to attract Williams. He told Williams, "You're going to inherit the worst team in baseball. If you don't do any better than last year's last-place finish, people'll say it's a lousy team anyway. If you do better than last year, they'll say you're a hell of a manager."

Short offered Williams considerable money. The salary was to be $65,000 each season for five years, with an option to buy ownership in the team. Short also named Williams the vice president of the team. The value of the package of salary and incentives was put at $1.25 million. Williams retained the more lucrative Sears commitments that required little of his time. He had an endorsements contract with Sears that was his main source of income, estimated at another $100,000 annually. Yet money was ultimately not the issue that led Williams to return to baseball.

Many believed at the time that Williams' time away from the game had been hard emotionally. His missed the game and the adulation it brought him. He had spent his time in retirement as a front man for Sears' fishing and outdoor gear. He appeared occasionally, leading fishing expeditions to exotic locales, and it worked for Williams because he loved the outdoors, hunting and fishing, almost as much as baseball.

As a baseball player, off-season fishing and hunting trips had always been a sanctuary from the spotlight. Now, after nine years of sanctuary, Williams needed the fanfare, the excitement and the challenge that baseball had always represented. Bob Short offered the perfect safe opportunity, one where he could not fail. Williams took the hook and ran with it, saying, "I've been sitting around doing very little for eight years except fishing." He said exotic fishing trips had been less fun recently, not as much fun as baseball, or at least not as much fun as it had once been.

Williams was also impressed with Short as a man. Perhaps he was a willing buyer from the beginning, but Short not only sold the idea, he sold himself to Williams. The two men were very close in age, and Williams said of Short, "He is a self-made man." That picture described Williams' view of himself. He said of Short, "He is a smart man." Both men had intellectual gifts that they brought to what they were doing, but it was the level of very focused energy and enthusiasm for the project at hand that united the two men ultimately. Williams recognized in the smaller Short something of himself.

On February 25 in Pompano Beach, Florida, Ted Williams stepped back onto the diamond for the first time in eight years. At the beginning of spring training for the Washington Senators, Washington and Boston press were all over the field for the event, watching as Williams fielded questions and spoke to his players, wearing his old number 9, taken from the Senators' great hitter Frank Howard. No one seemed to mind, though. Howard took the next available number, 13, and the equipment manager told him it had been good enough for Sammy Baugh. A superstitious baseball player, Howard ultimately settled on number 33 for the '69 season.

Shirley Povich described the scene as a three-ring circus with Williams at its center. The fans at Pompano's shabby little stadium applauded every time Williams set foot on the field or picked up a bat, applauding more for Williams than the players. There were more television and radio cables lying over the field than the new manager could contend with. But if he was confounded by the over-zealous press attention, there was not an angry word spoken. The press poured in from everywhere to see Bob Short's experiment. Some may have been waiting for a shot of the hot temper, the brash remarks, the blow-up that could happen at any moment. One predicted Williams would be gone within 90 days after his team slumped. But Williams handled the press well and made the story in the spring of 1969 about the new Ted Williams, the in-command, focused manager.

The new Ted Williams thought he could make a difference for the Senators. He was confident about two things. First, he knew he could teach his most consuming love in life — hitting a baseball. Said John Steadman of the *Sporting* News that spring, "Ted Williams can talk about the scientific theories of hitting a pitched ball in a way that makes every boy and man that ever played the game ashamed with himself that he never batted .406. The man has an enthusiastic desire to learn and teach."

Another writer said of the atmosphere around Williams that spring, "He gives off sparks. If you stand next to him long enough, you'll catch fire." If ever there was a team that needed to stand next to Williams, that needed to catch the sparks from Williams and the fire from his personality, it was the Washington Senators. As that fire caught hold, it began to spread all the way back to the fans in Washington, who had waited so long and been betrayed so often.

In 1968 the Senators' team batting average had been a lusty .224. Yet judging the team's offense by twenty-first century standards is unfair. The overall American League batting average in 1968 was .230, and the once-proud Yankees hit only .214 as a team that season. The advantage that had accrued to pitchers was very real, and major league baseball hoped that 1969 was going to be the beginning of a period in which the pendulum swung back the other way. It is fitting that one of the greatest hitters of all time would be there at the beginning of that historical shift. Ted Williams could teach hitting, and he knew he could impart more than a sense of excitement and electricity to the 1969 Washington Senators after their last-place finish in '68. But it was going to be a steep hill to climb, as his first spring training with the team would show.

3

Shine Your Light on Me

On the first day of spring training in Pompano Beach, Ted Williams was alone in the clubhouse. The players were staging their first real labor action in baseball history, setting in motion an era that would be dominated by rancorous disputes. At issue were the player pension fund and the growing pot of baseball television revenues that ownership had kept largely to itself. The nascent players union, led by Marvin Miller, wanted a fair share. Bowie Kuhn, the new commissioner, was dipping his foot into the labor issue for the first time. A patrician lawyer, he had served baseball's owners in earlier disputes over the anti-trust exemption. The labor issue would prove a more intractable problem, however, and would return time and again during his tenure as commissioner.

As Williams walked along the grass apron in front of the dugout inspecting his new realm, a reporter walking beside him opined that the Pompano Beach ballpark was hard to hit in. Williams replied, "It is 410 to center and 350 down the lines, but the prevailing wind is out and all you have to do is get the ball in the air." As a hitter Williams always knew where he was.

The Pompano Beach facility was little more than a college ballpark, according to the players, and the dugouts were as scant as a high school facility, barely below the surface of the field. The crowds at the games were thin, and a Friday night football game between two good high school teams might draw better, calling into question Bob Short's belief that Ted Williams would be magic for attendance. But the crowds that came to those first spring training games in 1969 were there to see Ted, and they let him know it as they applauded his every appearance.

The pension dispute was settled on February 25, and most of the Senators began to report for duty. Pitcher Jim Hannan, who would be the number three starter in 1969, remembers when the first group of players finally gathered for the first clubhouse meeting with their new manager at the end of February. "It was like a hero come to life," Hannan said. "When I was growing up, he was the greatest player there was, and all of sudden he was our manager, asking for quiet and standing there right before us. It was really hard to believe."

From the outset all of the players wanted to impress Williams and play well for him. Frank Howard was an established star in 1969 and his salary dispute with Bob Short kept him out of camp for two weeks. When he reported, he was no less in awe of Ted Williams. "He was such an icon of the game," Howard said, "that you really had to play your best for a man like that. We were all willing to listen to pretty much whatever he had to say, about hitting or anything else."

As important as the emotional and psychological lift was to the team, Hannan and others also credited Williams with a unique approach to managing. He was more than just a great hitter, according to Howard. Williams had a thorough knowledge of the game that he brought to bear on just about everything. "Even when he was talking to the press near the batting cage," Howard said, "he had an eye on everything that was happening on the field."

Hannan particularly liked how Williams delegated authority to the coaches and left the pitchers to pitching coach Sid Hudson. But as Howard said, Williams had ideas about everything, including pitching. "He told us from the beginning that he wanted us all to throw sliders — I think today it might be called a cut fastball," said Hannan. "It was the one pitch he had trouble with and he wanted everyone to learn to throw it. The job of teaching the pitchers and pretty much everything relating to pitching, he left to Sid Hudson."

Hudson was one of two very fine coaches Williams inherited from the previous year with the Senators. Besides Hudson, Williams retained Hall of Fame second baseman Nellie Fox primarily to coach infield play, about which Williams admitted he knew nothing. Williams was most concerned about his lack of expertise as a game-day strategist. He needed someone in the dugout who knew the demands of each situation that arose during the course of a game. He considered himself ignorant of the many maneuvers that might shift the fortunes of the Senators inning by inning.

Williams sought out old friend Johnny Pesky of the Red Sox for the position of bench coach. Pesky had experience in confronting game days from the dugout. Pesky, however, had a good deal worked out with the Red Sox and turned his old friend Ted Williams down.

The next choice was an unlikely one: Joe Camacho. Camacho's career seemed to have reached its logical conclusion as a high school principal in Connecticut, but he had been a minor league prospect for the St. Louis Browns and Cleveland Indians. He had played minor league baseball with Rocky Colavito and Herb Score and kept one foot in the game. Williams had brought Camacho in to run his boys baseball camp in Lakeville, Mass-achusetts. Camacho may have seemed less experienced than Pesky, but he had another very important quality, namely Ted Williams' trust.

Camacho may have been the first bench coach hired, although he was not certain a good team would have needed someone to perform his function, saying that a good team obviated the need for strategy or talk," Camacho said. Some writers have suggested that Williams gave Camacho the job so he could accumulate the necessary service time to get his pension. Given how loyal Williams remained to all of his friends, it would make sense.

Williams also hired former major league infielder Wayne Terwilliger as third base coach. Terwilliger had been pegged to manage the Senators' Triple-A franchise in Buffalo, but so impressed Williams that he wanted him for his own staff. Terwilliger and Camacho were the primary batting practice pitchers.

Former Red Sox coach George Susce rounded out the coaches. Susce was an old friend from Williams' Red Sox days who, at 61 years of age, had been around the game longer than anybody, and always reported to camp in better shape than any of the players. It was an eclectic group, but one that shared an important trait — a talent for teaching the game.

Although Williams attributed many of his managerial approaches to the Yankees great manager, Joe McCarthy, many of his methods were pure Ted Williams. As a remarkably acute student of the game, Williams brought a sharp analytic approach to managing that foretold many of the trends that would take hold during baseball's quantitative era, which would begin two decades later. In 1969 computers were still massive behemoths for the space and defense industries. The mathematicians who ran them were only just beginning to fantasize about their use to support predictive models about baseball behavior. It was more than a decade before stat heads and *Money-ball* interns would surface to war openly with old hands like Ted Williams.

Williams had been breaking down the process of putting bat to pitched ball since he was a kid obsessed with his swing, watching it endlessly in the mirror of his mother's house in San Diego. There has never been anyone to play the game of baseball who knew more about the science of hitting than Ted Williams, and when the players took the field in the spring of 1969, he began to teach the basics of hitting as only he knew them.

Mike Epstein, who would be the Senators first baseman in 1969, was a young, unproven major leaguer when spring training began. Williams was encouraged to have a left-handed power hitter in camp. "Epstein has the tools," said Ted, "he should be a great hitter." But he believed Epstein was swinging too hard. "Why the big swing?" asked Williams. He told Epstein he was trying to hit every ball 450 feet when the distance he was aiming for most of the time was only 380 feet away.

Epstein began an internship that March that would lift his game enormously, and during and after his playing career he would become one of the most ardent advocates of Williams' approach to hitting. He believes that Ted Williams had *the* greatest understandings of the rudimentary mechanics required to successfully hit a baseball. Williams broke the process down to three simple rules of hitting:

1. Let the hips lead the hands to develop torque.
2. Swing level to the ball, not to the plane of the field.
3. Stay inside the ball.

Ted Williams talked mechanics with Epstein, but he was slower to tinker with the approach of proven stars like Frank Howard. Howard believes that Williams' talent involved leaving his mechanics alone. Howard had endured two seasons of tinkering by previous managers Jim Lemon and Gil Hodges; it was understandable when Howard said that it did not make sense for Williams to try to change the swing of every player in spring training that year. For Howard, it was the extra batting practice. "Repetition is the most important part of learning to hit," said Howard, who valued the extra batting practice as much as anything else Williams provided that spring.

Every player began to take notice of the extra time in the batting cage. There had never been such long batting practice sessions as Williams held that first spring training in '69. Williams was asked after his career with the Red Sox if there was anything he would have done differently. Williams is alleged to have said, "Taken more batting practice."

Although Howard was a great hitter going into the 1969 season, Williams believed he was one of the easiest players to improve. One of the most persistent teaching methods Williams employed was needling his players into better performance. He called Howard into his office and asked him, "How can a guy hit 44 home runs but only get 48 base on balls?" Williams accused Howard of always going after that "first swifty, that first little fastball you see."

He convinced Howard he needed to learn to take a tough pitch instead of swinging at it just because he knew it would be a strike. Howard admitted to having a strike zone "from the bill of my cap to the shoelaces," but Williams got him to go deeper into counts, to get the count more in his favor before hitting, and to let the tough fastball that he would never hit go by even if it was a strike.

Williams tried not to curb Howard's aggressiveness completely, saying, "Heck, if you see one you can handle, Frank, come out of your shoes swinging at it if you want to, but take that tough strike, will you?" That was advice Howard would take often into the season to come.

Although Williams did not mess with the mechanics of the established hitters like Howard, his greatest success in 1969 was the change he wrought in Eddie Brinkman. Brinkman was the consummate good-field, no-hit short-stop. Every previous year in his career Brinkman had struggled to keep his batting average over .200. In his best two years — '63 and '66 — he had managed no higher than a lowly .229 batting average. Williams encouraged Brinkman to choke up on the bat so that he could more effectively slap the ball to all fields and to take the pitch where it was thrown by punching it into the outfield.

Brinkman had been a successful hitter before turning pro. He had played on the same Cincinnati high school team as a young Pete Rose. Though Rose would go on to hitting greatness, Brinkman was his peer with a bat in high school. Williams saw some of the old fire in Brinkman's bat and believed that his job was to restore Brinkman's confidence more than anything else. He told Brinkman to leave his glove in his locker and carry his bat with him at all times that spring.

"What he helped me with most was the mental part," said Brinkman, "not so much the physical stuff." Williams told Brinkman and everybody else, "Get a good pitch to hit. Don't swing at the bad balls." Brinkman, like Howard, credits the extra batting practice Williams provided in that first spring training in 1969. Yet it was also the intensity of it as much as the long sessions in the cage. Williams would stand by the batting cage watching Brinkman and would yell at him, imploring him to concentrate on the ball.

When Brinkman and other hitters came to the plate in game situations, they knew Williams was watching, and if nothing else, that helped them concentrate. The players agreed that "the immediate result in camp has been a unanimous effort to concentrate." As observers could see in Williams himself, focus led to enthusiasm and from there to success.

Williams was passionate about hitting, always intent on action in the batting cage, and could be counted on to critique an at-bat if some part of his teaching was being ignored. No one was safe from what John Underwood called Williams' probing interrogations. "His advice and admonitions from behind the batting cage are easily the educational highlight of the camp," wrote Underwood of Williams' approach in the spring of 1969.

Making believers of his players was relatively easy. None of them had ever seen someone with such a scientific approach to hitting. Williams is credited with saying, "In the first seven innings I always tried to hit the top half of the ball because I wanted to hit line drives, then after the seventh, I always tried to hit the bottom half for a better chance at a home run." Such statements were bewildering to his peers, and were no more enlightening to the '69 Senators. But they were indicative of the mental pictures of hitting that Williams brought to coaching the Senators, arguably the worst hitting team in the majors.

Williams believed the mental and physical war waged between pitcher and hitter in every at-bat was the mythic struggle upon which baseball's magic depended. The hitter had to command the plate, and any advantage that could be gained through study of pitchers was a necessary part of preparing for a game as a hitter. His banter in the Senators dugout was always about hitting.

"Hey, bush! What's the next pitch going to be?" Williams would demand of his players on the bench.

"Fastball" would be the reply, because it was the most likely pitch. Many hitters used the same simple logic in their approach at the plate, waiting for and guessing on the fastball.

"See, that's why you jaybirds will never learn to hit," Williams would counter, "always looking fastball."

Mike Epstein says the game of guessing pitches never ended. Years later when both he and Williams were retired from the game, just two old friends sitting in Williams' den in the Florida Keys watching a baseball game, Williams would still test him on every pitch during the game. "What's the next pitch gonna be Mike?" Williams would ask.

Epstein never understood how Williams could get a read on a pitcher and what they were throwing until much later, after those sessions with a much older and more patient Williams. But whether it was intuition or science, Williams always seemed to know, and it confounded and amazed his players.

Epstein's chance to mentor with Williams was a serendipitous event. Early in his career Epstein rocketed through the Baltimore Orioles' farm system as a much-touted minor league slugger. He was locked behind the Orioles great first baseman Boog Powell, and attempts by the Orioles to teach him to play the outfield ended in disaster. When Baltimore sent him back to the minors to start the 1967 season, Epstein refused to report, sitting out the first two months of the season. His first stroke of luck was being traded in May of '67 to the Senators, where he would catch on and slowly work his way into the lineup as a starter at first base in 1968.

Epstein's second stroke of luck came in the winter months of 1969. Senators general manager George Selkirk had all but completed a trade of Epstein and catcher Paul Casanova for Joe Torre, already an All-Star catcher with the Braves who would win the MVP award two years later at the zenith of his career. Torre would have added a much-needed bat to the Senators, especially at catcher where they had been historically weak. But Bob Short, in one of his first moves as the new general manager, nixed the deal and kept Epstein, who he believed Williams could mold into a star.

Short's failure to seek out or bring baseball knowledge to the table when serving as his own general manager began with the unconsummated Torre trade, but would continue during his tenure in Washington with disastrous results. Short was in the vanguard of businessmen owners to come, like Ted Turner and Peter Angelos, who were cocksure their business acumen was more important than the knowledge of baseball men who had played the game and evaluated talent for decades. Short continued during his years in Washington to serve as his own most trusted adviser on trades and personnel moves, often consulting no one other than Ted Williams, and often ignoring even Williams. Ultimately, it would lead Short to make one of the worst trades in baseball history.

As a rookie in 1968, Epstein hit 13 home runs in 385 at-bats, but managed only a .234 batting average. Like Brinkman, Epstein became one of Williams' key tests. Could he take an immense talent like Epstein's and shape it successfully?

There was no doubt about Epstein's talent. He had been a minor league player of the year with 37 home runs in 1966 as a first baseman for Triple-A Rochester in the Orioles system. Before that he had been a star on the '64 U.S. Olympic team. Some of Epstein's rough edges as a player had their origins in his late start as a serious baseball player. He signed a football scholarship to play at the University of California at Berkeley and ignored baseball. He was a big, strong kid playing both ways on the Cal freshman team as fullback and linebacker, never picking up a baseball bat until a chance moment in the spring of his freshman year.

Epstein and a group of Cal football players were coming back from spring workouts, walking past the field where the varsity baseball team was practicing. The Cal baseball coach noticed them and called out in a loud voice, "You know, football players aren't really athletes." The coach continued, "Heck, no. All a football player can do is grunt and keep moving forward." Looking back toward the group of baseball players he was addressing, the coach added with a nod toward Epstein, "Not one of those guys has the athleticism to hit a baseball." Epstein took the challenge and offered to hit whatever the coach could throw.

Epstein had played baseball in high school, but once in the batting cage, he couldn't hit a single one of the batting practice pitches offered by the coach, whiffing every time. On the verge of giving up, Epstein asked for one more chance. Finding his groove, he started hitting ball after ball over the fence. The astounded Cal baseball coach knew he had discovered a talent; Epstein discovered his true niche in sports. Baseball became the game Epstein grew to love for a lifetime, valuing it much, much more than football. His appreciation for football diminished over time to a level similar to that of the Cal baseball coach who challenged him one spring afternoon to take up a real game.

Epstein had great coaching along the way, playing for legendary University of Southern California coach Rod Dedeaux in the Olympics and Earl Weaver in Rochester. Yet in none of those experiences did he believe he was actually given instruction in hitting. Epstein's coaching fortunes went from rags to riches in 1969 as he began an intense tutelage with the greatest hitter ever. It was a learning experience that would continue throughout Epstein's lifetime, but it all started that spring in 1969, with Epstein, like everyone else in Williams' first camp as a manager, somewhat in awe, listening to the gentle ribbing from the great man.

"Come on, bush, get a good pitch to hit"

"Wait on the ball! Get on top of the ball!"

"What the hell are you thinking about up there, bush?"

There was amazing passion in that first spring camp in Pompano Beach, according to the players, and it flowed from a man who was doing something he had missed, something for which he had the most unique talent of any baseball player in history. And the '69 Washington Senators were the ones to whom he chose to pass that knowledge. Ted Williams, Eddie Brinkman, Frank Howard, Mike Epstein and the entire team started an affair in the spring of '69 whose ardor would not cool until the very end of that very unique season. For some, that passion would last a lifetime.

4

Going Where the
Sun Keeps Shining

Bob Short's great managerial experiment did not show immediate returns in the won-lost column. Activities heated up at the Pompano Beach complex, but spring training's first games revealed a Washington team still failing at the fundamentals, as hopeless as they had been at the close of 1968. Short's main concern, though, was not the team on the field. When the sun rose over the Atlantic Ocean each day, Short searched the horizon for a positive cash flow from his new venture. In that sense his biggest investment, Ted Williams, was showing good early returns.

Although the crowds at the little Pompano stadium were not impressive, the media were everywhere; never had such attention been devoted to the Senators' baseball fortunes in Florida. The press was bent to the plough behind conventional story lines that wondered whether Ted Williams would be able to control the frustrations of dealing with a cellar-dwelling team or would it drive him nuts? The gaggle of writers following him in Pompano watched for signs that the pressure was building, the boiler was about to blow, but there was little of that. Instead, the reports were about a passionate and energetic Williams working hard with his new team. Writers were starting to ask a different question: "Could Ted Williams teach the game of baseball to a bunch of major league ne'er-do-wells? Could he make something of them?" In the end it was a more compelling story line.

With the exhibition games in the Grapefruit League going full-tilt in the third week of March, the Senators had lost eight straight and had only a single win to show for almost a dozen games in the book. Williams dismissed it all as meaningless. Frank Howard's holdout for more money kept him out of camp the first few weeks and out of the lineup. He then developed nagging injuries that limited his playing time and was not sharp even as March wore on. He did not hit a home run in the spring exhibition games until the last weekend before Opening Day. The Senators' anemic offense was ghastly without Howard, who towered above the other players in every sense.

Yet nothing seemed to get Williams off the task at hand. He was unperturbed by the contract negotiations with Howard, the losing streak or the non-existent offense. He shrugged off the games as he focused on getting the best mix of players on the field and getting those players to perform at the highest possible level. Williams said after two weeks of spring training, "The kids are trying. They are really working hard."

Epstein was still struggling at the plate, hitting into double plays and flailing with runners aboard. Despite apparent ineptitude, progress was slowly surfacing. One reason Epstein looked so bad was that he was coming up with runners on base more often. Williams' favorite sermon about patience at the plate, taking pitches and getting the best pitch to hit was beginning to have an effect.

Though the hitting was still weak, the Senators were having better at-bats, seeing more pitches, and getting more bases on balls in the early games. The story was the number of men being left on base, but the belief was that Howard — known as "Hondo" from his minor league playing days — would start hitting home runs and the problem would solve itself.

Williams was teaching a more patient approach at a time when baseball was changing. Umpires were calling a smaller strike zone, and pitchers were adjusting to a new mound. The results each batter could see at the plate may have come from changes major league baseball had introduced. While the umpires were tighter with their strikes, it was hitters who were patient at the plate and willing to take the walk who were benefiting. Williams' ideas opened his players' eyes to the ways to gain from the rule changes. Although the timing of Williams' message and the strike zone change may have been a coincidence, the players were seeing results from Williams' approach. Confidence grew as the words of the great teacher bore fruit, and confidence was what Williams believed many of the Washington hitters needed most.

In the months to come, analysts who noted Williams' efforts with the Senators' offense would point out the rise in batting averages as the most common refrain. "Every player on the team hit for a higher average," they would say. A closer examination of Washington's offensive statistics provides the first kernel of a more complex story, one that affected not only the Senators, but all of baseball. It starts with the changes wrought by Ted Williams in his first year of managing. The table below details several key statistics for Washington's regular lineup that started the '69 season in Pompano with Williams.

TABLE 4-1. SELECTED BATTING INDICATORS FOR
SENATORS 1969 OFFENSIVE REGULARS WHO
STARTED SEASON IN POMPANO BEACH

	1968		1969		BAvg	OBP
Name	BAvg	OBP	BAvg	OBP	Increase	Increase
Bernie Allen	.241	.301	.247	.337	.06	.36
Hank Allen	.219	.265	.277	.312	.58	.47
Brant Alyea	.267	.317	.249	.346	-.18	.29
Eddie Brinkman	.187	.259	.266	.330	.79	.71
Paul Casanova	.196	.213	.216	.257	.20	.44
Tim Cullen	.230	.296	.209	.257	-.21	-.39
Mike Epstein	.234	.339	.278	.416	.44	.77
Jim French	.194	.281	.184	.352	-.10	.71
Frank Howard	.274	.340	.296	.402	.22	.62
Ken McMullen	.248	.327	.272	.354	.24	.27
Ed Stroud	.239	.285	.252	.353	.13	.68
Del Unser	.230	.284	.286	.351	.56	.69
All Senator Hitters	.224	.289	.251	.332	.27	.43
American League	.230	.299	.246	.323	.16	.24

Comparing the numbers for each hitter tells only part of the tale. It is the change in the league overall, evident in the 1969 totals at the bottom of the chart, that gives the first indications of the new direction major league baseball was mapping. The almost uniform rise in on-base percentage of every Senators player demonstrated an improved approach at the plate. The extra batting practice, the needling around the batting cage, and the increased focus of batters like Brinkman were all paying clear dividends. Instead of being well below the league average, the team was above the average, going from next-to-last in hitting in 1968 to tied for third in the league in batting average in 1969.

The rise in on-base-percentage for Washington's offense and its individual players is often overlooked. The 1969 Senators were fourth in the league in on-base-percentage. More than Howard's home runs, it was the additional men on base that led to the team's increase in runs scored. In fact, the Senators added more than one whole run per game in 1969 compared to 1968. They went from a weak 3.25 runs per game in '68 to an almost lusty 4.28 in 1969. Compared to the league average, it was a remarkable turnabout for any team, but for largely the same group of players who had played the year before, the transformation was astounding.

The data in Table 4.1 reveals almost every player hit for a higher average than in the previous year. But for those that did not, even they showed greater patience at the plate and consequently increased their on-base percentage. It is fair to ask, however, given the overall increase in hitting for the league as a whole and the changes in the game to favor the hitter, are the changes as notable as many have stated over the years?

What cannot be disputed is the change in key individuals in the Washington lineup. The heart-of-the-order hitters — McMullen, Epstein and Howard — made a remarkable turnaround in their approach at the plate. What had been a weak middle of the lineup for the Senators in 1968 became a powerful one that pitchers were careful when pitching to. The transformation of the Washington sluggers can be fairly credited to Williams, the greatest slugger of all-time.

The other key hitters in the lineup, those who got on base ahead of the sluggers, Eddie Brinkman, Del Unser, Ed Stroud, and Hank Allen, all improved significantly in almost every hitting category. It was a career year for Brinkman. Hank Allen was not an everyday player and would never have a year like '69 again. Del Unser achieved success for the first time under Williams, and it would carry forward for his successful 15-year career in the majors.

The most noteworthy statistical differences in the chart are those for Epstein and Howard. Howard, the very good hitter at the middle of the Senators lineup, became a great hitter in 1969. Williams' early meeting in his office and ongoing coaching paid very big dividends for the "Capitol Punisher," as he was called by the writers. Howard's increase in batting average is probably outside the normal swing of change from year to year that a player may experience.

Early in his career, Howard had hit for better average and less power. But as his early coaches in Los Angeles tinkered with his swing, he became more accomplished as a slugger; he concentrated more on hitting for distance. He saw hitting as an either/or choice he had to make. Either he hit for power or he hit for average, and as a big man from whom slugging was expected, it made sense to focus on hitting the long ball. Williams taught Howard that he could have both; he could hit for power and for average, and as a bonus, he could get on base more often. He could do it by being more selective at the plate, getting better pitches to hit, and "coming out of his shoes" when he did.

The change in Howard and other players reflect the constant nagging of Williams around the batting cage to "get a good pitch to hit, bush." They reflect his dugout sessions emphasizing the need to anticipate and concentrate on what the pitcher will throw. Howard had an on-base percentage of .402 in 1969, a 60-point jump and exactly the figure Williams had in mind

when he called Howard into his office in the spring and told him that anyone who could hit 44 homers should be getting twice as many walks.

Howard was a proven hitter, but the changes Williams wrought elsewhere — with Epstein and Brinkman — created success that had never been
there. Epstein became a legitimate major league hitter for the first time in
1969 while working with Williams. He would take the lessons to heart for
several years to come, playing on the Oakland A's world championship team
in 1972, and remaining a devotee of Ted Williams' hitting techniques his
entire life.

While Ted Williams' influence on the Senators' offensive production
drew praise from everyone and made Bob Short beam, the phenomena was
not limited to the hitters. As anemic as the run production had been in 1968,
the pitching had been worse still. It ranked at the bottom of the American
League, and no one was even close. In the "year of the pitcher" in '68, the
Senator staff had the worst team ERA in the American League. With the
league ERA at the unfathomable level of 2.98 earned runs per nine innings,
the Senators could manage a team ERA of only 3.64. If they had been that
bad pitching from an elevated mound, then elemental fear might have been
a reasonable emotion as they trudged to the new lowered mound in 1969.

It made sense to believe that Williams might improve the hitting around
the edges, but the Splendid Splinter never much liked pitchers and was
thought by many to be clueless on the subject. In the spring of '69 Williams
said if he had his way, there would be so many pitchers in camp for batting
practice that the hitters would get tired of hitting. Williams saw pitching as
just a necessary evil to hitting.

Jim Hannan, who would pitch in 1969 as the number three starter in
the Senators rotation, saw it differently, as did Frank Howard. Both men
came to understand that Williams was as good at handling the pitching staff
as he was the hitters. Joe DiMaggio concurred that spring as well, saying "I
don't think too many people realize it, but he studied pitchers and pitching
just as intently as he did hitters and hitting." Williams' study of Washington pitching and pitchers began with evaluating what he had going into the
'69 season.

In '68, a 34-year-old Camilo Pascual had one of his better seasons with
a record of 13 wins and 12 losses for the cellar-dwelling Senators and an ERA
of 2.69. Pascual had been the mainstay of the last Senators team that left
town in 1960, going to Minnesota. As a Minnesota Twin, Pascual had back-
to-back twenty-win seasons. He had been traded back to Washington after
injuries sidelined him in '65 and '66, but after throwing more than 200 innings
in '68, Williams could hope he had the anchor for the rotation in Pascual.

The number two starter turned out to be a young, hard-throwing kid from Boston named Joe Coleman. Coleman had broken into the major leagues at age eighteen late in the 1965 season. Like most power pitchers in their youth, Coleman struggled with his control, and over two minor league seasons at York, Pennsylvania, of the Eastern League, he showed only marginal improvement. But the Senators had few options, and late in '67 Coleman was summoned to the major leagues for good to hone his craft in that most demanding of venues.

Coleman was the hardest thrower on the team with a great fastball, called "the hummer" by teammates. He also featured a solid curve and a change-up, standard repertoire for the high-mound era. Coleman's first full season in the majors was 1968, and he pitched well, but was only twenty-one years of age and still learning his craft. It was the state of Senators pitching at the beginning of the 1969 season that the best Washington had to offer came from a 35-year-old veteran with a history of recent injury and a 22-year-old still very much feeling his way.

Williams knew the young Joe Coleman. Coleman's father was a big-league pitcher of the same World War II generation as Williams. The elder Coleman had sent his son to Williams' baseball camps in New England — the ones run by Senators coach Joe Camacho. Williams in 1969 had two new things to teach Coleman. The first was to throw a slider, which Coleman refused to do at first, and the second was to throw fewer innings in a game, which Coleman fought against as well. Coleman and Williams were a generation gap in reverse, with the younger man clinging to the time-worn approach and his manager, the fifty-year-old World War II veteran, insisting that he give new ideas a chance.

Though Coleman was young, he believed himself to be following in the footsteps of the great pitchers before him, those of his father's generation who pitched nine-inning complete games whenever they could. But those days were gone. The lowering of the mound and the diminishing size of the strike zone made those great pitchers dinosaurs from a distant past.

The change in the world of pitching in 1969 was as radical as the new astrophysics being taught on college campuses that year. Lowering the mound five inches meant that pitchers were confronting a new physical reality, and the change, according to Washington starting pitcher Jim Hannan, was a significant one. William Leggett, writing for *Sports Illustrated* early that year, said the lowering of the mound might have an effect as profound as "lowering the net in tennis." In typical analytic fashion, Williams said of the mound change that it meant a "5½ percent difference in hitting." Williams had calculated the difference for an overhand pitcher 76 inches tall and the reduction of five inches. He estimated the difference in the angle of delivery would be directly proportional to the change in hitting.

Pitchers were more articulate in assessing the damage. Larry Moffett, the Cardinal pitching coach, believed, "It is going to take a lot of work for some people to get used to this new mound." Gaylord Perry of the Giants discovered he had to make adjustments immediately to his delivery to compensate for the reduction in height. He believed, though, that pitching from a lower angle would help, and that pitchers who pitched from a three-quarters motion would be less affected. Larry Shepard, the Pittsburgh Pirates manager, said it was resulting in pitchers throwing the ball high. Moffett agreed that his pitchers were struggling to adapt. Pitchers around both leagues were remarking on the change and were troubled by the lower strike zone and the reduction in the mound's height, both of which were causing havoc in their approach as they started the season in 1969.

Pitchers use the downward slope of the mound to gain leverage. As their front leg drives down the slope of the mound, it allows them to push hard off the stiff rubber behind them. The arm follows, coming over the top, and the additional slope of the mound provides a longer follow-through and greater leverage. Some pitchers threw from a side-arm or three-quarters arm slot. They tended to work down in the zone anyway and were not as affected by the change, but that approach was not as dominating in the pre–'69 pitching world as the big overhand pitcher who threw hard.

The great pitchers of the early 1960s were more likely to look like Juan Marichal or Sandy Koufax, whose exaggerated leg kicks allowed them to thrust forward their long leading leg far down the slope of the mound as they pushed off. The effect was to gain enormous leverage and force as they torqued the ball down from a tall overhand position. The greater the drop-off to the mound, the further the leading leg goes down the hill and the greater the torque added by the finishing rotation of the pitcher's body.

Mike Epstein, who has studied hitting techniques since leaving the game, believes that lowering the mound gave the hitter a bigger advantage than most understood in 1969. He believes that it led to a whole new approach in pitching that has evolved over the last few decades. Pitchers lost some of what they called "tilt." The search to regain the extra downward movement of the ball as it flashed through the hitting zone ultimately led them to experiment with different pitches, different arm angles, anything that could give them the advantage they enjoyed with the higher mound, anything to get back what Mike Epstein called the old "tilt."

Jim Hannan described the higher mound as adding "more spin and better leverage" on pitches such as big overhand curves. It added more force as well, causing the late break to be sharper on other pitches. Gaylord Perry admitted that it was his curve that seemed most affected by the lowering of the mound. He said in the early months of that year it was harder to get his curve to drop through the strike zone. Mickey Lolich blamed his arm problems that year on the change.

Hannan said it was not as though the curve lost a full five inches from its break, "but the old curves broke off sharper, there is no doubt about that. There was just more downward motion in the strike zone." The bigger arc to the curve put more stress on the batter to track the break across the strike zone. The new lower mound put the stress on the pitcher to find a way to get that extra break on the ball back. That search for the advantages lost in 1969 would change pitching for decades.

The changes in the defensive aspects of the game created by the lower mound were exacerbated by the change in the strike zone mandated by the rules committee. Pitchers in 1969 confronted a new reality that was just beginning to be understood, but the struggle to adapt to the change would last for many years. Over the decades it would produce consequences that were unforeseen by the rules committee.

An important but unintended result of lowering the mound was the increasingly watchful efforts by baseball officials to keep the mound heights uniform in every ballpark. Before the rule change, little attention was paid to the height of each team's pitching mound. Some teams had opted for even higher mounds. It was conventional wisdom that teams like the Dodgers, who depended on great pitchers like Koufax and Drysdale, allowed their groundskeepers to set the pitching rubber at the top of the mound even higher, perhaps as much as four to five inches higher. Stan Musial estimated that the Dodgers mound may have been as high as 25 inches during his playing days. Each additional inch of height the Dodger pitchers were given increased the speed of the pitches thrown and the tilt on the breaking pitch as it planed downward through the strike zone.

The rule changes produced improved batting and power statistics in 1969 and beyond, which did not go unnoticed by baseball experts. Over time scouts, managers, and coaches looked for ways to change the equation back toward the pitcher any way they could. Scouts began to look for taller pitchers. In the first six decades of the twentieth century, baseball hurlers were of average height. Clark Griffith and other early pitchers were short. In the middle of the twentieth century, pitchers without notable height, such as Eddie Lopat (5'10"), Bobby Shantz (5'6"), Elroy Face (5'8") and Whitey Ford (5'10") achieved considerable success.

With the lowering of the mound, short pitchers — those significantly under six feet in height — almost disappeared from the game, as the conventional wisdom became that a pitcher had to be over six-feet tall, and the taller the better. The idea was that adding the five inches taken from the mound to the height of the pitcher would get the old edge back. The more height added to the pitcher, the closer to the old point of release from the higher mound and the better the chance to get the tilt back.

The other compensation was to add to the advantage in the pitches thrown. Pitchers began to throw more sliders — the pitch that bothered Ted Williams the most. The slider moved across the plate, but a good slider had later and sharper downward movement. Off the new mound, the more late, downward movement a pitch had, the more deceptive it was to the batter. Sinking fastballs could add downward motion back into the equation, as could forkballs and split-finger fastballs. After 1969, the repertoire of pitchers expanded considerably over time as they searched for ways to regain the advantage that Marichal, Koufax and the great pitchers of a bygone era got with their long first step down the higher pitching mound, generating the big overhand rotation that created more force and greater speed and tilt.

Many of the new pitches added unusual torque to the arm of the thrower, creating significant stress to the pitcher's joints, specifically the shoulder and elbow. The additional stress resulted in more frequent injuries. Teams began to structure their pitching completely differently. Teams cut back on the number of innings a pitcher threw each time out and the number of times they pitched during the season. The effect was to significantly lower the number of innings a pitcher threw each year of his career.

The effect on teams was a need to spread the total innings of the season over a larger group of pitchers. Teams went from what was at times a four-man starting rotation to a five-man rotation as the norm. Relief pitchers were taking a larger role in 1969, but after that season, the role of relief specialist became increasingly more prominent.

Joe Coleman wanted to emulate the pitchers from his father's generation who threw 300 or more innings each year. The '69 Senators were moving into an era when only the best pitchers would exceed 200 innings each year, and even those were likely to incur injuries that would limit the number of years they reached that new benchmark. The standard of three hundred innings for a pitcher over the course of the season disappeared during the next decade. The number of starts possible for a member of the rotation went from forty to the low thirties. Complete games, which during the 1950s and '60s were commonplace, almost completely disappeared by end of the 1980s. For each year after 1969, the number of pitchers achieving the old high watermarks in strikeouts, innings, and complete games diminished.

The first indications of change show up in 1969, and they are not inconsequential. The effects of the lower mound height and reduced strike zone in '69 can be seen most decisively in the average number of runs scored per game that year. The average number of runs scored per game in the American League went from 6.81 in '68 to 8.18 in '69. That is a 1.37 runs per game difference in one year. Some have argued that the expansion of the league diluted the talent in the league and accounted for the rise. But expansion in 1961 had seen a far less dramatic increase, with average runs increasing only .3 runs per game.

Baseball set out to juice the game in 1969. The only surprise might be how quickly the change occurred. The lower mound and smaller strike zone may have been helped by a talent pool diluted by expansion. Teams like the White Sox, who moved in the fences and added artificial infield turf, helped the hitters as well. There is no denying that the effects in 1969 were cumulative. But regardless of where the greatest emphasis is placed, there was a measurable increase in offensive production in 1969.

The edge to the hitter that baseball had sought was obvious in every area of the game, including the reduced number of shutouts (the bugaboo that had Shirley Povich wincing before the '69 season began), the number of runs scored, and the number of home runs hit. Like an election with stuffed ballot boxes, the increased advantage to the hitter could be seen early and often. It was there in the statistics at the end of the first month and at the end of the year.

In the American League alone — the junior circuit unable to score a single run in the '68 All-Star Game — there were 545 more home runs hit in '69 than the prior year. Even discounting the 225 hit by the two expansion teams, there were more than 300 additional home runs hit in the American League. The National League saw sharp increases as well, though less dramatic. In both leagues there was more offense for the fans to see, and there would be more fans to see them. The equation worked, though it would take time to win back the fans who had grown bored.

The compelling point is that as this offensive juggernaut was launching, Ted Williams' pitching staff was improving. At a time when pitching statistics overall were declining precipitously, the Senators found the strike zone and did so consistently. The overall earned run average (ERA) for the American League went from 2.98 in 1968 to 3.62 in 1969. The Senators staff ERA went from 3.64 in 1968, the worst in the league, to 3.49 in 1969 — fifth-best among the twelve teams that year.

The strike zone was reduced in '69 as well, which compounded the lowering of the mound. No longer would the letter-high fastball be a strike, nor would the picture of the great hitters in full stride swinging at it be a baseball postcard. In 1969 batters would garner more bases on balls, walking eleven times for every hundred at-bats, as opposed to nine times per hundred at-bats in '68. Pitchers had struck out hitters 18 times per hundred at-bats in '68, but would manage only 16 times per hundred at-bats in 1969.

The odds were tipping in the batters' favor in each at-bat, ever so slightly, but with remarkable overall results.

It was as if in 1969 the baseball gods decided to lean on the playing field that had been tipped in the favor of the pitcher in order to tip it back toward the batter. The game of football with its constant exciting action was posing a threat to what had been America's pastime for three-quarters of a century. The baseball gods wanted a more exciting game, and they took an important first step in 1969 to that end.

It was into this new and more offensive-minded baseball world that Ted Williams ventured in 1969, probably unknowingly. He was teaching patience at the plate in a year that umpires were squeezing pitchers and the strike zone. It was not surprising that he achieved significant success in getting his batters to take advantage of those new directions. Yet it is more compelling that a manager so gifted in teaching hitting could affect similar positive changes in his pitching staff. More intriguing is how the approach Williams advocated fit so well into the new paradigm. Teaching his pitchers to throw the slider with its additional tilt would be a first step in the direction baseball would take for the next four decades.

TABLE 4-2. SENATORS 1969 PITCHERS
(WITH MORE THAN 50 INNINGS PITCHED)

Name	Innings Pitched 1968	1969	ERA 1968	1969	Strikeouts to Walks 1968	1969
Dave Baldwin	42.0	67.0	4.07	4.03	12/34	34/51
Dick Bosman	139.0	193.0	3.69	2.19	63/35	99/39
Joe Coleman	223.0	247.2	3.27	3.27	51/139	100/182
Casey Cox	7.2	171.2	2.35	2.78	0/4	64/73
Jim Hannan	140.1	158.1	3.01	3.64	35/63	39/99
Dennis Higgins	100.0	85.0	3.24	3.49	46/56	56/71
Bob Humphreys	92.2	79.2	3.69	3.05	30/56	38/43
Darold Knowles**	41.1	84.1	2.18	2.24	12/37	31/59
Barry Moore	117.2	134.0	3.37	4.30	42/56	67/51
Camilo Pascual	201.0	55.0	2.69	6.87	59/111	38/34
Jim Shellenback**	N/A	84.2	N/A	4.04	N/A	48/50
Senators Totals	1440	1447.1	3.64	3.49	826/517	835/657
American League			2.98	3.62	9634/4881 (2-to-1)	8988/5819* (1.5-to-1)

*Statistics for Kansas City and Seattle — the expansion teams — are withheld to maintain a constant baseline of the same ten teams for both 1968 and 1969.

**Darold Knowles did not join the team until May 1969, and Jim Shellenback joined the team in late April from Pittsburgh.

The chart on page 44 provides a glimpse of how the pitching changes affected each member of the Washington staff in 1969. The changes in work load — innings pitched, the number of runs allowed (ERA), and the strike-outs-to-walks comparisons — give good insight into how the Senators pitchers fared in adapting to the new mound and new strike zone.

For most of the Washington pitching staff, the changes are not as arresting as with the hitters, and some of the numbers suggest the pitchers were heading in the wrong direction. Joe Coleman's ERA remained constant, but his overall walk total would double in 1969 from the previous year. As a young hurler projecting himself into his father's world of pitching, looking to achieve what the great pitchers of that era had done, he was not able to adapt as quickly to the demands of a new era. In addition to Coleman initially balking at throwing the slider, the changing strike zone was one reason he had a noticeably higher number of bases on balls.

In his defense, no other pitcher on the staff relied more on the big overhand fastball and curve. He used a repertoire of pitches most diminished by the lower mound. More experienced pitchers like Lolich and Perry stated at the beginning of the season their own problems with the change. However, while veteran pitchers were able to adapt, Coleman's strides as a young pitcher slowed in '69 as he learned to experiment with new pitches and a new strike zone. His strikeouts were up noticeably as he learned how to pitch, but as they say, the walks will kill you.

The rest of the staff did improve, however, and that can be understood only in comparison to the league as a whole and the falloff in pitching stats overall in 1969. The Senators pitchers went from being the worst pitching team in the league in '68 to a more respectable fifth overall in '69. It is a notable feat and attributable to the large turnaround of two players, Casey Cox and Dick Bosman. Like the impacts Williams had on Brinkman and Howard, the emergence of Bosman and Cox would offset many of the problems that the Senators pitching staff would face in '69.

Bosman and Cox came out of the Senators bullpen, and it was here that Williams made great strides as an innovator in 1969. Believing that his starting rotation was weak, Williams devised a strategy to limit the damage they could do. He began to suggest early in spring training that he would not take his starters as deep into ballgames, as tradition dictated. He was hoping to find capable arms that spring, but the pickings were sparse. He needed a strong bullpen to underwrite his theories, but he was unsure whether the pitchers on hand were up to the task.

There was a notable problem in the bullpen. Darold Knowles was the best reliever the Senators had and was unavailable to start the season. He remained on active duty with the Air Force in Japan, where he spent most of the '68 season. Patching together something until Knowles returned required Williams to evaluate a group of what he called "soft tossers."

The reliever of the greatest importance was Dennis Higgins, who had filled the shoes of Knowles when he departed in '68. Higgins was a veteran pitcher who had knocked around the minors for almost a decade before sticking with the White Sox in 1966. Coming to the Senators in '68, he took the opportunity to sub for Knowles and used it to carve a solid niche for himself, saving thirteen games and posting a respectable 3.25 ERA over ninety-nine innings of steady relief.

Much of the bullpen was young and had limited major league experience. Bosman was only twenty-five and had a little more than a year under his belt as a major leaguer. He stuck for the first time in the majors with Washington in '67. In '68 he proved an invaluable swing man, starting 10 games, but pitching more as a long reliever and notching 139 innings. The other candidates for the bullpen included the 26-year-old Barry Moore, who as a left-hander was a rare commodity for Williams' staff. As Williams cast about for the necessary pitching parts to start the season, he was most in need of a lefty in the starting rotation and in the bullpen.

In 1969 Casey Cox was a twenty-eight-year-old right-hander with almost no major league experience. He was joined in the bullpen by two veteran journeyman pitchers, Bob Humphreys and Dave Baldwin. They could be counted on to eat innings in relief. Humphreys was especially durable since he threw a knuckleball, but he had been inconsistent over the course of his long major league service. Cox would start thirteen games as well and would have the best season of his short career.

The only other bullpen pitcher to make the team out of spring training was Frank Kreutzer, who would be gone in the first weeks of the season, traded for Jim Shellenback. Shellenback was the big left-hander that Williams knew he needed. Only twenty-six and with limited major league experience, he would get his baptism by fire with Washington in '69, and along with Humphrey and Baldwin, would provide important depth to Williams' pitching staff. It was a staff that would undergo changes during the season, not so much in personnel as in the roles each was expected to play.

The starting rotation Williams was evaluating in the spring of 1969 had no more proven commodities than the bullpen. Pascual was the certainty as a starter. For a veteran like Pascual, the changes in the strike zone and the lowering of the mound may have been more than he could handle. In the spring Pascual said he was "having trouble forcing my arm and body down into the ball" because of the mound difference. He said, "It isn't so much a matter of getting stuff on the ball so much as getting oomph." Pascual would have considerably more difficulty finding the "oomph" in 1969.

Behind him were talented youngsters like Coleman and smart young pitchers like Hannan. Jim Hannan, described by *Washington Star* columnist Bob Addie as a freckled "Huck Finn, aw shucks" type who eschewed the limelight, had established himself as a member of the rotation in 1968. He was a ten-game winner with one of the better ERAs on the staff at 3.01. A smart player too, Hannan was a graduate of Notre Dame, taking an uncommon route to the majors for that era.

The other member of the projected starting rotation was Frank Bertaina, a left-hander who had come over with Epstein from Baltimore. Bertaina had great minor league numbers at Triple-A Rochester, but had no track record of success in the majors. Given the shortage of good lefties, he was given every opportunity to fail.

Williams believed from his experience that hitters gained an advantage against pitchers the more times they saw them during the game. Bringing in a fresh arm in the sixth or seventh inning could limit the exposure and the damage. It would become an increasingly conventional approach within baseball over the next decade, with all pitchers cutting back on their overall innings and the frequency of their starts. Teams would expand their starting rotations from four to five pitchers to limit the work on their starters as well as the stress on arms proving increasingly fragile.

With pitchers throwing more breaking pitches, putting greater stress on their arms with each pitch, fewer starts and fewer innings were a logical answer to a growing conundrum. The end result over time — the next two decades — was that every major league team employed the same strategy as Ted Williams introduced in 1969. Williams began immediately in the spring of 1969 to press his pitchers to throw the slider, a pitch that would help them in the search for the old tilt.

The pitchers thrived as they fit into Williams' new scheme and started to put emphasis on his pitch of choice, the slider. But more than anything, they did what Casey Cox did, who said, "I just listened to everything he said to the hitters and turned it around. If this was the situation they wanted to create, the 2–0, 3–1 count, then it was the situation I wanted to avoid. The important thing was to throw strikes." The needling, the constant reprimands to focus when in the game, all of Ted Williams' work with the hitters affected the pitching staff as well, just an equal and opposite one.

Williams did not look consciously to add tilt back for his pitchers when he expanded their repertoire to include the slider. Nor did he knowingly anticipate the future in looking for a deeper bullpen and fewer innings for his starters. He was simply looking for ways to compete with the meager cards he was dealt. As a hitter Williams was seldom ahead of the curveball.

He was always able to wait on the pitch because he could pick up the spin on the ball with what many considered to be the best eyes in baseball. As a manager in 1969, he was way out in front of the tactical curve, teaching his players to adapt to a changing environment before most recognized anything dramatic was afoot.

5

Do You Want to
Know a Secret?

Maybe it was Frank Howard's first homer of the spring on March 27. Maybe it was the 10–6 thumping of the Astros that followed a game later. Or maybe it was getting Ken McMullen healthy. Whatever the reason, suddenly the hits were coming in bunches. The hitters who had been struggling to find their rhythm were walking to the plate with greater confidence as spring training wound to a close.

McMullen had been the starting third baseman for Washington since coming over from the Dodgers with Frank Howard to start the '65 season. Nearly every day since the trade, he and Howard had been the heart of the Washington lineup, and for most of the time McMullen was the only other power source in the Senators lineup to complement Hondo. In 1968 he had his best year with 20 home runs, and as the team broke camp, it looked like he could be counted on again.

There were signs up and down the starting lineup that Ted Williams' lessons were having an effect. The cumulative batting average for the regular season starters during spring training was nearing .300, and Williams was expressing optimism. The pitchers were beginning to show signs of hope as well. Coleman went six innings and was almost untouchable in one of his last starts of the spring, followed by Bosman, who was equally sharp. Camilo Pascual had an ERA under two, though some observers were concerned that he had not hit his stride yet. Del Unser had a 15-game hitting streak going, and everyone was showing signs of coming around.

Several of Ted Williams' rookie favorites, Jim Mason and Jack Jenkins in particular, were part of the final roster trimming as the team readied to leave its modest Pompano Beach home to head north for the final exhibition games of the preseason. Williams was mulling how to platoon his players to get the most out of what had been a weak hitting crew in '68. Ed Stroud and Hank Allen looked to be the platoon in right field, and Tim Cullen and Bernie Allen the platoon at second base. Although Williams was impressed with the progress Mike Epstein had made in the spring, he was concerned about the player's ability to handle left-handed pitching. His thought was to let Frank Howard play first base and sit the young slugger Epstein against lefties.

The *Washington Post* announced a "big four" rotation of Pascual, Coleman, Bertaina, and Hannan, and it appeared the pieces were starting to fit together. The last day in Florida was trademark Ted Williams when a long session of extra batting practice was held for the regulars who would be making the trip.

It had been an exciting spring, one that energized the players. The excitement had spread to the hometown fans and writers in Washington who were hopeful that despite the rough going in the first few weeks, a better team was emerging. The Washington papers were touting last-minute changes and trade talks.

Perhaps the most fortuitous moment of the 1969 season came when attempts to trade Frank Howard to Cleveland were nixed by Bob Short. Williams began to see promise in the four-for-one trade being proposed by the Indians. Ted was formally the vice president of the Senators and was in charge of most of the baseball moves, all the way down to the hiring of the new Buffalo manager, Hector Lopez. He was the only sounding board Short had on trades, but this time he was wrong, and grateful fans were happy to see Williams overruled.

Short was easily talked out of the trade because he was busy elsewhere. The papers back home were giving vent to the hue and cry of fans whose ticket prices were being hiked by as much as twenty-five percent. Short was launching a new marketing campaign — "It's a Whole New Ballgame." He was fighting a two-front war, trying to wrestle lucrative parking fees and concessions away from others and defending his ticket hikes against the press and patrons.

Part of Short's argument on parking was that the area around the stadium was unsafe and that increased security was needed, something the Stadium Armory Board, which controlled the stadium and its parking lots, could not afford. The need for additional safety would become a recurring rant for Short; it was a fair concern. The sharp reductions in attendance in '68 were attributed by many to the riots and public perceptions that the city was not as safe as before. Because ticket sales just prior to the season were brisk, the concern drew some skepticism in the press.

At the end of 1968 with the announcement of the sale imminent, Short had been quoted as saying, "I'm not committed to keeping the team in Washington if D.C. Stadium is not made safe for the fans." Some atmospheric change was accomplished when the stadium was renamed to honor Senator Robert F. Kennedy in January. The Armory Board relented on most of Short's demands about safety leading up to Opening Day, yet he continued to growl about safety, leaving his motivations as an open question.

Local writers took note of a spring scheduling change as the team prepared to leave Florida. The final two spring training games were exhibitions that for several years had been played in Louisville, Kentucky, but suddenly they were shifted to a new location — Dallas, Texas. Dallas was one of three cities that had been unsuccessful finalists in the contest in 1968 to land one of the expansion franchises that went to Montreal, Seattle, San Diego and Kansas City. It was therefore not surprising that it was one of two cities named early on by Short as possible relocation sites when grousing about safety and lack of fan support at D.C. Stadium. Those who were paying attention saw the connection immediately. Although a damp field was the official explanation, *Washington Star* writer Merrell Whittlesey raised the red flag first among the home crowd. He asked in his daily column whether Washington fans would tolerate a threat to move the Senators before there was any chance for fans to demonstrate their support for Ted Williams and the improved team he was promising to put on the field.

The exhibition games in Texas were a bust. The crowds that showed up on relatively "short" notice were scant, and the Senators lost them both after a string of winning games ended the Grapefruit League season in Florida. In the first game Frank Bertaina was roughed up by the Pirates, costing him his position in the starting rotation. Williams demoted him to the bullpen and announced a shift to Jim Hannan to start the third game of the season against the Yankees.

The Senators ended the exhibition season with a dismal record of eight wins and 19 losses. But spring exhibition records were forgotten in the excitement as the team arrived in Washington. Hopes were still high that Ted Williams could pull off some form of magic with the Senators, and for the Washington press corps Williams' celebrity status got almost as much ink as the royal family in the London tabloids.

The official opening of the 1969 baseball season was set for April 7. Washington would host the Yankees for the Presidential Opener. The tradition was for the president of the United States to throw out the first pitch of the season, often in Washington, D.C. It was "America's Game," after all, and the honor that year fell to the new president, Richard Nixon. The program for the game being hawked at the front gate to souvenir-minded fans had a compelling cover, featuring the face of Ted Williams grinning ear to ear in his new Senators uniform and bright red hat, with the words, "Welcome back to baseball" as the title.

During the pre-game warm-ups, Nixon was sitting in Bob Short's field-level box seats, ready for the pageantry. More than anything, he was waiting to see Ted Williams, beaming like a kid at his first game. Nixon had lettered in varsity football for tiny Whittier College, played basketball, and run track. Although he had not a kernel of athletic talent, according to his fellow students, he brought boundless school spirit to the games. Nixon's enthusiasm for sports remained undiminished, and he transferred that fervor to Washington during his long years in Congress and as the vice-president. As much as anything, the new president was a fan of the new manager, Ted Williams.

Williams made no secret of his conservative bent in political matters, and was frank with Bob Short about his aversion to Hubert Humphrey and his support for Richard Nixon. A baseball legend and a war hero, Williams was larger than life, even for the president. The start of the baseball season also provided an opportunity to shift the focus away from troubling and sad events that had occupied the president and the nation in the run-up to the beginning of the baseball season.

Former president and World War II hero Dwight Eisenhower had died only days before the Senators' home opener. At the service Nixon had eulogized the man who had vaulted him into national prominence. Eisenhower had not always been an avid supporter of Nixon, so there was some irony in the passing of the torch of leadership from the beloved war hero who had brought the Republican Party back from its nadir of popularity when he was elected president in 1952. Eisenhower won that election on a campaign pledge to end the Korean War and had eschewed American involvement in Vietnam when pressured by the French after their defeat at Dien Bien Phu in 1954.

Now Nixon was the hope for peace in a new era, not just a peaceful end to a dreadful war, but peace in American cities, peace as an end to the social upheaval of 1968 — riots after the death of Martin Luther King, the long hot summer foretold by King, and the riots at the Democratic Convention. Nixon referred to his supporters as the "silent majority." They were Americans "who viewed the scene of the sixties with disquiet, fear, bewilderment or disgust," and who "cried out for the return to stability, respect for authority, and the primacy of traditional values." Ted Williams was solidly in the Nixon camp, regardless of what it was called.

Opposite: Richard Nixon's first pitch lofted high into the air. Library of Congress, Prints & Photographs Division, U.S. News & World Report Magazine Collection, LC-USZ62-106488.

The mood of the country that April did not match the cheery smiles beaming from the dignitaries that day at RFK Stadium. A new spring offensive by the communists in Vietnam shouted from the headlines, "GI War Toll Highest in Ten Months" and "Reds Burst into American Base, Kill 21." Nixon's early attempts to get the Russians involved in brokering a peace agreement — his secret plan — was unraveling. Nixon underestimated the independence of Ho Chi Minh from his Russian sponsors and did not appreciate the ferocity of the small country's desire to free itself from foreign domination at any cost. American casualties in 1969 would reach new highs, and hopes for Nixon's success would sour as the fighting maintained a horrible intensity.

There was another secret plan afoot in Washington. The Yankees were in town for the unveiling of Bob Short's scheme to divest baseball of its roots in Washington, D.C. The press noted how both Short and Nixon were declaring war on crime, but the worries about crime, the war, and the business plans of Bob Short were swept aside. It was Opening Day. The sun was shining and the smiles were out at RKF Stadium for the turning of one page in the national drama — a new baseball season was beginning. Ted Williams was in town and it was Bob Short's "A Whole New Ballgame."

Nixon's ceremonial first pitch lofted high into the air to the cheers of the sell-out crowd of over 45,000. The pitch was caught by Hank Allen, one of the Senators lining the foul line for introductions. Two more tosses by the president were chased down, Williams shook the president's hand, and the crowd roared as the 1969 season was officially begun. The fans stood longer and cheered loudest when the name of the new manager was announced.

To the standing ovation of the largest Opening Day crowd in Washington history, Williams did what he had never done in Boston throughout his long career — he doffed his hat to the crowd. The simple act was noted by the attending press who knew Williams' reputation and temperament in years past. It marked a new beginning for the man and endeared him to all.

Bob Short's happy countenance was focused on Williams the entire time, smiling like a school boy with the answers to Monday's test tucked in his pocket on a Friday afternoon. The other face in Short's box that Opening Day in 1969 was Bowie Kuhn, the new commissioner. Opening Day of 1969 marked the centenary celebration of America's pastime. Professional baseball had begun one hundred years earlier when the Cincinnati Red Stockings set out in the spring of 1869, a group of players openly boasting of their salaries from the parent club and playing as a professional enterprise.

It was a momentous occasion. Kuhn had appeared on the Sunday television news show *Face the Nation*, where he had talked about the history of the game and the opener the next day. Kuhn was faced with a larger task, more daunting than even the labor unrest that was brewing. Kuhn and baseball's elders wanted to restore the game to its heyday, when it alone reigned supreme as the sport of choice for Americans from every walk of life. Football was capturing the fancy of Americans, and many said baseball was too slow, too boring.

The pace of life was picking up, attention spans were growing shorter, and entertainment was more fast-paced. The question was, how could baseball compete in such an atmosphere? The answer was to "soup up" baseball like it was a '57 Chevy, to boost power, add offense — especially more home runs. Babe Ruth had created the modern era of baseball with his celebrity in the 1920s. So baseball chose a smaller strike zone and lowered the mound to bring the offense back alive. Now the greatest pure hitter in history, Ted Williams, was back, too. Kuhn had reason to smile that day at RFK, looking out hopefully as a new season began, and a new era maybe as well.

The dignitaries and fans settled in as Yankees ace Mel Stottlemyre started the game. Stottlemyre was coming off his first 20-win season in '68. He would reach that mark again in '69, and his first win came that day against a bumbling Senators team that had two errors that were marked in the official scorecard. Base-running blunders and overall play in the field that was less than sharp marred the game. The Senators had not won a home opener since 1962, and starter Camilo Pascual did nothing to change that. Pascual was in trouble from the first inning and had departed before the end of the third with the Senators behind, 4–0.

Bob Humphreys replaced him and gave up another four runs in the next inning. With Washington behind, 8–0, there were no moves Williams could make except to change pitchers. He did so three more times. The Senators showed signs of life, though, rallying behind fourteen hits off Stottlemyre for four runs. The final score was 8–4, and it was not a happy dugout celebrating Ted Williams' return to baseball.

Frank Howard hit a home run in the ninth inning to delight the president, who had called the shot, telling Bowie Kuhn that before the game was over Howard would hit one out. The real story line may have been buried in the fourteen-hit attack. Weak-hitting Eddie Brinkman started his season with two hits, Tim Cullen with three, and Del Unser had three hits as well as the leadoff batter. The banjo hitters were coming alive. They had roughed up one of the best pitchers in the American League. Although Howard, Epstein and McMullen would fail to bring them around, the hitters that had closed out the long extra batting practices at Pompano Beach showed their coach that they had been paying attention.

It would be the pitching staff, however, that brought home the first win

Frank Howard became the most popular player on the Senators. National Baseball Hall of Fame Library, Cooperstown, N.Y.

and gave the Washington fans something to cheer about. In the second game of the season against the Yankees, Joe Coleman went the distance for the win. Ken McMullen finally caught fire after his slow spring, and Paul Casanova had a two-run homer to clinch the game. But Frank Howard was the hero again. He hit his second home run in as many days, and the Opening Day loss was forgotten in the happy dugout with everyone clapping the big man on the back after the win.

Howard was the biggest man who played the game in 1969. He stood 6'7" and weighed 290 pounds. He had such a mammoth appetite that he avoided eating in public for fear he might embarrass his family. He had six kids — a Frank Howard-sized family. He would report to camp in the spring invariably overweight and then take on an ugly self-imposed regimen to shed the pounds. The problem had been particularly acute in the spring of '69 after his holdout delayed his spring ritual for two weeks.

Howard was a corn-fed Ohio boy, sporting the same flat-top haircut and jughead look as Johnny Unitas. Born in Columbus, Ohio, Howard had gone to his hometown school, Ohio State, to play baseball and basketball on scholarship. A standout in each sport, he was recruited by the great Red Auerbach of the Boston Celtics, but chose baseball by signing with the Los Angeles Dodgers. After a prodigious minor league season in 1959 where he hit 43 home runs for Spokane and Victoria, Texas, Howard was up with the Dodgers' major league team to stay in 1960. He was the National League Rookie of the Year in 1960 with 23 home runs.

Howard had huge potential that everyone saw and at which many marveled. Yet by dividing his time with basketball, Howard's coaching in the finer points of baseball started late. Buzzie Bavasi, the Dodgers' general manager for much of the 1950s and '60s, made sure that Howard had the best coaching, bringing in former big-leaguer Pete Reiser specifically to coach Howard's minor league team in Victoria, Texas. When Howard came up to stay with the Dodgers, he was the only slugger in a lineup that included Tommy Davis and Maury Wills, but no significant power source.

It was Howard's relationship with Walter Alston, the great manager of the Dodgers, that was the problem. Both men respected the other, but Howard chafed when Alston continued to platoon him even after his great 1962 season, when he had 36 homers and 119 runs batted in. Howard hit the game-winning home run against Whitey Ford to clinch the sweep of the 1963 World Series against the Yankees, but when Alston would not assure him of more playing time, Howard demanded a trade. The trade never happened because Bavasi believed Howard would become a great ballplayer with time. The Dodgers and Howard put aside the rancor for the '64 season, but Howard's numbers continued to fall.

The trade finally came in December of 1964. Bavasi would deal Howard to Washington because he felt comfortable sending the player once considered the "next Babe Ruth" to a team in which he believed the trade could not come back to haunt him. Houston and other National League teams made attractive offers for what they saw as a box office bonanza. Bavasi wanted Howard on neither a National League team nor a contender. Washington was a perfect fit.

Howard responded well to the trade, particularly to the assurances that he would be playing every day and that the pressure to provide power to the Dodgers lineup was gone. Saying that he preferred to play every day for a cellar dweller than part-time for a contender, Howard gratefully reported to his new team in 1965 and asked for not a penny more than the Dodgers paid him. The trade did cost the Senators one of their best pitching prospects, Claude Osteen, and in the first years after the trade, Howard struggled with his batting average. Although he was much beloved by the fans in Los Angeles, he was booed by Washington fans when he went into a prolonged slump and struck out, which he did quite often.

Another reason Bavasi chose Washington was his close relationship with former Dodger great Gil Hodges, who was the new manager of the Senators. Hodges worked with Howard on his stance, moving the big man closer to the plate and cutting down on his prodigious swing. He hit 36 homers in 1967 and his average rose. Jim Lemon, his manager in 1968 helped as well, and Howard led the league in home runs in 1968 with 44. The boos were forgotten as Howard became the most popular player on the Senators, a great player on a mediocre team.

Howard remained a Midwesterner even after his salary could have afforded a more exotic lifestyle. He lived in Green Bay, Wisconsin, and preferred small-town America to big-city life. Known in Washington as the "Gentle Giant," his mammoth home runs were discussed in D.C.-area households, in the press and among ballplayers, all of whom speculated whether they were the longest of all-time. The writers called him "the Capitol Punisher" and "Hondo," but fans just called him out of the dugout after his home runs, and he was willing to oblige as he settled into being the face of Washington baseball.

Frank Howard never betrayed the love of Washington, D.C.'s baseball fans. Howard became the greatest slugger ever to put on a Washington baseball uniform, hitting with 237 lifetime home runs for the Senators. He broke a Babe Ruth and Hank Greenberg record of 10 home runs in a week that had stood since 1930. The great teams of the first three decades in Washington, featuring Hall of Fame hitters like Goose Goslin, Sam Rice, and Heinie Manush, never produced anyone who could hit with power like Howard.

As many great feats as Howard accomplished, his leadership of the 1969 team would go down as his best, and he would be the player Washington fans would remember the longest.

The Gentle Giant started the 1969 season with four home runs in the first three games against the Yankees at RFK. His friend Eddie Brinkman would homer in the fourth game, and the early evidence was overwhelming that 1969 would be the year that offense made a comeback in baseball. Shirley Povich noted in his April 10 column, "There are signs that the joyous sound of the base hit is returning to the game." He noted the hitting carnival in the week's opening games compared to the dreary shutouts in last year's openers. Frank Howard, with Ted Williams smiling in the dugout, would lead the charge.

6

Getting Better All the Time

The win in game two was matched by another win against the Yankees in game three. Suddenly the hope for a turnaround was running a bit higher, the smiles at RFK a bit brighter, and life was just that much better for Ted Williams and his new Washington team. The third game of the season against the Yankees continued to showcase the revamped Washington offense when it banged out a 9–6 win. It was early, but against the Yankees, the Senators certainly looked like a stronger hitting team.

In the win everyone in the lineup had a hit, including Jim Hannan, the pitcher. The big news was Frank Howard's two home runs as he went 3-for-5 and drove in three of the nine runs. The rest of the team looked very good as well. Del Unser had three hits in the lead-off spot and Brinkman had a couple while hitting second behind Unser. The other big hitting star of the day was Brant Alyea, who had three hits and his first home run while hitting down in the bottom half of the batting order.

Howard's two home runs gave him four in three games to start the season. Everyone in town was talking about his start, wondering what a new retooled Frank Howard could do over the long season with the greatest hitter of all time behind him in the dugout.

Bob Short was counting the money and patting himself on the back. With the same team as in 1968, and by adding only a new manager, he had pulled in 25,000 more fans for the three-game Yankees series than the opening series had in 1968. Ted Williams was not worrying about attendance, but about pitching. After the Yankees series, the team would play 22 games over 21 days, including three double-headers, two of which were against the Baltimore Orioles. Baltimore had been the second-best team in the AL in 1968 and had probably the best pitching staff in baseball. Williams was considering going with a five-man rotation. The concept was relatively novel at the time, but there was really no choice as Williams saw it. He only had to find the candidates from among the weak Washington staff who could start.

Barry Moore was a twenty-five-year-old from North Carolina. As a twenty-three-year-old rookie in 1966, he had established himself with the Senators. Not overpowering, he had been a starter when he first came up, but had shifted back to the bullpen in '68. Of Williams' choices, Moore had the most experience as a starting pitcher. Dick Bosman was the second choice. He had broken into the majors with Washington in '67 and shown flashes of brilliance, but moved back to the bullpen in '68 for most of his 139 innings that year.

Williams chose Barry Moore for the fourth game of the season in Memorial Stadium, up the road in Baltimore. Moore was replacing Frank Bertaina, who had pitched his way into Williams' doghouse and did not pitch at all in the first two series. Williams wanted a left-hander in the rotation, and Moore, coming off a good spring, was moving himself into that slot. Starting for the Orioles for the first game of the series would be Jim Hardin, who had been outstanding in 1968, winning eighteen games. However, 1968 would be his only successful season in the major leagues.

Against Hardin and the Orioles, Barry Moore proved to be the better pitcher that day in Baltimore. He rewarded Williams' vote of confidence with six innings of shutout ball. Moore had two hits as well and scored a run on a day the offense was mostly quiet. Tim Cullen continued to hit well, but the offense could only eke out four runs. It was enough for the Senators to win their third game of the year against only one loss — the Opening Day defeat.

The headlines in Washington touted the 3–1 record of the Senators that had them in first place ever so briefly. But Barry Moore's win would be the last for the Senators during their first trip to Baltimore. The second game on Saturday saw Dave McNally — coming back from his first 20-win season in 1968 — pitch a masterful four-hit shutout. McNally would win twenty games in the 1969, '70, and '71 seasons as a crucial cog in the Orioles' greatest run in their short baseball history. During that time span they won three AL championships and a World Series.

They would continue to look like champs in the Sunday double-header that April. Jim Palmer, who was on his way to greatness, pitched a five-hit shutout in the first game, besting Joe Coleman for a 2–0 win. In the second Sunday game, Tom Phoebus pitched the best game of all, throwing a two-hit shutout. The game ended in the fourth inning for all practical purposes after the Orioles scored six against Dick Bosman following an error by the pitcher. The three straight shutouts left the faithful wondering about Ted Williams' new offense.

Bosman's poor outing left Williams worried about his ability to maneuver the pitching staff though April. Bertaina came on in relief of Bosman, going four capable innings to close out the otherwise lamentable 9–0 loss. The effort got him out of the manager's doghouse, and along with Barry Moore, gave Williams hope that he could keep his pitching staff afloat.

Washington moved on up the East Coast to New York City for a rematch with the Yankees. The first game of the series was the Yankees' home opener. Instead of Richard Nixon, the Yankees would have singer-songwriter Paul Simon throw out the first pitch. Simon wrote the song "Mrs. Robinson" that became a number-one hit for him and Art Garfunkel in 1968. Its lyrics about Joe DiMaggio were really about Mickey Mantle, who was Simon's boyhood idol. Simon admitted later in his career that he could not make Mantle's name fit into the song.

Whether it was Mantle or DiMaggio mattered little to Yankee fans; neither was in center field anymore. Bobby Murcer, the rookie center fielder, was trying to fill their shoes. A former infielder, he had the New York fans hopeful, but he was a pale comparison to the old days. He had neither Mantle's power nor speed. When Murcer began the '69 season with a display of power, most in the organization were more surprised than hopeful.

Yankee fans had reached the depths of despair as their team slipped in 1966 to the basement of the American League. Paul Simon provided young New York fans with more to think about than the Yankees, and cultural interest was moving toward the music of the era; baseball stadiums were bringing in more fans for rock shows than for the American pastime.

Joe Pepitone was one of the few links back to the great 1964 Yankees team of Maris and Mantle. Batting clean-up, he was all that was left on the '69 roster. His season was off to a good start as he and Roy White anchored the heart of the Yankee lineup. Coming off a big game against Detroit, Pepitone and White would continue the Washington slide.

At the beginning of the Yankee game in New York City, a curious thing happened. When Ted Williams' name was announced as the new manager of the Washington Senators during the pre-game ceremonies, the New York faithful rose to their feet in appreciation of Boston's great slugger with a long and loud ovation. They certainly hadn't loved him when he was the heart of the hated team from the Commonwealth to the north, and he was frequently booed at Yankee Stadium during his heyday as a player. Perhaps it was the mention of Joe DiMaggio in the opening Paul Simon song, but the fans were reminded of the a golden era for baseball in which Williams played a huge part. Fans missed the post–World War II era of the game during the late forties and fifties when Ted Williams' name was so much a part of the magic.

The home opener that day pitted the same two pitchers from Washington's 9–6 victory a week earlier, Peterson and Hannan. Peterson looked like a different pitcher as he hurled a complete game. Aided by the Washington hitters who hit into four double plays, he limited the damage to two runs, only one earned.

The outcome might have been different except for a scary event in the third inning. Rookie Jerry Kenney hit a screaming line drive back through the box that caught Hannan on the pitching hand. Though he stuck with the play and threw the runner out, he was clearly in pain and was removed from the game immediately by Ted Williams. Hannan wanted to stay in the game, and Williams may have regretted his decision to lift his starter as the bullpen was horrible. Four relievers gave up eight runs in the 8–2 loss.

The same two teams played a double-header on Thursday. The first game was a loss to Mel Stottlemyre, and coupled with Hannan's defeat and the losses to the Orioles, it gave the Senators a five-game losing streak. Again it was the bullpen that gave up the game. Camilo Pascual had his first decent outing of the year, but the game went into the 10th inning tied 3–3 when Dennis Higgins coughed up four runs that doomed the effort.

Barry Moore continued to be the stopper for Williams. He ended the losing streak with a well-pitched 5–2 win. The Senators' offense was keyed by a remarkable eight walks they coaxed from Yankee pitchers. The smaller strike zone was taking its toll, and Washington hitters could see the advantage they could gain by using it against their opponents.

The team limped home to Washington to face the Orioles, who had humiliated the Senators in Baltimore scant days earlier. Tom Phoebus made it look like déjà vu all over again with another shutout, this time by a 6–0 count. Daily columns questioning the Senators' offense and the magic of Ted Williams were surfacing. Washington's baseball writers were noting the long string of zeroes being pasted on the scoreboard by the Orioles pitchers and too many others.

The writers had forgotten Frank Howard's great start from the opening series, and the Gentle Giant re-emerged as an offensive force after slumping for almost two weeks. Howard got the entire team back on track with his first home run since the opening series against New York. It almost made the Orioles seem human as Washington roughed up Mike Cuellar in a 7–5 win.

The teams split the double-header the next day. Dave McNally beat Jim Hannan, 2–1, in the first game despite Howard's sixth home run, but in the late game, Frank Bertaina made his first appearance as a starter and won against Jim Hardin, 5–2.

Shirley Povich, writing in the *Washington Post* after the game, lampooned Bob Short's war on crime, noting that the only robbery occurring at RFK that he could see occurred when Don Buford stole a game-winning hit from Hank Allen in the first contest. The same morning papers showed

Allen among the league leaders in batting average and Howard's six home runs atop that race as well. But it was the Orioles that were getting the rave notices. They were sitting atop the American League East, and it looked like they would be the biggest beneficiaries of the new divisional structure if Povich was correct that the Tigers could be had.

Going into the season it looked as if the East would be the tougher division in the American League. Boston still had Yastrzemski and many from its 1967 pennant winner. Detroit had wowed the baseball world in '68 and was accorded respect, if only for that. But Baltimore's lineup presented a daunting challenge. Frank Robinson was looking like he might have another MVP year, and Washington had seen how tough the Baltimore pitching was.

Washington baseball writers were noticing the tilt toward the East in the American League and wondering if their team had not drawn the worst hand. With Baltimore, Detroit, and Boston, the AL East looked like the toughest division in baseball. The Senators could take solace from the lowly Cleveland Indians, who looked pale in the early going and occupied the cellar. Washington was left to contest the now-weakened Yankees for the other spots in the division.

Shirley Povich on the day of the game said of the new league divisional alignment, "Now the home team doesn't have to beat the whole world, just half of it. The creation of two small puddles has enabled baseball's small fish to look bigger." Povich saw the ability of the new divisional play to maintain fan interest not only during the pennant drive, but over the entire season. But he was not impressed with the upper tier of the American League East and saw the Tigers' pitching as thin behind Lolich and McLain. Teams were starting to look up the ladder of the standings, and seeing only five other teams, not nine, it was easier to rationalize one's way into the thick of the fight.

With Detroit coming to town, there was a chance to evaluate the Senators against the best, the world champion Tigers. But if Washington had been reading Povich's assessment of the Tigers, it did not show. In the first game the Senators reverted to the form they took in Baltimore, shut out again, this time by the Tigers' Joe Sparma. Sparma was hardly the equal to Dave McNally and the Baltimore staff, and the shutout called into question the strides the Washington lineup was making.

The second game saw Camilo Pascual pitch extremely well, but not well enough as Pat Dobson came out on top of a 4–2 score. Williams' managerial prowess was questioned the next day for leaving Pascual in the game to start the ninth inning. The Senators had a precarious 2–1 lead and Pascual had a one-hitter going. The only hit had been a Bill Freehan home run, but the veteran pitcher looked worn out in the ninth and could not get a batter out, surrendering a three-run triple to Dick McAuliffe that won the game. The pundits thought Williams should have pulled the old war horse, and that maybe a more experienced manager would have done so.

Washington's record was not dismal at six wins and ten losses, but the lack of offense was beginning to wear on early advocates of Williams. He was the focus of all the attention when the schedule brought the team into Boston for a single mid-week game. It was Williams' first return to Fenway Park, where he had starred for nineteen glorious seasons, spanning three decades and two wars.

Though Williams was sixteen times an All-Star, the Fenway faithful had only one championship to share with Williams, that of 1946. However, the old disappointments did not dim the memories as fans poured out to remember a hero. Jim Hannan described the atmosphere with the outpouring of national as well as local press that was on hand for the event, saying, "It was the closest thing I ever saw to a World Series game."

For all of the enthusiasm and warm, rousing welcome, Williams gave no overt sign of recognition to the fans. He shooed young fans pleading for an autograph from the dugout roof, but he was smiling the whole day. The high point for Williams may have come when he saw his old teammate from the 1946 championship team, Bobby Doerr. They took time to reminisce, but the greatest fun came when Joe Coleman, another player with Boston connections, silenced the Red Sox and gave Williams' Senators a 9–3 win.

The win was clinched by three-run homers from Ken McMullen and Mike Epstein. Many of the players' averages had slipped during the tough stretch of games against the Tigers and Orioles. Eddie Brinkman's batting average was sliding back toward .200. The twelve hits the team recorded for Williams in front of the hometown Boston crowd marked a turnaround and gave the Senators' skipper something to crow about, to show the skeptics in Boston what their best player ever could do as a manager. His team was about to embark on a winning streak that would make Williams' status as a capable manager a more compelling one.

7

Coming Into Los Angel-lees

The Senators used the win in Boston to leverage a five-game winning streak that pushed their record above .500 for the first time since early in the 1968 season. The wins came during the last week in April on the road against the cellar-dwelling Cleveland Indians. It was the awakened offense that was driving the team forward. Frank Howard got it started with his seventh home run in the first game of the Cleveland series. In the same game, Eddie Brinkman snapped out of his slump with three hits, scoring three times in front of Howard's torrid day at the plate. The win went to Dick Bosman in relief of Jim Hannan, who struggled in the early innings. Bosman came on in the fifth and his four-plus innings of scoreless relief finished out the game.

The second Cleveland game witnessed a similar scenario. Barry Moore, who had been so good in the early going, walked the first four batters. Nothing got under Ted Williams' skin more than a pitcher walking hitters, and with one run in already and the game about to slip away, he pulled Moore, bringing in Casey Cox. Williams may have remembered the game against Detroit when he let Camilo Pascual face one batter too many, so despite the impending stretch of consecutive games, he took his starter out before it was too late.

Like Bosman, Casey Cox pitched the rest of the game without giving up another run. He made an impression on Williams by throwing strikes all day long and never walking a batter. The offense took advantage of eight walks by the Cleveland staff and made them pay by scoring eight times for the 8–1 win.

The back-to-back wins by Bosman and Cox out of the bullpen marked a turning point for Williams and his pitching staff. The bullpen was starting to perform after many rough outings in the first two weeks of the season. Casey Cox began to see the value of turning Williams' hitting philosophy on its head. He set the batters up with strikes early in the count and got them out swinging at pitches away or down in the zone.

For the first few weeks of the season, Bosman had been trying without complete success to find the pinpoint control upon which he relied. As the weather began to warm up, Bosman began to get the sharpness back in his slider, and the results were winning the confidence of Williams. Bosman's only start against Baltimore, on the thirteenth of April, had been a disaster, yet Bosman was not only the kind of pitcher Williams liked — he threw a great slider and kept it in the strike zone — but also one who was not impacted by the lower mound or the smaller strike zone.

Bosman said that the lowering of the mound actually helped him. He considered himself a sinkerball pitcher whose target was the bottom half of the strike zone. If the rules committee wanted to reduce the top part of the zone, it helped him because he tried to keep his pitches low and breaking lower. If umpires were looking to call more low strikes and fewer high ones, then pitchers like Bosman who relied on keeping the ball down would not be hurt and probably benefited from the change.

Bosman said it was Sid Hudson who helped him refine the slider and adjust to the new realities of pitching in 1969, but it was Williams who encouraged his pitchers to move from side to side on the rubber, based on whether the batter was right- or left-handed. By moving the point of delivery further across the mound, it was easier to work the slider in on the hands of left-handed batters or break it more sharply away from right-handers. The change helped Bosman to refine what may have been his best pitch. It may have also been important that both Bosman and Cox were tall. Cox, at 6'5" was especially tall for a pitcher at that time. He could throw the slider and keep most of the tilt that some pitchers had lost with the reduction of the old mound.

"Ted Williams made me a successful pitcher in 1969, there is no denying it," said Bosman many years later. "He taught be to pitch from the neck up," repeating Williams' oft-repeated allusion to the various parts of the game requiring intense concentration as much as physical adeptness. Bosman believes that Sid Hudson taught him the mechanics of pitching. Hudson had been working with Bosman since his days as a roving instructor in the Senators' minor league system and was excellent at explaining how to hold various pitches to increase their break across or down through the strike zone.

Bosman is now a pitching coach himself and says he still uses and teaches many of the same techniques that Hudson taught him. "Those basic elements of pitching haven't changed a whole lot since then," says Bosman.

Bosman was headed for the starting rotation. Even an old hitter like Ted Williams could see the value of having Bosman pitch more innings for the Senators. Bosman's teammates in the bullpen won the last game of the Cleveland series in relief of Frank Bertaina. Bertaina's three-run homer provided much of the early punch, but it was Dave Baldwin's spotless relief and Dennis Higgins' save that won the game and gave Washington a sweep against the lowly Indians. It was the last win against Cleveland that finally got the Senators back to the .500 mark with ten wins and ten losses. The season was at a tipping point, and the road trip continued with two games against Detroit as the first month of the campaign was drawing to a close.

Detroit had beaten the Senators in Washington a week earlier, and Williams' offense looked dispirited after the long stretch of games against the Orioles. The Tigers hardly looked like the team Povich said could be had. Yet when Washington ventured to the Motor City at the end of April, once again the Senators did not have to face either McLain or Lolich, and Detroit's pitching looked every bit as thin as Shirley Povich had claimed early in April. Washington pushed across six runs against Earl Wilson and Bosman again was flawless across four innings of relief to nail down the win. Camilo Pascual earned the victory, but now Williams pulled him as soon as the veteran appeared winded. Hank Allen had a big day at the plate and continued to rank among the league leaders, hitting at a .432 pace.

The road trip ended with a 5–4 loss to Detroit to put the team at .500 again, but there was a five-game homestand coming up. Boston and Cleveland were coming to D.C. and the first game would pit Jim Hannan against Dick Strange. Since the opening series against the Yankees when he notched his only win, Hannan had pitched well only once, in a loss to the Orioles in which he had given up only two runs in eight innings. Like Bosman, Hannan was a sinkerball pitcher who should have been the least affected by the lower strike zone and mound.

Hannan was at his best the last day of April against the Red Sox. He gave up a single hit to Carl Yastrzemski and two to Tony Conigliaro, but he held Boston off the scoreboard for seven innings and turned the game over to the rejuvenated bullpen. Hannan's sinker kept Eddie Brinkman busy, but the shortstop's sparkling defense helped keep Boston from scoring. Dennis Higgins pitched two shutout innings to save the game. Frank Howard's eighth home run was really all that was need as the Senators ended April with a winning record.

The Senators' record at the beginning of May was 12 wins and 11 defeats. They were bunched with the Yankees, Tigers and Red Sox, with the Orioles sitting firmly astride the division standings. But Howard's strong month and the new signs of life in the pitching staff had the team and its fans excited again.

The Senators swept the two-game series against Boston with a 7–6 May Day triumph as Casey Cox came out of the bullpen, with the relievers getting the win again. The *Washington Post* headlines read "Senators Climb to

Second." Howard had another home run — his ninth — and the team was suddenly charging, putting space between themselves and the Yankees, Tigers and Red Sox, all of whom were sliding. Cleveland was ensconced in last place after a dismal April that saw the Indians win only three games. The Indians were coming to Washington for a three-game series — a great opportunity to create momentum for a Senator club just starting to believe in itself.

Dick Bosman received his second start of the season in the first game of the Cleveland series. After a nice run of relief appearances, he deserved another shot at the starting rotation and was excited about the opportunity. Bosman's outing was an inspiration as he pitched the best game of the early season by a Washington starting pitcher. Bosman went the distance — nine innings — and gave up only a second-inning single that was blooped off the bat handle for the hit along with three walks. Sid Hudson, the pitching coach, called it a masterpiece. Eddie Brinkman's clutch hit in the second inning pushed across the winning run in the 5–0 game.

Luis Tiant, pitching for Cleveland in 1969, still had the high leg kick and gave up four walks in five innings. The Cleveland bullpen pitchers then gave up four more. The Indians' staff was struggling early with the new strike zone, and the Senators were once again able to make the most of it.

Bosman established himself in the rotation to stay against Cleveland and was on his way to becoming the staff ace of the '69 Senators. He turned it around by listening to Ted Williams' advice on pitching. "Ted and I had a relationship that a lot of guys didn't, and a lot of pitchers didn't," Bosman said. "I learned how to use my breaking ball to set up my fastball." Some of the pitchers like Joe Coleman chaffed under the new pitching regimen, but Bosman and Cox were making the most of it.

Washington won the next two games against Cleveland. Camilo Pascual pitched only five innings again, but allowed only a single run in a 6–1 victory. Williams was babying the veteran, saying Pascual looked to be tiring early in games. The bullpen continued to pitch much better. Dave Baldwin pitched three and two-thirds innings of scoreless relief behind Pascual to save the game and hit a home run as well.

The home series sweep of Cleveland put the Senators only three games behind the Orioles, firmly fixed in second place with a record of 16 wins and 11 losses. The Senators' early success was overshadowed by the Kentucky Derby. Richard Nixon — ever the sports enthusiast — was among the Churchill Downs crowd picking winners again; this time Majestic Prince was the president's choice and a good one. Williams was worried about the Senators' most-trusted thoroughbred, Camilo Pascual. To Williams' practiced eye, his ace was looking worn, and he was worried whether Pascual could make his next start.

Mike Epstein hit a solo home run in the last Cleveland win, only his third of the season, but his platoon with Frank Howard at first base was causing problems. Howard had never been a good fielder. He was a lumbering outfielder, but he compensated for his lack of speed with hard work and hustle, and surprised runners with the strength and accuracy of his throws. Around the first base bag, however, he could be wooden. He had soft hands, but was committing numerous errors in the early games, including two in the last Boston game that had almost cost Washington the win. Only an outstanding play by Eddie Brinkman had picked him up.

Epstein was better around the bag. Although he was a big, strong ox himself, he was more of a natural defender around first base and was destined for more playing time as he chafed under Williams' platoon system. The last game in the Cleveland series saw both Epstein and Howard homer. It was Howard's tenth, and he was on a pace to hit over sixty home runs for the season.

TABLE 7-1. AMERICAN LEAGUE STANDINGS, MAY 6, 1969

Eastern Division

Team	Wins	Losses	Pct.	GB
Baltimore	20	8	.714	—
Washington	16	11	.593	3½
Boston	14	10	.503	4
Detroit	11	13	.456	7
New York	11	15	.423	8
Cleveland	3	18	.143	13½

Western Division

Team	Wins	Losses	Pct	GB
Minnesota	16	7	.696	—
Oakland	14	10	.583	2½
Kansas City	13	11	.542	3½
Chicago	8	11	.421	6
California	8	13	.381	7
Seattle	8	15	.341	8

Despite the heady winning streak in which Washington had won ten out of eleven games, the writers and fans were cautious. Everyone remembered how the 1968 team had played well to start the season, going 11–7 in April before beginning a long and dismal plummet into the cellar. As a result, fans in Washington were not ready to accept the sudden spurt as a long-term trend. They had been teased by Washington's spirited baseball devil before and were not taken in easily, but the current season did seem different. The middle of the order was not just Frank Howard and Ken McMullen; now there were Williams' other pupils Epstein, Unser, and the rejuvenated Eddie Brinkman. They provided the supporting cast that had been missing in 1968.

Washington packed its equipment and headed on a long road trip out west. Everywhere the Senators landed, in every ballpark and every airport, the press was waiting with microphones and cameras and a litany of questions for Ted Williams. It was as if he were a one-man celebration of the baseball centennial traveling the country.

One rationale for the decline of baseball's offense suggested by writers was the new long flights between the East Coast and West Coast after the expansion of baseball to California. The argument suffered from a notable weakness — that whatever effect extended flights might have had, they were faced by the pitcher as well as the batter — but it was bandied about nonetheless. The new schedule put in place to accommodate the separate East and West divisions had the teams in both leagues start and end the season with head-to-head play against their divisional rivals. The month of May was the first venture of the new Senators into the newly formed American League West.

The first stop for the Senators was Oakland, California, home to the Athletics — formerly of Kansas City and before that Philadelphia. Owner Charlie Finley had moved the team to Oakland only a year earlier, bringing his signature bright green and yellow uniforms with him. The attendance in Oakland had so far been uninspiring, but the team itself looked good if one could get past the uniforms.

The Athletics had been bad almost as long as the Senators, but the new Oakland team had a young 22-year-old named Reggie Jackson, who could hit the ball as far as Frank Howard, and a young pitching staff with talent equal to their colorful names: Vida Blue, Blue Moon Odom, and Catfish Hunter. Those were the starters, who were followed by one of the best relievers to practice the specialty, Rollie Fingers, he of the great handlebar mustache.

Hunter pitched a gem in the first game for a 4–1 Oakland win, and when the Senators got close in the second game, Fingers shut them down for a 5–4 win. That sent Washington on to Seattle still looking for its first West Coast victory and girding for the press gaggle around its new manager.

The new expansion Seattle Pilots were an ill-fated venture that would last but a single season before relocating to Milwaukee in 1970. But in May of 1969, they had a young pitcher named Mike Marshall, whom they had drafted from Detroit. Marshall would go on to become one of the few players to get a Ph.D. after leaving the game. He pitched a two-hitter against Washington, while winning, 2–0 and Frank Howard had one of the two hits.

The second game was one of the most depressing ballgames of the young season and may have marked its low point. With Camilo Pascual, ostensibly still the ace of the staff, on the mound, and with an 11–3 lead going into the bottom of the sixth inning, the wheels fell off the train. Against an expansion team and with everything pointing toward a win, the Senators could not close the deal.

Pascual started the sixth inning but retired no one, reminding Williams again that his veteran was running out of gas sooner in each game. Pascual did not help his cause by getting no one out and throwing a lot of pitches. For the five-inning outing, he walked five batters, but when the bullpen came on, the relievers ran into the same problem. They had bailed Camilo out in prior starts but could get no one out in Seattle, walking an additional seven batters over the last three innings. Casey Cox, Dave Baldwin and Dennis Higgins allowed ten runs to score. There were men clogging the bases in every inning as Seattle came back for a 16–13 win. Washington out-hit the Pilots, but for once the Senators could not match Seattle for patience at the plate. There were an amazing seventeen bases on balls issued during the game.

The most excitement in the Seattle series came when Frank Howard exploded in frustration at the new strike zone. With the game on the line in the ninth inning and two men aboard, a pitch down and away was called a strike. Howard had checked his bat, but the umpire ruled it a swing. He walked back to the bench but began a tirade against Ron Luciano from the dugout steps that did not end until his ejection.

The Gentle Giant looked anything but gentle as he came back to discuss the matter with the equally large Luciano. It may have been the animated third-strike call that Luciano practiced — pumping his arm several times and then shooting his hand out — that irked Howard. Luciano was in only the second year of a very long career, and Howard may have been unaccustomed to the gesture. Whatever the cause, when the two men stood jaw to jaw, the ground appeared to shake, but ultimately it was no contest. Luciano won on a decision. The *Washington Post* asserted that it was the first time the normally peace-loving Howard had been ejected from a game since the referees tossed him while playing basketball for Ohio State.

Before he was tossed, Howard got back on track with a three-run homer, but that and Bernie Allen's big night were wasted. The Senators completed the trip to Seattle with another loss, Jim Hannan struggling for his second straight start out west, giving the expansion Pilots a sweep of the series.

A sweep to what was one of the worst teams in the American League did nothing for the self-esteem of Washington's regulars. They had lost five straight games and were back playing .500 baseball again. It was starting to look like 1968 all over again: a successful April followed by disaster. The road trip got no easier by going to Los Angeles for another three-game series.

The pitching was better against the Angels. After dropping the opener, 3–2, the losing streak was staunched at six as Barry Moore and Dennis Higgins beat Andy Messersmith, 2–1, to square the team's record at 17 wins and 17 losses. But the next night they lost again, and with a losing record, the team was headed to Chicago for the final four games of the road trip.

As was the case everywhere, Ted Williams held forth with a large bevy of reporters around the batting cage at Comiskey Park during the pre-game activities. On the South Side of Chicago, he talked hitting, telling the reporters how much he had hated hitting against the White Sox in Chicago, and why the park was better suited to a player like his coach, Nellie Fox.

There were questions about the new shortstop, Eddie Brinkman. Who was this guy people were talking about as a candidate for the All-Star Game in July? Was it the same player that barely hit his weight in prior years? Williams did not respond to the questions favorably, telling the reporters brusquely, "I'll give you the whole story, you ready? He has choked up on the bat, is waiting on the ball, and concentrating on hitting it on the ground. That's your story."

Williams got back on his favorite subject quickly, though, talking about Comiskey Park and how difficult it had been for him to hit there. He asserted it was the most imposing park for Teddy Ballgame and that he had considerable difficulty hitting one out of Comiskey during his playing days. Then he asked the reporters if they had noticed another young hitter with the Senators, Mike Epstein. He told the reporters to keep an eye on him "because he's gonna hit 40 home runs one of these days."

Epstein overheard the remarks and took inspiration from them into that first game in Comiskey. Batting against Sammy Ellis in the first inning, he hit a long, deep homer with no one aboard. Then in the sixth inning, he nailed Ellis again, sending another one out of the park. In the eighth inning against knuckleball pitcher Wilbur Wood, Epstein hit his third homer and was smiling ear to ear when he came back to the dugout, remembering how Williams had said it was the toughest ballpark to homer in.

Williams was not amused. He turned away from Epstein as he walked down the dugout steps. Williams refused to talk to him for the rest of the game and the rest of the day, telling him later that Epstein had shown him up. Williams had told everyone how hard it was to hit a home run in Comiskey Park, and then Epstein hits three in a row. No one mentioned

Mike Epstein hit his third homer and was smiling ear to ear. National Baseball Hall of Fame Library, Cooperstown, N.Y.

that the walls at Comiskey Park had been moved in for the 1969 season for exactly the reasons Williams was talking about.

None of it helped. Epstein was in Williams' doghouse, at least for the day, and the Senators lost the game, 7–6, after Joe Coleman staked the White Sox to a 6–1 lead in the first three innings. Even with Epstein's home runs and Howard's 14th of the season, the Senators continued to lose. They had lost eight of nine games on the road trip, and they lost the next day as well by a 6–0 score, shut out on a single hit by young flash-in-the-pan Jerry Nyman. Camilo Pascual could not get out of the fifth inning; the bullpen was being over-worked by his struggles.

Williams' refusal to talk to Epstein may have had its root cause in his general frustration with losing and his growing sense that maybe the nay-sayers were right. Maybe the Senators could not be taught to win. Yet on the following day, the Senators managed to eke out a 3–2 win against Chicago. Then on the last day of the horrible road trip, they managed another win by an identical 3–2 score against the White Sox to bring them closer to .500. They headed home with a record of 19–20.

Dick Bosman was the stopper, throwing six innings of one-run ball in the first Chicago win. The bullpen was able to hang on for the precarious victory. Regardless how ugly or cheap it may have been, it was a win and a badly needed one that prevented a total collapse. Even with the final two victories against the White Sox, the road trip had been a disaster. Washington managed only three wins in twelve games and squandered the great April start. The Senators limped home to play the same two expansion teams, the Pilots and Kansas City Royals.

While the team's grip on its early enthusiasm was fraying, Bob Short could not have been more pleased with the bottom line, which was looking better all the time. He was asked in late May about running a team in Washington, D.C., with all of its racial tensions. Short responded, "Baseball fans don't notice each others' color." Los Angeles writer Melvin Durslag continued questioning Short about the safety of baseball in Washington, and Short responded, "How do we make our area safe? I checked one night on the safest place in Washington, the White House. Do you know how they make the White House safe? With fences, lights and gate security, and that's the way we'll be doing it at our ballpark."

The remark came in an interview that also explored the effects of the new manager. "How can I complain? Ted took a cellar team and he is playing around .500 ball. You don't have a right to ask for greater improvement than this." Although low expectations might have been what Bob Short was selling in the press, he was more cheered by the attendance. Short was making the streets safer and fans were turning out to see Teddy Ballgame. Attendance was running well ahead of the 1968 season, 36,000 ahead of the best year the Senators had seen at the new RFK Stadium. And it was only the middle of May. The great experiment was working for Short.

Seattle and Kansas City were teams starting down a path trod by the Senators for nine seasons. Nine years into a process of building a team, Washington had little to show for its efforts. Dick Bosman said that the pre–Bob Short years in Washington featured a team just treading water. Bosman had spent several years in the minors playing for Washington affiliates and had been in the majors since '66. In those years he saw an ownership group that was content to try to hang on, to maintain President Eisenhower's commitment to keep a team in the nation's capital, but one that either had no money to invest in the team, did not know what it took to build a winning franchise, or simply believed like everyone else that Washington could not support baseball.

A fiercely competitive man, Bosman believed that Short's hiring of Ted Williams was the only progressive step the team had taken during his years with the club. Bosman saw it as the only thing separating the Senators from the lowly Royals and Pilots, but it was a belief put to the test by the road losses to a team of little more than expansion draftees.

Although the Seattle Pilots did not have a legend managing them or providing inspiration, they had Tommy Davis batting clean-up, who with Frank Howard had led the Dodgers to the World Series in 1963. Still only 30 years of age, Davis joined another familiar face, John Kennedy, who had been traded to the Dodgers along with Claude Osteen for Howard and McMullen. Kennedy was a defensive specialist whose offense was unspectacular. A solid professional, he typified the Pilots, mediocre but respectable.

In the first game, though, Seattle gave the Senators all they could handle. Jim Hannan got roughed up after several bad outings on the road, but the bullpen gave Williams six strong innings of relief. A towering ninth-inning home run by Mike Epstein that went over the center-field scoreboard at RFK Stadium won the game by a 6–5 margin.

Over the next two days, the Pilots were clearly the better team. Joe Coleman's funk deepened. He lasted only three innings, but it was the lack of hustle that lost the game and got Williams' ire. Coleman broke for the first base bag late on a grounder in the third. He missed the bag with his foot as he hurried, and the Pilots went on to score three runs in the inning. The miscue earned Coleman a trip to the manager's office for a tense lecture and almost cost him his spot in the rotation.

Mike Epstein was on fire, however. He hit his tenth homer and would add another the following day in a 7–6 loss to Seattle. The last game of the

Seattle series was the beginning of the end for Camilo Pascual. He pitched two short innings, giving up four runs. Both he and Jim Hannan were struggling, but Pascual's problems had gone on all season.

The Royals were the next expansion team to visit Washington, and although Barry Moore pitched well in the first game and Epstein continued on his home run binge, the Senators kept sinking, losing a close game, 4–3, in the ninth. Williams tried Frank Bertaina in the second game, but despite four hits by Eddie Brinkman and another Epstein home run, the team lost, 5–4, this time in the tenth.

In the last game against the two expansion teams, Williams left Jim Hannan in the rotation despite his run of bad outings. He responded with seven strong innings, but again the game went into extra innings and Washington found a way to lose. The close 3–2 loss put them five games under .500 with a 20–25 record.

Williams' frustrations were beginning to show. He banged around the clubhouse after the loss to the Royals, letting his team know what he thought. "We're dead," Williams announced in the *Washington Post* the next morning. "Our pitchers can't hold anyone on base." He added, "We are playing back when we should be charging. We can't hold a lead and we can't hit with men on base." The team had won only four games against fifteen losses since early May. It was a video replay of 1968.

8

Can't Rewind,
We've Gone Too Far

Controversy erupted near the end of May like a small volcanic atoll in the South Pacific. It came from a new source, but one that would become famous for frequent upheaval. Billy Martin was the fiery first-year manager for the Minnesota Twins who in late May made his initial trip to Washington. Shirley Povich wrote a long piece about Martin's early success with the team and his dealings with former Senators owner Calvin Griffith, who was now Martin's boss in Minneapolis.

The article ran several days before the series began on Monday, May 26. Povich was correct in saying that Martin had the Twins well positioned in the race. What fascinated Povich was the dark side of Billy Martin, the battler who was always in a scuffle with someone. Martin would have a long, colorful and winning career as a manager of ball players, but in 1969 he was a rookie like Williams. Martin, like Williams, brought a new perspective and innovative approach to the task of crafting a winning team.

In the Washington papers on the day before the game, Martin announced a new tool that he believed could revolutionize game preparation for players — the use of videotape. Martin was using camera studies of his pitchers to discover flaws in their deliveries. Each pitcher would work with a cameraman who filmed their movements on the mound while other pitchers charted the pitches, making notes on the game action to go with the videotape.

This small announcement was quickly lost as controversy descended on the two men. While talking to the press about his managerial approach, Martin managed to get in a jab at the man in the other dugout, saying, "Williams was not my kind of player." The remarks began a shouting match in which the two men used sportswriters to deliver their punches.

Billy Martin, whose best years as a player came with the Yankees, spent eight seasons working his way through the Minnesota farm system after his playing days ended. He had started as a scout, and then became a minor league manager before getting his shot with the Twins' major league job. While Ted Williams was fishing in exotic locales, Martin was earning his job, and there may have been some resentment as the press contrasted the two men's styles.

In his first year as manager, Martin seemed to rock from one controversy to another, and at the end of the year he would lose his job after getting into a fistfight with a player outside a bar. He picked the fight with Williams, saying, "He was one of the worst players I ever saw." Martin elaborated to say that Williams did not play the game hard, that he never tried to take Martin out on the double play, while accusing Williams of running out of the baseline rather than get into it with Martin.

Martin was a great second baseman who had to work hard at every aspect of his game. But Martin had a lifetime batting average of .257, more than eighty points below Ted's. To small guys like himself, it may have seemed as though sluggers in the mold of Williams were born with their talent and never labored at the game like scruffy infielders. Williams responded politely to Martin, saying he respected him as a player, but added a jab that "players like me used to carry players like Billy Martin."

The bickering might have delayed Williams' use of videotape, at least publicly. Williams told the press that his hitters should be able to guess the pitch without watching videotape. What he said to the writers for Martin's benefit was one thing, but he went to Bob Short shortly thereafter to inquire about purchasing the equipment.

It made eminent sense. The Sears ads in the Sunday *Washington Post* offered "$2 Off, Ted Williams Fly Casting Rod, $8.45," and right next to it was an offer for videotape of Ted Williams giving expert advice on hitting a baseball, tossing a lure, and shooting a gun. So Williams was familiar with the lucrative use of videotape.

It was Williams' competitive nature to be concerned that Martin would somehow gain an advantage from video. Williams knew it could help his hitters as well as his pitchers, and he convinced the miserly Short to make the meager investment of $10,000 in the new technology. Short whined but gave in after Williams sold him on the ability of pitchers and batters to improve their game by studying tape. Short would pay for only selected use, not in all games, but coaches and players alike began to make use of it that May.

Martin and Williams were two of the first to use videotape. The technology was not widely used in 1969, but it would gain popularity gradually and become one of the most important tools available to competitive teams in the modern baseball era. Buzz Bissinger details its use by the St. Louis Cardinals and Tony La Russa in his book *Three Nights in August.* Bissinger said in the book, written in 2003, "Of all the changes in baseball over the past decade, the rise of video is the most significant." The best Cardinal players were portrayed by Bissinger as using video to study opposition pitchers and anticipate the movement of the ball when thrown by a certain hurler in various game situations. He used the singular work ethic and intense game preparation of Albert Pujols to underscore how the best players were benefiting.

As late as the 1990s, some teams were still struggling to put expensive video technology to work for them. When Williams started looking at how to employ the tool, he was ahead of the curve. He had always studied his swing in the mirror. As an adolescent he learned to break down its components and analyze ways to make it better. Now the advent of technology would make that process easier by providing the pause button to stop the player in the middle of his motion and the rewind button to play the same mistakes over again so that remedies could be found and put into action.

Sid Hudson's work with the new technology showed very positive results, according to Jim Hannan. Hudson told Hannan he was rushing his delivery. Hannan had heard it before, but despite his Notre Dame diploma, he was having trouble internalizing the criticism and visualizing exactly what Hudson was saying. The issue became more important as Hannan went through an extended rough patch in the early months of '69 after a breakout season in '68. He feared he would be sent down unless he could right himself. His record had fallen to two wins and five losses in early June, and he was walking way too many hitters to keep Williams happy.

His initial understanding of Hudson's criticism was that he was not taking enough time between pitches. He took the mound consciously seeking to be more deliberate between pitches. He then would come in and ask Hudson at the end of the outing if he was doing better. It was not until Hannan literally saw for himself what Hudson meant that he was able to turn his season around. Because Short did not allow the expense of taping every game, Hannan had to wait until the tape was rolling when it was his turn in the rotation. Finally, he had a chance to watch himself on tape.

"I burst into laughter as soon as I saw the tape," Hannan said. "I looked like the silent movie comic Charlie Chaplin on the mound." Hannan recognized the problem easily and began working with Hudson to slow down his arm motion so that he would get better command of his pitches. Once he got his motion under control, he showed dramatic improvement. He went 5–1 for the rest of the season, losing only to Dave McNally by a 1–0 score in late September.

Ultimately Williams' use of videotape became a point of significant controversy. Williams began to set the camera up in center field, directly behind the pitcher, and shooting into the catcher's mitt. The Kansas City Royals later in the year accused Ted of using the cameraman and the person beside him to steal signs. They demanded that the camera be removed, and it was. Williams appealed the ruling, but decided to put aside the technology for a time.

In May of 1969, Americans were fascinated by pictures of a different sort. The Apollo 10 astronauts had flown close enough to the moon to take breath-taking pictures of the surface, its craters and rivulets shown in stark black-and-white close-ups of a world where color seemed a luxury item. Although Apollo 10 was but a warm-up for an actual landing on the moon that would be attempted in July, the mission was successful in every way, and the astronauts landing back on earth were covered with a fanfare that had been missing in recent space ventures. The precision that marked America's space exploration was something that Williams could only marvel at from afar as he watched the clumsy play of his team in late May.

The Twins' former life as the old Washington Senators was a fact lost on some Washington fans, or maybe it was just too painful for them to remember. The Twins — sitting proudly in first place in the AL West as they came to town for three games — had once called Washington home. Fans hated to remember Harmon Killebrew's great 1959 season as a Senator when he led the AL in home runs. But in 1969, he was still the most dangerous hitter in the league, unless of course you were paying attention to the year Frank Howard was having.

Killebrew was preceded in the order by Tony Oliva and Rod Carew, two gifted hitters in their own right. Carew's 3,000 hits and lifetime .328 batting average would land him in the Baseball Hall of Fame. In the first game against the Senators, a rare show of power by Carew was the difference in the outcome. He had two home runs — he would hit only eight all year — in a 7–1 Minnesota win. More impressive to Williams was Carew's batting average, which sat only points off the .400 mark.

The loss in the series opener to the Twins was made worse when Joe Coleman lasted only three innings. He had not won since April and had not gone farther than three innings in his prior three starts. He followed Camilo Pascual to the bullpen, with Williams calling Coleman his biggest disappointment of the year. Dick Bosman was still injured and unavailable, though he was sent out on a rehab assignment to test his shoulder. Without him, the pitching staff was disintegrating rapidly.

There was good news, a saving grace of sorts. Darold Knowles returned to action. Back from Air Force duty in Japan, he pitched an inning of perfect relief against the Twins in the first-game loss. Frank Howard hit his 15th homer and Ken McMullen was heating up, going 3-for-3, but there was little to show for their efforts — a single run.

The most amazing thing about the loss to the Twins was what Shirley Povich noted in the *Washington Post* after the game. The team was mired in a terrible slump in which the Senators lost fifteen of nineteen games. Povich took note of the irony that Williams was "not acting out, or bursting out, as the Senators' manager, because two of his governing forces will not permit it. He is stubborn and he is proud." The predictions that Williams would be gone by May — too angry and frustrated at losing — were proving shortsighted.

Williams was too engaged in the action in 1969 to lose focus. He knew that many of the losses before the Minnesota series had been close, lost by a single run. Williams remained upbeat, saying that it proved the Senators "we're not really a bad team." Williams opined that what the Senators needed was one more good ballplayer to even the odds. His words fell on deaf ears. Bob Short was not interested in paying for anything additional.

Darold Knowles, however, was free, and he could make a big difference on the pitching side. The pitching was in disarray, but what Williams wanted was another slugger. Knowles improved the situation, but with Bosman out and Pascual looking like he might be done, the team needed more than a great relief pitcher. Although Williams wanted more, his batting order was more respectable than he would acknowledge. With the two sluggers — Howard leading the league in homers and Epstein close behind — and Ken McMullen healthy again and hitting behind them, it might be enough.

A change of fortune came the next night. Barry Moore pitched a complete-game six-hitter to shut down the Twins, and Brant Alyea, part of Williams' platoon for Epstein, had three hits, including a three-run homer that proved to be the clincher. The game changed the flow. A starting pitcher went the distance and rested the overworked bullpen. The platoon worked and made it look like Williams had the right man in the lineup at the right time for a change. Alyea was leading the team in batting average at .347, so it was not difficult for Williams to write his name into the lineup; it was hard to take Epstein's bat out.

The next night was even more upbeat as Washington won again, this time on the sweet end of a one run, 4–3 margin. Howard's run-scoring single in the ninth inning and a solid relief performance from Dennis Higgins were the margin of victory. Billy Martin might have liked a play in the ninth most of all. With the Twins still up by a run, Hank Allen doubled and sat on second base when the Minnesota catcher fired a pickoff throw into center field. Allen not only raced around third with Martin speed and daring, but he knocked the catcher off his pins to score the tying run.

After their dust-up to begin the series, Williams must have darted a glance over at Martin to see how he liked the Washington style of play under Teddy Ballgame. The win gave Washington a series win for the first time since the beginning of May, and it was a win against the Twins, league leaders and significant rivals to Washington fans and their manager. After the game Martin was almost conciliatory toward Williams, saying, "He was the greatest hitter I ever saw, he was without peer. But there is more to baseball than just hitting."

The two men were from two different sides of the baseball coin. Both were known for a passionate commitment to the game, but as managers they were on very different tracks. It was hard to tell then that Martin was the better manager, and would become one of the most accomplished skippers in major league history. He stayed in hot water constantly while Williams emanated an almost patrician aloofness. The key difference was that Martin's team was in first place. The Senators were stuck just above Cleveland, four games below .500 and holding on precariously.

The homestand continued with a Memorial Day doubleheader against the White Sox. In the first game Camilo Pascual's career reached a crossroads when he was taken out after only two innings. Williams announced he would use Pascual only for mop-up appearances. Williams was all brusqueness when talking about the former Senators ace. He said he would not use Pascual unless it was absolutely necessary because he didn't have anything left. Williams' remarks overlooked a successful career of 174 wins, but the former star's performance over the first two months left the manager little choice.

Darold Knowles bailed the Senators out, getting the win in the first game when Howard led a late-inning surge for a come-from-behind 5–4 win. Knowles pitched another two innings of perfect relief in the nightcap, but his mates in the bullpen dug too deep a hole for the offense to climb out. The Senators walked away from the double-header with a split. Knowles' win in the first game was his second in as many days, coming less than a week after re-joining the team. Asked if he noticed the lower mound when pitching, Knowles said he could not tell the difference.

Williams, who was still fuming over Jim Hannan's five walks in the first three innings of the game, preferred to talk about Darold Knowles in his post-game comments. He said his new relief pitcher got the ball over the plate and had a good low fastball for double plays. He also fielded his position. George Minot observed that Knowles was the "only Senator who hasn't said that he owes it all to Ted."

Dennis Higgins was grateful for the help as the bullpen looked ragged and overworked in the double-header. Part of the problem was Dick Bosman's continued absence. It was hurting the team, but the trainers announced he was ready to return from injury.

The real pitching star as June began was Barry Moore. With a 1.69 ERA, the left-hander led the league, ahead of Jim Palmer, Dave McNally, Mike Cuellar and the rest of the talented pitching at the other end of the Baltimore-Washington Parkway. Joe Coleman was pressed back into service as a starter and responded in the last game of May with seven decent innings that gave the offense a chance to win. His batterymate, Paul Casanova, in a rare offensive display, went 3-for-5 with a home run and five runs batted in. He attributed the outburst to extra work with Williams.

With four wins to close out the month, the team was nearing .500 again, and the pundits were taking a look back over the first two months with decidedly mixed reviews. The Senators' record was much improved over 1968, but it wasn't just the won-lost record; there was a competitive edge to the team that hadn't been there the previous season.

Washington's political pundits were marking the first one hundred days of the Nixon administration, giving it uneven marks at best. Merrell Whittlesey in his column offered his expertise on non-sports related topics when he opined that Nixon "created controversy from coast to coast and around the world." Former Vice President Humphrey was more sanguine, saying that it was unfair to expect the new president to end a war in only a few months when the prior administration had fought it unsuccessfully for the better part of four years.

Merrell Whittlesey had critical things to say about Ted Williams as well. "Williams is probably the worst dresser in the game. He has a confessed profanity problem." Yet the column was intended in the spirit in which Williams approached the game — disciplined good fun. When he had ripped Paul Casanova for his casual wear upon leaving the clubhouse after a game, Casanova retorted, "Well, it's better than that white shirt you wear everywhere." Williams spun around grinning, threatening Casanova with an opportunity to dress out in Buffalo, the Triple-A Senators' affiliate where Bosman was rehabbing.

Whittlesey saved his most critical remarks for Williams' management of the pitching staff and his quick hook for the start. The remarks steered clear of the dreadful statistics for those starters, and concluded with a swipe at the controversial 15-minute rule. Williams had initiated a rule at the beginning of the season that reporters were not allowed in the clubhouse until fifteen minutes after the game. The idea was intended to protect the players from making remarks before they had time to reflect on the game and cool down — something that would have benefited Williams during his long career.

The press had given the rule a rude reception. The most heated confrontation over it had naturally occurred in Boston in April, where the press still barked Williams' name. Others in the press corps chafed about it as well, lamenting it as an infringement on free speech, as if the Berkeley student movement were their real milieu.

Shirley Povich penned his own reflections, looking at "Ted Williams' First Fifty-Six Days," a tongue-in-cheek reference to Nixon's first hundred days. He gave Williams passing marks both for his perseverance and results, noting that Williams had taken the same personnel that finished last the year before and had crafted a "respected team." Povich said that the leadership Williams provided went beyond the hitting instruction, citing the increased discipline he brought to the team, the superior conditioning he demanded, and the generally higher expectations that created a winning atmosphere and had been met positively by the players.

The demise of the starting pitching with the top three of the rotation, Pascual, Coleman, and Hannan, had challenged Williams, Povich said, but gave Williams good marks for managing the staff. It was the small things accomplished with hitters like Casanova, Brinkman and Epstein that Povich said made the difference. Of Casanova, Williams was quoted as saying, "Dammit, I know I can help that guy." That same passionate determination and confidence marked his approach with the team as a whole. It was, in fact, the extra offense Williams had managed to squeeze from the lineup each day that was keeping the team afloat, not the least of them the changes to the Gentle Giant. Frank Howard was eager to tell how much attention he was paying to Williams, who "took an undisciplined hitter" and was suddenly "getting more hitters' counts — 2–0, 3–2."

Overall Williams' report card looked much better than Richard Nixon's. Williams had made a few humble promises to bring Joe McCarthy's discipline and professionalism to the Senators. He was doing that and making it succeed. Unlike Nixon, Teddy Ballgame's plan was no secret. It was more and more batting practice, and it was working exactly as he had laid it out in the spring.

9

June, She'll
Change Her Tune

Everything changed in June. Before the month was out, the team would have turned like an ocean liner, slowly embarking on a new direction neither the fans nor the franchise had experienced in decades. It all started with the first game of the month, another masterful complete-game win for Barry Moore. Rounding into the staff ace, ahead of all of the "Big Four" the *Washington Post* had touted in March, Moore won his fourth game of the year, allowing only two runs in nine innings of work.

Once again Moore's outing gave the bullpen a day off and the starting rotation another productive day to work toward the return of Dick Bosman. Frank Howard supplied the offense with a 3-for-5 outing that included his sixteenth home run of the season and three RBIs that gave him 40 for the season. His .299 batting average put him in the top ten in the league.

Eddie Brinkman had an excellent game and pushed his batting average to .273, which ranked him as one of the Senators' best hitters through the first two months. Ken McMullen, who was still suffering lingering effects from injury, was quietly effective, hitting his fourth homer. Brant Alyea added another home run, his sixth.

Alyea was locked into the Epstein platoon. When Washington faced a left-hander, Epstein sat on the bench — much to his chagrin — while Alyea played left field and Howard played first. Alyea was becoming the standard option, although Williams was pushing him to shorten his stroke and wait for the ball longer. Alyea described his approach as "swing hard and hope." He believed the money was in the home run, and baseball's front office, including Bowie Kuhn, was in total agreement.

The month of June saw a push by the Commissioner's Office to focus fan attention on the Baseball Centennial celebrations. The *Sporting News* and local newspapers around the country were touting the voting for "Greatest Ever" teams. Fans in each major league city were voting on player listings that looked back over the first 100 years of baseball for their team.

Chosen as the Senators' "Greatest Player Ever" was Walter "Big Train" Johnson. The fans selected the award and named a lineup to play behind Johnson that included the following:

TABLE 9-1. GREATEST WASHINGTON SENATORS PLAYERS, JULY 1969

Position	First Team	Second Team
First Base	Mickey Vernon	Joe Judge
Second Base	Bucky Harris	Buddy Myer
Shortstop	Joe Cronin	Eddie Brinkman
Third Base	Ossie Bluege	Ken McMullen
Left Field	Goose Goslin	Frank Howard
Center Field	Clyde Milan	Del Unser
Right Field	Sam Rice	Heinie Manush
Catcher	Muddy Ruel	Rick Ferrell
Right-handed Pitcher	Walter Johnson	Al Crowder
Left-handed Pitcher	Earl Whitehill	Tom Zachary

From: *The Sporting News*

The inclusion of several current Senators players — like Ed Brinkman and Ken McMullen — over players with better statistical credentials, like Cecil Travis at shortstop and Eddie Yost at third base, showed the bias of current events and to some degree the limited memory span of the fans who voted.

Heinie Manush made only the second team and was the only Hall of Fame player slighted. At issue was Clyde Milan's selection. Milan was a speedy center fielder whose defensive skills were without peer, but Manush was a much better player overall whose impact during the best years of the franchise were difficult to ignore. Milan's career did not intersect with the championship teams in 1924–25, nor did he play on the great teams in the thirties that had featured Manush. Milan *did* manage to lead the league in stolen bases with 88 in 1912 and 74 in 1913, and had 494 over a sixteen-year span that predated the age of Maury Wills and Lou Brock by forty years.

Raising the issue of the all-time great Senators gave some perspective to Washington fans. Only older fans had seen any of the greatest names on the list play. Most fans had only witnessed the post–1933 teams fielded by the Griffiths, or worse yet, the expansion Senators of the '60s. But the only modern-era player on the all-time greats list was Mickey Vernon, who nudged out Joe Judge, another of the great players in the '20s.

C.C. Johnson Spink, the editor and publisher of the *Sporting News*, decried the low level of participation in the "Greatest Ever" series being promoted in major league cities around the country. Only 5,216 voters selected the Senators' all-time greats, and Spink was concerned that the new commissioner and his lieutenants would be unable to organize a celebration befitting the centennial of baseball and the great players in the first one hundred years of its history.

Spink's worried whether the formal announcement of player selection, scheduled to be made the night before the All-Star game in Washington, D.C., July 21, would generate the warranted pomp and circumstance. A dinner at the Omni Shoreham Hotel in Washington would host the celebration. But with balloting running at low levels, Spink was understandably anxious that another opportunity to pump life into the game was slipping from major league baseball's grasp.

One person whose popularity could not be higher was Ted Williams. Williams was named the greatest Red Sox player in history, and sportswriters were just warming up their pens on the issue of who were the all-time greatest players at each position,

Frank Howard's 1969 season was not complete, but at its end he would move into consideration for the list of all-time Washington greats. Howard was named to the same second team with Manush, but the problem was fitting him into a single position. Although Howard is the greatest Washington slugger, his lack of fielding prowess and his prodigious strikeout totals and lower batting average diminish his standing. The 1969 season marked the first time in his career that he was hitting for average and keeping his strikeouts low. The consistency of his approach at the plate — no long slumps — was also new.

The streakiness that had plagued him in Los Angeles was gone. In prior years Howard could carry a team — the Dodgers or Senators — for weeks, only to bury himself with strikeouts and bad play in the field for other long stretches. In 1969 the tinkering that Williams did was keeping Howard focused patient at the plate, thereby moving his career to a point where he deserved consideration as one of the elite players in Washington history.

On the actual field of play — away from lofty considerations — history was again being made. The Senators' victory on June 1 against Chicago gave the team three of four against the White Sox and their second consecutive series win. They were nearing .500 again, and no Washington expansion team had been this good this late in the year.

The Senators went on the road against a Kansas City team that had swept the Senators at home in May. Washington had an abysmal record against the Royals and Pilots — the two newest expansion teams. They had managed only one win against eight losses in the nine games they had played against Seattle and Kansas City. Everyone knew that if the team was going to be as respectable as Shirley Povich was saying, the Senators would have to beat the low-ranking teams.

The Senators' offense provided the margin to defeat the Royals in the first game of the Kansas City series as Hondo scored four times to fuel a 7–6 win. Epstein, McMullen, and Bernie Allen banged out the hits to bring Howard around to score, and Dennis Higgins closed the door after Kansas City scored two in the bottom of the ninth to bring the Royals within a run. The win was the sixth in seven games and put the team a single game below .500.

It was the best winning percentage the team had seen since prior to the long and disastrous West Coast road trip that had pushed the Senators five games under .500 early in the season. The Royals won the second game behind young pitching phenom Wally Bunker, who struck out ten in a complete-game win. Another exciting Kansas City rookie by the name of Lou Piniella drove in the winning runs.

Piniella was a crucial figure in the next day's game as well, but it was Mike Epstein's 13th home run that gave Washington the win. All of the starters got hits to plate three runs, but it was the return of an effective Joe Coleman on the mound that keyed another victory. Coleman went the distance and was happy that the win would get him back to his old spot in the rotation. He wanted to be a big-game pitcher and nothing could make the case for him like a masterful performance he turned in against the Royals.

Coleman incurred the wrath of Lou Piniella, the feisty Kansas City rookie, in the bottom of the third inning when he tagged Piniella running down the first base line. Piniella turned on Coleman after the play, and still holding his bat in hand, tried to connect with any part of Coleman he could find. Fisticuffs would have ensued had Mike Epstein — the former Cal linebacker and fullback — not stepped in between the two hot-headed young ballplayers.

George Minot, the *Washington Post* beat writer, observed that it was the first time the Senators had been involved in anything approaching a brawl that he could remember in quite some time. He seemed to relish the sight of the bullpens emptying onto the field and the prideful display by teams battling only to stay out of the American League cellar. Washington was able to walk now with a little more swagger, a little more glide in its stride, as the win gave the Senators another series win, their third in a row.

More importantly, the team was moving up in the standings, this time ahead of the Yankees in the American League East. Washington was again but a single game below .500. The Baltimore Orioles were running away with the American League. They were twenty games over .500, and only Boston was hanging with them, three and one-half games back. Detroit was proving Povich right when he guessed early in the season that the Tigers did not have the pitching to repeat. Denny McLain was not having the same kind of year he had in 1968, and the Tigers were now only three games ahead of Washington.

The Senators continued their road trip to Minnesota to visit Billy Martin again. It was an important game for Washington, and Ted Williams pulled no punches in trying to keep his team winning. He started Barry Moore, who was his best pitcher, to begin the series. Pitching for Minnesota was Jim Kaat, another of the old Senators who had found considerable success in the Twin Cities. Kaat gave up nine hits in six innings and another four walks, but Washington could manage only a single run. Darold Knowles pitched the final four innings in relief of Barry Moore and together they limited the potent Twins lineup to only four hits to walk away with a tight 1–0 win. The tense win brought the Senators back to even, 28 wins and 28 losses.

Minnesota came back and won a lopsided game the next day, 10–1, against Jim Hannan, but Washington would not give in and came back to win the rubber match, a 12-inning contest decided by a rare Del Unser home run. The game was the kind of slugfest that had the baseball gods smiling as Howard and Epstein homered for the Senators and Killebrew connected for the Twins. Camilo Pacual was given one last chance by Williams. Pascual went five innings, giving up only two runs, but Shellenback and Higgins allowed the Twins to tie the score in the eighth. Knowles and Casey Cox kept Minnesota off the board for four innings and set the stage for Unser's two-run shot that settled the affair, a 7–5 win for Washington.

The two victories over the Twins marked the fourth straight series win. Shirley Povich's idea that the Senators were now a respectable team had a more sober sense of reality to it now. Not only was this team better than the 1968 Senators, it was maintaining a .500 record, even threatening to win consistently. They were winning against the best of the west and had a long homestand coming at RKF Stadium against the other West Coast teams.

The Oakland Athletics were making a serious run in the new Western Division behind young slugger Reggie Jackson. Jackson was hitting them out just as fast as Frank Howard. The two men were tied atop the American League in the home run race. Epstein was not far behind, and it was becoming more common for the two men to hit back-to-back homers, with Epstein now hitting third in the order and Howard fourth on many nights.

In the first inning of the first Oakland game at RFK, Howard hit his eighteenth and was followed by Ken McMullen with his fifth. The victim was Blue Moon Odom, who got only one batter out in the inning before being replaced by Lew Krausse, who was part of a very good Oakland bullpen trying to hand the game to Rollie Fingers — the more deadly version of Darold Knowles from Oakland. Reggie Jackson and Sal Bando pushed across six runs for Oakland, and their bullpen shut down the Senators after the first inning. Fingers closed out the game and the A's won, 6–4.

Joe Coleman continued to look good back in his role of starter, allowing only three runs over six innings, but Dennis Higgins gave up the winning runs in relief. The crowd at RFK booed Williams when he went out to the mound in the seventh to remove Coleman, who had thrown only 90 pitches. It was the quick hook that Ted made famous that year, but Coleman supported the move in the press the next day by saying Higgins had been so good all year long that with only a one-run lead, it made sense.

The A's won the next night by the same score as Epstein and Howard went 0-for-11 against Catfish Hunter and the Oakland bullpen. Barry Moore took the loss. It was his first bad outing in many weeks. Reggie Jackson hit two home runs in the game to supply the offense. He took the lead over Frank Howard with nineteen home runs for the year. Frank Bertaina gave up the second home run to Jackson in relief and was placed on waivers after the game.

The big news in the second Oakland game was Richard Nixon attending the contest with his daughter Julie and David Eisenhower, the son of the former president and Nixon's son-in-law. When the president called Ed Doherty and said he wanted to attend, he got the same box seats from which he had thrown the first pitch on Opening Day. Ticket holders in the area had to make room for the president and his secret service contingent, but everyone was smiling.

The president had not been to a game since the opener in April. He had been traveling extensively in April and May, pursuing a negotiated peace to the war in Vietnam. Merrell Whittlesey wrote in the *Sporting News* that Nixon showed a remarkable grasp of the game. He gabbed to Doherty, who sat with the presidential party, about his favorite players over the years. At the top of the list was Ted Williams. Whittlesey said that Nixon spotted Bob Humphrey's knuckleball when he came into the game, but it was the young David Eisenhower who had the greater knowledge of the A's players, pointing out rookie slugger Reggie Jackson to his father-in-law.

Nixon responded to the sight of Reggie Jackson's home run with a personal letter to him on White House stationery. The letter later appeared in the *Sporting News* and spoke of his daughter and son-in-law as the more rabid Reggie Jackson fans. Nixon informed Jackson, "Although I always root for the home team, I have nothing but admiration for your performance on the night that I saw you."

Nixon was clearly a Senators fan and applauded the team when it came back late in the game to tie the score. Both Eisenhower and Nixon were avid enough fans to stay until the very end of the long thirteen-inning game, and Nixon promised to return when the Orioles came to town two weeks later.

Just days before the game Nixon had been on the historic island of Midway in the Pacific Ocean trying to end the long and deadly struggle in Vietnam. Nixon announced in press articles that "the Communists are more serious about negotiations than ever before." The *Washington Post* announced the day before the Oakland series that fighting was leveling off and the casualty rate lower.

Nixon took advantage of the lull in fighting to order a pullout of 25,000 American troops, saying that the South Vietnamese army was growing strong enough to allow American troop reductions. The strategy would backfire on Nixon as his growing reliance on the South Vietnamese convinced him to move away from direct negotiations with the North. The strategy would continue for the duration and diminish much of the support he still enjoyed in June.

While baseball may have come as a relief to the president of the United States, relief was hard to find in the Senators' bullpen. Ted Williams had used six relievers in the long losing effort against Oakland with the president looking on, and three the night before. Overuse was taking its toll. And there was no sign of Dick Bosman on the horizon yet. The bullpen pushed forward an unlikely hero for the last game against Oakland.

Jim Shellenback started the last game of the series against Reggie Jackson and company and did what few others had been able to accomplish: he pitched a nine-inning complete game, keeping Williams in the dugout and the boo-birds in check. It must have been a tough day for Ted. Shellenback walked five and gave up seven hits. There were base runners in every inning, but Eddie Brinkman's magic bailed Shellenback out three times on double plays. Brinkman walked, singled and scored two of the Senators' four runs in the 4–1 win.

Dick Bosman said of Ted Williams' managing in 1969 that he had remarkable luck. There were periods when every move he made seemed perfect for the situation, when whatever Williams called for seemed to click whether it was a hit-and-run or a squeeze. Whatever button Ted Williams pushed, it worked. The selection of Shellenback to pitch against Oakland when the team so desperately needed a win would have to qualify as one of his better calls.

Yet it was still the offensive resurgence of the team — an area where luck played far less a role — that continued to keep the team afloat. Eddie Brinkman was exhibit A. A growing chorus in Washington was touting Brinkman as an all-star for the mid-season classic that was looming on the horizon. Brinkman was still hitting over .270, and his glovework had no equal in the league.

Exhibit B, and more amazing still to the fans who had booed Howard's strikeouts when he came over from the Dodgers, was Hondo hitting .310. It was the best average on the team and fifth-best in the American League. Darold Knowles' numbers were getting notice around the league as well. Since joining the team he had pitched fourteen innings and had yet to be scored on. He was still reporting to Andrews Air Force Base for duty periodically, but was not letting the distraction interfere with his pitching.

Washington sports fans were watching another local player with fascination. Deane Beaman, the resident professional golfer at the Bethesda Country Club outside D.C., shot a 68 and was tied for third in the U.S. Open on its first day. More startling was the presence of a black golfer on the PGA tour. Lee Elder was in the U.S. Open as the first African American golfer ever to play in the event in its 73-year history. Beaman took the lead in the Open on the second day as the Los Angeles Angels teed it up at RFK for a two-game series.

The only starters for Washington who had remained healthy were Joe Coleman and Barry Moore. Injuries were pressing hard on Williams, and he was forced to start Camilo Pascual in the opener of the California series despite the knowledge that the veteran had nothing left. But there were few options. Williams had persuaded owner Bob Short to evaluate what the trade wires might bring, and with the Angels in town, the two teams talked about a pitching trade.

The word was that Short wanted to shock the baseball world with a headline-grabbing trade. Merrell Whittlesey wrote that Short was trying to pry Reggie Jackson away from Oakland for Epstein and Howard. Critics believed that Short was hamstrung by having no general manager, but he dismissed such talk, saying Williams was all the expert advice he needed. The Angels were willing to trade pitching but wanted Mike Epstein and Ken McMullen in exchange. Discussions widened to Boston, but talks provide futile. There was no pitching help to be had.

Dick Bosman may have been the ace of the staff, but he was getting no one out from the disabled list. Pascual was not the embarrassment Williams had described a few days earlier. Pascual yielded only a single run in two innings and the bullpen rose to the task, with Bob Humphreys and Dennis Higgins pitching seven innings of relief as Washington got a 6–2 win. Frank Howard's 19th home run provided the excitement as the Senators muddled their way back to .500.

After losing a 3–2 game to the Angels and wasting another good effort by Joe Coleman, Washington had to face the league-leading Orioles, who were coming for another visit to RFK. Casey Cox came out of the bullpen to start the first game. Washington had played its most determined baseball against Baltimore, which increasingly looked like the best team in baseball. The Senators had beaten ace Jim Palmer, but Williams' ability to patch together a pitching staff was beginning to look more and more like smoke and mirrors; the fishing line that held it all together was spinning to reveal an empty spool.

TABLE 9-2. AMERICAN LEAGUE STANDINGS, JUNE 10, 1969

Eastern Division

Team	Wins	Losses	Pct.	GB
Baltimore	39	16	.709	—
Boston	35	18	.660	3½
Detroit	27	23	.540	9½
Washington	29	29	.500	11½
New York	28	29	.491	12
Cleveland	18	32	.360	18½

Western Division

Team	Wins	Losses	Pct	GB
Minnesota	29	23	.558	—
Oakland	25	24	.510	2½
Seattle	24	28	.462	5
Chicago	21	28	.429	6½
Kansas City	23	31	.426	7
California	17	34	.333	11½

Source: *Washington Post*

10

How Many Times Must
The Cannon Balls Fly?

Professional baseball pitchers had reason to look a little shell-shocked as the 1969 season moved towards its midpoint. A single game and a single player provided anecdotal evidence as to the turn baseball was taking and the firepower that was confronting the once-dominant American League hurlers. Reggie was single-handedly giving AL pitchers something more to think about. He was carving his name across the headlines, taking the home run lead in the American League with two Ruthian shots against Boston on June 14 for his 22nd and 23rd round-trippers on the year. It was the sixth time in the season that the young slugger had hit two homers in a single game.

On that June day Jackson had ten RBIs in a remarkable performance that saw his Oakland teammates score a total of 21 runs. Carl Yastrzemski in the same game had two homers as well, and the Red Sox scored seven overall. Five home runs were hit in the game and 28 runs scored, totals that many major league teams in 1968 might have been hardpressed to meet in a week or more. Less than a week later, Oakland scored 16 runs to beat Kansas City, 16–4.

The rules changes in 1969 — the smaller strike zone and lower mound — were creating more excitement. If home runs and runs scored per game were the formula for added thrills, then the game was on its way to becoming a theme park ride. Runs per game in the middle of June were up by more than a run and a half per. The ultimate baseball thrill, the home run, was tracking well ahead of 1968 levels at almost two per game, compared to slightly more than one per game in '68. The dreaded baseball snooze, the shutout, was occurring much less often.

Whether it was the lower mound or the strike zone, something cost pitchers their edge. It could be seen in the ERAs, as well as the numbers of walks and strikeouts. The only team in 1969 with an ERA below 3.00 was the Baltimore Orioles at 2.40. No other team was even close, and the second-best team ERA belonged to the Twins at 3.21. Three teams had ERAs over 4.00 and only one was an expansion team. Teams were allowing 3.7 walks per game in 1969 as opposed to less than 3.0 per game in '68. Strikeouts were down only slightly at this point in the season, but they were down nonetheless.

The Senators pitching numbers put the team in the middle of the pack. What critics might call mediocrity was a remarkable accomplishment for a staff that had been so bad in '68, and had experienced such adversity in the first few months of '69. When factoring in the problems encountered by the pitchers in '69 — the ineffectiveness of Camilo Pascual and the injury to Bosman — Ted Williams' ability to nurse wins from the staff was uncanny. Washington pitchers were giving up only 3.58 earned runs per game, which represented a notable improvement from the prior year when their 3.82 norm was the worst in the league, even as the season neared a halfway point.

The staff was no longer last in the league in strikeouts. Washington had upped its total because Williams' emphasis on breaking pitches like the slider was having an effect. A statistic that must have caused Williams some consternation was the number of walks. The Washington pitching staff had allowed 100 more walks than the league-leading Baltimore Orioles and was the worst in the league in this respect.

Although Casey Cox said years later that he had success in '69 by inverting the lessons taught by Williams to the hitters, the other pitchers were not there yet. The idea that hitting success revolved around patience and getting a good pitch to hit meant to Cox that pitching success was achieved by getting ahead of the hitter and never giving the batter that good pitch to hit. Cox was having success with the formula by posting an ERA of 2.29, second only to Dick Bosman and Darold Knowles.

Cox in a June article laid the credit for his improved numbers squarely at the door of his manager. "Ted Williams has helped me gain the confidence and concentration that a pitcher needs in a situation like that," he said, referring to pitching against Harmon Killebrew with the game on the line in the eleventh inning. Cox said that the confidence helped him throw more strikes. It was not a lesson that was being passed around the staff yet.

The pitcher who was having the most difficulty making the adjustment to the new mound and strike zone was Jim Hannan. His ERA of 3.91 was one of the worst on the team, and he was walking batters at an alarming rate. In 69 innings he had issued 48 bases on balls. It was more alarming statistically that he had fewer strikeouts than batters walked.

Oddly enough, the same could be said of the best starter during the first few months of the season. Barry Moore had walked more batters — 38 —

than he had struck out — 31. The numbers presaged difficulties that Moore would have in the second half of the season. Contrastingly, Hannan would put the lessons of pitching coach Sid Hudson to good use in the second half and turn his season around.

The statistics bore out the larger reality that Washington was more than holding its own. It was June 17 and the Senators were still in the middle of the pack, ahead of the Yankees and looking up at the Tigers, who sat just ahead in third place in the Eastern Division standings. At a similar point in 1968, the team had been twelve games under .500 and on a hopeless slide that did not end until the season mercifully concluded.

Now the primary problem Washington had was the Orioles were next on the schedule. The Senators indeed had their work cut out with Baltimore in town, but Bob Short could not have been happier. He figured the local rivalry and the presence of the league leaders would bring out good crowds, and he was right. The three-game series brought out 46,000 fans for a mid-week series, and overall attendance was significantly up from '68 levels.

Despite all the good news, despite the 22,000 fans who showed up for a Tuesday night game, Short was telling sportswriters that he stood to lose a half-million dollars. That calculation, according to Whittlesey, was based on drawing 700,000 fans. He was also complaining about radio and television broadcast rights, saying that Oriole-Senators games should be blacked out locally, and Short was pushing for a more lucrative radio contract.

Having the president attend another game — this time to see the Orioles — was another marketing tool that was free of charge to Short. Nixon was no lucky charm for the team. The Senators lost the third game that he attended, and the Oriole series was not a good one on the field in any way. The league-leading Baltimore pitching staff limited Washington to only two runs over the course of the three games as the Orioles swept the series. Joe Coleman, Barry Moore, and Jim Hannan pitched well against Baltimore's offense that featured Frank Robinson, Brooks Robinson, and Boog Powell, but they received no support. Darold Knowles extended his string of scoreless innings as well, but it was for naught.

The Orioles' record stood at an amazing 47–17 at the end of the series in Washington. It was an unprecedented winning percentage of .734. Washington was only grist for the mill, able to look competitive against the best in the league, but unable to close the deal.

The best news was the return of Dick Bosman. He threw two scoreless innings of relief against the Orioles and proved to his manager that he was ready to go. With Bosman in tow for the first time since May, the team left for a series in Detroit. With both Darold Knowles and a healthy Dick Bosman, the mediocre pitching could only get better.

The press and pundits were saying if there were just another arm or another bat, it might tip the balance in the Senators' favor. Short was criticized as a naïve trader, that the general managers of other teams were toying with him to see if they could steal him blind. But on June 20, the team announced the acquisition of Arthur Lee Maye from the Cleveland Indians for slightly more than the waiver price of $25,000. Ted Williams may have wanted more, but he was happy that Short had finally gotten him some help.

Maye was an intriguing figure, who had starred first as a rhythm-and-blues singer. He sang at times with the well-known group The Platters and had hits of his own with his group The Crowns during the early sixties. In 1964 his greatest hit song, "Halfway Out of Love," topped the charts. It was also his best year with the Milwaukee Braves. He hit .304 in 588 plate appearances with ten homers while playing both at third base and in the outfield.

Picking up Maye was a shrewd move by Short, who finally found a trading partner more desperate than himself—the Cleveland Indians. Although Maye was not a top-tier talent, he was a solid ballplayer. At thirty-five years old, he was at the back end of his career, and the Indians had been willing to take cash for a veteran who was blocking the path of younger players the Indians would need to build around for the future. Washington sent to Cleveland right-handed pitcher Bill Denehy from its Triple-A Buffalo franchise to complete the deal. Cleveland was spiraling downward and a prospect like Denehy coupled with cash were welcome additions.

Functioning as his own general manager, Short made one notable assertion never heard before about the ability of race to impact the game of baseball in Washington, D.C. He was continuing to claim in the press that he wanted Reggie Jackson from the Oakland Athletics, saying again that he would give up both Epstein and Howard in the trade. Short said a talent like Jackson could have great appeal in a town like Washington, DC. He explained that Washington's large black population did not support the team as well as might be expected and that adding a black superstar was economic common sense.

Short admitted, "I am no expert." Calvin Griffith might have agreed, but much had changed since Griffith had pulled up stakes and fled to Minnesota. In the final analysis, Lee Maye could not change the racial dynamic the way a Reggie Jackson might have, but it was an important acquisition for the team nonetheless. Maye was a left-handed hitter who gave Ted Williams more interesting platoon possibilities.

Maye started the first game of the Tiger series on June 20, batting second against the right-handed Denny McLain. The game was a pitchers' duel with Joe Coleman matching McLain until Williams removed the young pitcher in the seventh and brought in Darold Knowles. Knowles out-pitched McLain, and the Detroit bullpen surrendered five runs in the first extra frame to give the Senators the win, 7–2.

Frank Howard ended a brief dry spell in the first game in Detroit, hitting his 20th homer of the year. Reggie Jackson and the Oakland Athletics continued their offensive binge, one that would have been beyond the dulled mind of the '68 baseball fan. In a one-week period beginning on June 14, the Athletics scored seventy-one runs — an average of more than 10 per game. They put more points on the board than the Oakland Raiders football team and won by scores of 21–7, 13–5, and 16–4. Jackson was at the heart of the tear, hitting six home runs over the span of a week. The outburst put him ahead of Howard and Rico Petrocelli in homers. Howard took solace in his batting average that had climbed to .308, which put him in the top five in the league.

Mickey Lolich proved that the great pitchers of 1968 were not flukes as he pitched nine innings to win in the second game of the series, giving up only two earned runs. Brant Alyea and Frank Howard homered again and the Senators' offense took the last two games in the four-game series, scoring nine runs in a double-header on June 22. Mike Epstein was continuing to prove himself with the bat, and Eddie Brinkman was hefting heavy lumber as well. Steady Eddie pushed his batting average over .280 in the double-header, going 3-for-6 with four RBIs. The fans back home were calling for his selection to the All-Star game, and given his talent with the glove, it was not an outlandish expectation.

Dick Bosman continued his return from injury with six innings of shutout pitching in the first game of the double-header. He did not get the win, but the Senators could now boast a consistent rotation of Bosman, Moore, and Coleman, all of whom were pitching well as the month of June rolled toward its end.

Every winning streak the Senators put together seemed to end with the Orioles. Washington left Detroit and headed back to the East Coast to confront Baltimore once again. Taking three games of four in Detroit came on the heels of losing three to the Orioles, and Washington was still two games below .500 with 34 wins and 36 losses. For a moment in the first game of the series, it looked like the curse might be broken and the team ready for a real climb.

Casey Cox wanted to join Ted Williams' rotation, and he took the mound in his first major league start against Dave McNally. The Senators pitcher used his sinker and command of the strike zone to best McNally, going into the sixth inning with a 2–0 lead. But when Cox ran into trouble in the sixth, Williams handed the ball over to Darold Knowles to protect the lead. Knowles was arguably the best pitcher on the team. The heat and humidity were sapping Cox's stamina, so Williams' move to the bullpen made sense. Knowles got the side out in the sixth inning, but while pitching in the seventh inning, a rainstorm descended upon Memorial Stadium and interrupted play. When Knowles returned to the mound to finish out the inning, he was not the same pitcher.

It seemed as if the odds or the gods or something was opposed to the Senators beating the Orioles. The decisive blows were home runs by Davey Johnson and Frank Robinson in the bottom of the eighth inning as the Orioles scored five runs in the final two innings to win their 51st game of the season. With seven days left in the month of June, they were on a pace to win 118 games.

The next day the Orioles again won on the strength of Frank Robinson's bat. An eleventh-inning home run provided the margin of victory in a 6–3 Orioles win. This time the fine efforts of Jim Hannan were wasted. It was the first strong outing in more than a month for Hannan, who limited the league leaders to three runs over eight innings of work. Jim Shellenback was Robinson's victim as the Senators failed to push home the winning run on several occasions.

The Orioles' spell was finally broken in the last game of the series. Behind Frank Howard's 22nd home run, the Senators built a 6–1 lead, but Joe Coleman could not hold it. The Orioles came back to tie the score in the fifth inning, and the momentum seemed to shift just as it had in the prior games. But a three-run home run from Del Unser put the Senators ahead, 10–6, and Bob Humphreys and Knowles were able to hold the lead this time for the win and a final score of 11–8.

Baltimore won both of the two June series, but for the Senators, the hard-fought win in the final game on the 25th of June provided momentum. They had beaten one of the best pitchers in the league in Mike Cuellar, stood toe-to-toe with the division leaders, and punched back until they won. They returned home for a four-game series against the Red Sox and then back on the road against the Indians. They had their dignity intact and were still only three games below .500. They remained several games ahead of the Yankees, firmly in fourth place in the Eastern Division. Nearing the halfway point in the season, their record would be a low water mark as the tide began to rise for the Senators and lifted the career of almost every player to new heights.

11

The Heat Is On

Whenever the Senators returned to RFK Stadium, Bob Short had one thing on his mind, attendance. He set the bar for success at one million fans and said that was the level at which he could build a winning team. In Short's mind, winning did not happen on the field, but in the till of the cash register. He did not want to hear whether winning was the chicken or the egg, whether he had to have a winning team before he could bring in more fans. That was not important. He knew he did not have the money to build a winner and would have to draw fans through sheer bluster.

Short ignored the steady climb in attendance that could be seen at RKF and impatiently called for more. He claimed again that as things stood, the team was on track to draw no more than 700,000 fans, and he said that was not good enough to keep the team in Washington.

The Senators had not drawn a million fans since 1946, after the team had finished second in '45 and fourth in '46. There was a Catch-22 of which Short was keenly aware. Fans only came in great numbers to see winning teams, and winning teams cost money. Short was not going to put out the money for a winning team, so he put the onus on the fans to provide the money to improve the team. As the team improved in 1969, attendance had climbed steadily. There was proof in those figures that the city would support a winner.

"Ted Williams wants me to buy $1 million worth of ballplayers," Short said, "but I need help, I cannot do it alone." To attract more fans, he responded with promotional gimmicks like a milking contest between backup catcher Jim French and a local dairymaid. French won the pre-game contest handily, and attendance was topping 25,000 for most weekend games.

Winning teams were drawing record crowds in cities like Chicago, where the reversal of fortune for the Cubs produced sellouts at Wrigley Field. They literally had fans climbing over one another for access to the team. Detroit drew more than 50,000 to one of the games with Washington in

101

June, a year after the World Series and two years after the worst urban riots of the decade.

In Washington, Short said that although attendance was up over the prior year, "If I had stayed with last year's ticket prices, I would be broke." When asked whether he was just a carpetbagger in D.C. for a fast buck, Short replied in late June, "I'm no fool and no carpetbagger either." He remained concerned about his ability to milk profits from the concessions. Claiming he had never had a "hot hotdog," Short threatened to sue to gain control of the concessions. He was equally concerned about the parking that he continued to say was unsafe without additional lighting.

Attendance was boosted for the weekend homestand that featured the popular Red Sox, and the first game pulled in almost 30,000 paying customers to see a contender. Boston manager Dick Williams still talked hopefully about his team's chances of catching the Baltimore Orioles for the Eastern Division championship. The Red Sox were leading the league in home runs with a meaty batting order led by shortstop Rico Petrocelli, Carl Yastrzemski, and Tony Conigliaro. They were all established sluggers who had played on the championship team in 1967. The lineup also included two young power hitters in Reggie Smith and George Scott.

For all the power and box office draw Boston provided, the pitching was thin. Jim Lonborg was hurt and ineffective and never would regain the Cy Young form he had flashed in 1967. Ray Culp had replaced Lonborg to lead the rotation. Behind Culp there was not much help or consistency, and Dick Williams' problems became apparent during the series in D.C.

The large crowd in attendance at RFK for the Friday night game was disappointed as the Red Sox's worst pitcher — Bill Landis with an 8.76 ERA — held the Senators to only a single run over six innings. Barry Moore was unable to find the early-season form that had made him the ace of the staff, and he slipped to 6–3 after giving up four runs in five innings. The final score was 4–2 as Sparky Lyle pitched the final three innings in relief for Boston and got the save.

On Saturday slightly less than 10,000 fans were in attendance as the temperatures hit 100 degrees and the humidity made it seem much hotter. The *Washington Post* blamed the weather for the lack of attendance. The crowd that stayed for the entire ten-inning contest saw the Senators win one that even Ted Williams said, "We didn't deserve to win." Two Boston errors in the ninth inning on weakly hit balls allowed Washington to push across the tying run and knot the score at 3–3.

Ken McMullen was the hero of the game when he hit a game-winning home run in the 10th inning to send the noisy, cheering crowd to cooler climes. His home run barely cleared the fence and the glove of left fielder

Reggie Smith. It was in stark contrast to one hit earlier in the game by Frank Howard. Howard's 23rd home run of the season came in the eighth inning off Ray Culp. It landed in the third row of the left field upper-deck seating, where other seats are painted to celebrate Howard's moon shots. Dick Bosman continued his run of effective starts after being out with an injury, but the victory went to Darold Knowles, who returned to form for a scoreless tenth inning.

The last two games of the series were a Sunday double-header, and the heat was near intolerable as temperatures hovered near 100 degrees again on the field. Mike Epstein powered the sweep of the two games with homers in each game. In the nightcap, Epstein's homer traveled even farther than Howard's homer the prior day. David Bourbon, writing in the *Washington Post* the next day, said the shot was the first to reach the "binocular belt" all year, home to Bob Short's two-dollar seats. The homer was estimated at 475 feet, and one fan claimed that the ball had such force that it broke the seatback's wooden slats on impact.

Washington stroked fifteen hits in the second game and won by an 11–4 margin. Frank Howard and Del Unser had home runs, and Joe Coleman pitched a complete game that allowed a beleaguered bullpen a well-deserved rest from the heat. Lee Maye had played in all three of the wins and collected hits in each to make his first meaningful contributions after arriving from Cleveland in the trade.

The three-game winning streak put the Senators within a game of .500 at the end of June. They had played the best teams in the American League East to a draw and their status as a competitive team was not disputed by anyone. The dismal 1968 season was forgotten, and now the Senators had the Cleveland Indians coming to town for four games.

On the last Sunday in June, the ball was flying out everywhere in the American League. Reggie Jackson hit his 29th homer as Oakland took two games from the White Sox to stay ahead of the Minnesota Twins in a West Division race that was proving far more exciting than the East. Minnesota second baseman Rod Carew was leading the league with a .378 batting average a year after Carl Yastrzemski had won the batting title with a .301 mark. Yaz had only managed to get his average over .300 in the final week of the season.

In 1969, six others, including Frank Robinson of Baltimore and Rico Petrocelli and Reggie Smith of Boston, were over .300 as the season neared the halfway mark. The Senators were led by Frank Howard who was hitting .297. Buzzie Bavasi in Los Angeles must have been thinking how wise he had been to trade Howard to the American League.

The *Washington Post* noted two historic events the following day with no baseball action taking place. Several decades later it is still easy to see the historic import of Arthur Ashe seeking to play tennis in a tournament in South Africa. In 1969, Ashe was playing in his first Wimbledon tournament, and it was there that he announced to the media that he had applied to play in the South African Tennis Championships in March of the next year. He told the gathered sportswriters he had been told he would not be granted a travel visa to get into the country.

Ashe was at the height of his game, having won the U.S. Amateur Championship as well as the U.S. Open within a single year —1968. He then led the USA's Davis Cup team to victory. Ashe turned professional in 1969, and as he went out on tour, he used his status as an international tennis star to highlight the racial oppression of the South African government. He was successful in pressuring the International Tennis Federation to keep South Africa out of the professional tennis circuit and led a lengthy campaign against apartheid.

The Senators crafted their own historic statement that day. The Senators had never had a winning record as late in the season as July since expansion. With the cellar-dwelling Indians as opponents on their home turf, the Senators' chances for a memorable moment in the history of the young franchise were in place. Washington fans could experience winning baseball in the hot days of June and July and hope that it would continue. Washington had beaten Cleveland all six games the two teams had played in 1969 and wanted to keep that streak alive.

The mid-week series began with a Tuesday double-header. The Senators were sending out an unlikely champion in Casey Cox to start the first game. If he could win, the team would be at .500, and Barry Moore would start the nightcap with a chance to move back into the winner's circle. In his only prior start, Cox had been magnificent and hopes were high that he could repeat. Sid Hudson said that if Cox could develop a third pitch, he would make an excellent starter. He remained, however, only a two-pitch pitcher, throwing only a sinker and a slider. The 6'5" Cox had used the repertoire to great effect throughout the season.

The pressure would be on Moore in the second game to win and put the team over .500. He had been slipping steadily since his first six wins. Only a month earlier, at the beginning of June, Moore looked as though his career was taking off, but now after several consecutive bad starts, his early domination was being called into question. The problem was control. In the year of the new strike zone, control was at a premium, and Moore could not consistently command his pitches. He did not have overpowering stuff, and without an ability to locate his pitches effectively, batters were beginning to wait him out, and it was working.

The first game was a well-played affair from the Senators' perspective. Casey Cox was at his best. Although he walked six batters over the course of nine innings, he kept the sinkerball low and got two double plays to help keep Cleveland off the board. He gave up only a single run, and Frank Howard's mammoth 450-foot homer was the margin for victory in a 4–1 game. Eddie Brinkman and Mike Epstein also homered and set the stage for history to be made.

Barry Moore did not manage to turn it around in the second game. In the third inning, he gave up a home run to Tony Horton, and Cleveland managed to score four times in the inning to take a 5–2 lead. But Frank Howard continued his season-long siege of American League pitching with a 3-for-5 night that included his twenty-sixth home run and a game-winning, seeing-eye single in the ninth that gave the team a 7–5 win.

Eddie Brinkman added two hits in the second game and raised his average to .269, stratospheric regions for the great gloveman so late in the season. The fans were chanting during the game that he should be an All-Star, though Rico Petrocelli was having the better offensive season. In Washington, having a great year was measured differently. Brinkman, Mike Epstein, and Casey Cox, to name just a few, were having seasons filled with starry ambitions. Frank Howard was having the kind of season his early supporters in Los Angeles had always known was within his grasp. Despite the accolades of the fans for Brinkman and others, the Gentle Giant was the one player on the Senators roster who was truly having an All-Star season.

Even Howard was facing considerable competition among American League outfielders for the All-Star team. Carl Yastrzemski was the reigning batting champion and the twenty-three-year old Reggie Jackson had already hit his 30th home run to pace the division-leading Oakland A's. Frank Robinson was among the league leaders in batting average and home runs and was the leading hitter on an Orioles team that looked unbeatable in the Eastern Division. Although Frank Howard had been a starting outfielder for the American League in 1968, the field had grown more crowded in 1969 with the addition of the young Jackson.

In the third game of the Cleveland series, Dick Bosman held the Indians off the board until the sixth, and then Darold Knowles pitched two perfect innings for a 5–1 victory. The light-hitting Tim Cullen, who fought all season against Williams' ideas and the man himself, went 3-for-4. Brant Alyea knocked in two runs with two hits to provide the rest of the offense. The team stood at 41 wins and 39 losses. The next day would mark the midpoint of the season, and it was a certainty that Washington would have a winning record at that milepost.

In the jubilant celebration, Shirley Povich led his next column with a nomination for Williams as manager of the year. Claiming Williams had "brought the city joyously alive ... at the sudden success of the Senators," Povich raised the stakes for the newly ascendant manager and his team. He said a crucial difference between the '69 team and prior incarnations was the grittiness with which they battled back, and he laid the credit for that trait at Williams' doorstep. Povich called forth the ghosts of past seasons and the more than three decades of futility to which Senators fans had been subjected. He described Williams as performing in his first year of managing with "the self-assurance of old war-dog managers."

Povich noted the profound change in Ted Williams from a player to a manager. He said that as a player, Williams had been more profane with the scribes than the umpires, but as a manager, he raged at the men in blue and worked the scribes like the wily hitter who knew the umpires could be his friends. Williams was now more patient than disruptive, more sage than resentful. Povich accused the players, a bit tongue-in-cheek, of playing to please their manager, of being "apple-polishers" to the Hall of Famer they knew was back in the dugout watching them when they went to bat or out into the field.

Favorite teacher or not, Williams was taking the show on the road two days hence, to Beantown, where the ghosts and goblins of his past indiscretions awaited him. Everyone in baseball would be awed by the transformation in Williams when he greeted the Boston fans. And the fans themselves had a special treat in store for Teddy Ballgame.

Before leaving on the fateful trip, the Senators showed a modicum of mercy to Cleveland, losing the getaway game to Luis Tiant, 7–2. Tiant in two years would be headed to Boston as well, where he would perfect his peek-a-boo delivery and establish himself as one of the more memorable Red Sox hurlers. Camilo Pascual took the loss in what would be his final appearance as a Senator. He was sold for slightly more than the waiver price to the Cincinnati Reds. He had been a fan favorite in Washington in two different decades. He had been the Opening Day starter for the Senators on five occasions, and his 36 shutouts were tops among all active American League pitchers. Even to Ted Williams, he was more than just another pitcher.

Shirley Povich noted in his morning column the changing of the guard for the Senators as Bosman replaced the departing Pascual as the team ace. He noted how difficult and unfair it had been for the immensely popular Pascual to accept the booing that had begun at RFK when he departed after an unsuccessful start. "My coorve ball," he quoted the great Cuban pitcher as saying, "I dunno, I do not get it over the plate." More importantly, he cited the record-breaking performance of Pascual in 1960 when he had broken Walter Johnson's record with a 15-strikeout outing against the Red Sox in the final season of the old Senators. He ended the column saying that Pascual was the "finest fielding pitcher of his time," and one who also could handle the bat. The release of a great pitcher was fittingly noted by a great columnist.

Major league teams were part of the centennial celebrations in 1969. In Boston, the All-Time Great team that had been voted on by the fans was named in the papers on the morning before the July 4 game with the Senators. For fans at-large, it was just more of the ongoing centennial celebrations leading to the July 23rd All-Star Game, but to the Boston fans, it was something more. With Washington in town that day, and with Ted Williams in the visiting dugout, it was something more indeed.

The event started with all of the old players named on the list called one-by-one to stand along the foul line in a heart-warming pre-game ceremony reminiscent of a World Series or All-Star game. In what may have been a bit of a surprise given the nature of the relationship between Boston and Ted Williams, Williams was named the "Greatest Player Ever" to put on a Boston uniform by none other than those same Red Sox fans with whom he had shared such a long and complex relationship.

It was a compelling tribute given the many great players he was competing against. Ted's teammates Bobby Doerr and Joe Cronin took their place on the field along with Lefty Grove, who would be voted one of the greatest pitchers of all time. Carl Yastrzemski and Frank Malzone from the more modern era stood along the foul line as well. The applause rained down so thickly on the Red Sox that it almost needed to be brushed aside like confetti.

When Williams' award was announced last, the ovation grew and the crowd of 25,000 fans rose for a long and loud standing ovation. Wearing his dark blue Senators uniform and warm-up jacket, he jogged out to receive the award at home plate from Commissioner Bowie Kuhn. After years of animosity between Williams and the Boston fans, all was forgotten and forgiven. Williams even waved the cap he held humbly in his hand. Williams was so overwhelmed by the events that he claimed afterward to have been unaware of the intensity of the crowd's applause.

Ted Williams' team did not hold back on Boston for the nation's birthday, even after the gracious award for its manager. In the first game of the holiday double-header, Frank Howard went 3-for-3 with his 28th home run of the season. Ken McMullen was even better, going 4-for-5 with three runs batted in, and Jim Hannan and Dennis Higgins combined on a six-hitter. The 5–1 win for the rookie manager may have been the icing on a very sweet cake.

The Boston series ran for five games — a rarity that included back-to-back double-headers on July 4 and 5. Washington threw its entire rotation at the Red Sox over the course of the series, and it was now a very different group than what had been forecast in April. Without Camilo Pascual, the rotation included Jim Hannan, Joe Coleman, Barry Moore, Casey Cox, and Dick Bosman. Coleman followed Hannan in the Friday twi-night double-header but lost the game, 7–4, as Reggie Smith and Carl Yastrzemski homered — for Yaz his 23rd.

The Saturday double-header began with Barry Moore regaining his form to win his seventh game, but Casey Cox struggled in the nightcap, taking the loss. It was up to Dick Bosman, who went out to defend the new status of the team in the rubber game of the series. He was cementing his reputation as the ace of the staff each time he pitched. His game on July 6 was an ace's. He won it by going all nine innings, throwing a shutout against the very potent Red Sox batting order.

Bosman's command was so keen that even with the restrictive strike zone, he did not walk a batter. When he was right, his ball stayed in the bottom half of the strike zone, and in Boston, he hit the low target all day long on what was a hot Sunday afternoon.

The decisive victory put the team back to two games over .500. The Tigers had climbed into second place, and Washington was a scant three games out of third place behind Boston. The two six-team divisions engendered a palpable new sense of possibility. The problem for Washington was Baltimore, who like St. Louis in 1968, was running away from the pack. No one was going to catch Baltimore, and the rest of the teams were just playing for pride.

Years later various members of the team would recall the pitching staff as the glaring hole in what came to be a very competitive team. "We were just one good pitcher away from being able to really make a run," said Mike Epstein. It may not have been an idle boast. With an additional starter, Cox could have remained in the bullpen to shore up what was a very good core of relievers and what was rounding into a fine team at the midway point in the season.

Frank Howard continued his spree with two home runs in the middle game of the series. Howard sat on 30 home runs, with Reggie Jackson still keeping pace ahead of him. The two men were starting an exciting race where they would match one another with one long clout after the other in the weeks leading up to the All-Star Game. It was as though the two men believed they might be competing for the last outfield spot.

In the first game of an 11-game homestand that started with Cleveland, Frank Howard gave Reggie Jackson something to watch in his rearview mirror. The Gentle Giant hit two home runs in the first game, his 31st and

32nd, one of which measured at 486 feet into the center field upper-deck seats. Mike Epstein hit a very quiet 20th homer of his own. Casey Cox came on in relief of Frank Shellenback — the newest spot starter — and pitched a masterful six and two-thirds innings in which he gave up neither a walk nor a hit to take the 7–2 win.

The team was euphoric. A crowd of 1,700 fans had come to meet them at the airport when they returned to start the homestand. They were unused to such adulation. Jim French, the backup catcher and milking champion, was quoted in the *Washington Post* the next morning as saying, "This was the best game I've played in. It had everything — great plays, good execution and great pitching. We all did our part." French went 2-for-2 in a rare start. Shellenback drove in the first run in the second inning. Caught up in the noisy dressing room fever, he said, "It was only my second major league RBI ever."

Shellenback and Cox were both able to step into the fifth starter role at this point in the season. Had it not been for Baltimore's seemingly insurmountable lead, even Bob Short might have seen his way clear to invest in a fifth starter to bolster the team and send Shellenback and Cox back to the pen where their contribution would have been even more important.

As if on cue, in the second game of the series, Washington squandered an early lead with its bullpen and lost a 6–5 heartbreaker. But the Senators came back the next day behind Joe Coleman, who had his best game of the season. It was a complete-game shutout in which he struck out 11 Cleveland batters. Coleman was continuing to struggle with his control, but he was quiet and controlled about his tutelage with Ted Williams on throwing more breaking pitches. As long as it was working and the team was winning, the advice looked extremely good.

Howard and Epstein were batting third and fourth now in almost every game. The platoon of Epstein was fading as his home run total and batting average against lefties rose through the season. Lee Maye and Del Unser batted ahead of them, and the combination was responsible for steady offensive production. With Ken McMullen in the five hole, the Senators were a tough team to pitch to.

The Cleveland series put the Senators three games over .500, and there were still four games with the New York Yankees, who had been struggling all season. But they *were* still the Yankees, and they were only a few games behind the newly respectable Senators. The Yankees had an excellent left-handed pitcher in Fritz Peterson, who was starting the first game. Lefties caused the Senators problems. As good as Brant Alyea was looking at midseason, the lineup was not as strong when Ted Williams platooned for Epstein and Unser.

TABLE 11-1. SENATORS MIDSEASON STATISTICS

Hitting

Player	G	AB	R	H	2B	3B	HR	RBI	SB	AVG
Alyea	52	119	20	37	3	0	10	31	1	.311
Howard	86	324	62	99	12	1	30	62	0	.306
Epstein	73	217	43	61	11	0	19	48	2	.281
Unser	81	304	35	83	8	1	4	31	4	.273
H. Allen	74	216	34	59	7	2	1	15	11	.275
Brinkman	86	340	44	91	11	3	2	25	0	.265
McMullen	83	300	40	76	11	2	6	36	2	.255
B. Allen	64	186	19	47	9	3	5	25	0	.255
Maye	57	154	14	38	5	0	1	18	1	.247
Stroud	65	122	19	30	4	2	2	10	5	.246
Cullen	65	142	12	30	2	0	0	6	1	.211
Casanova	71	222	10	45	6	1	3	25	0	.203
French	28	68	6	11	3	0	2	7	0	.162

Pitching

Player	G	CG	IP	H	BB	SO	ShO	W	L	ERA
Cox	30	0	76	61	34	34	0	5	1	1.89
Knowles	16	0	19	23	8	21	0	4	1	1.89
Bosman	16	1	67	61	22	39	1	5	2	2.15
Baldwin	25	0	39	27	19	31	0	2	2	3.23
Humphrey	25	0	52	47	22	28	0	2	2	3.12
Higgins	30	0	53	52	29	49	0	7	7	3.23
Moore	17	3	87	70	43	36	0	6	3	3.41
Hannan	17	0	80	66	50	48	0	2	5	4.05
Coleman	17	3	110	110	45	73	0	4	6	4.34
Shellenback	13	1	29	25	20	10	0	1	3	4.65
Pascual	14	0	55	46	38	34	0	2	5	6.28

TABLE 11-2. AMERICAN LEAGUE STANDINGS, JULY 8, 1969

Eastern Division

Team	W	L	Pct.	GB
Baltimore	56	25	.691	—
Detroit	44	34	.564	10½
Boston	46	37	.554	11
Washington	45	42	.517	14
New York	40	46	.476	17½
Cleveland	32	59	.390	24½

Western Division

Team	W	L	Pct.	GB
Minnesota	47	34	.590	—
Oakland	42	35	.545	3
Seattle	36	45	.444	11
Chicago	35	45	.438	11½
Kansas City	35	47	.427	12½
California	30	50	.375	16½

Source: *Washington Post/Sporting News*

12

Moon Dance

As the nation headed into the Fourth of July weekend, the *Washington Post* ran a dramatic front-page photo showing the Apollo 11 spacecraft in all its quiet elegance silhouetted against the early morning sky just before the Florida sunrise. Americans had been fascinated by the space program since the beginning of the decade, had witnessed ten prior moon missions, and were trying to wrap themselves around the idea and magnitude of the historic moment. Mankind as a collective entity would set foot upon a foreign object in the sky, our own moon. True believers in the space program viewed the success of the Apollo program as a first step in a journey that would take mankind further into space.

The American moon mission was initiated by President Kennedy in a speech before a joint session of the Congress on May 25, 1961, when he laid out the goal for the "landing of a man on the moon and returning him safely to the earth." After three astronauts — the popular Gus Grissom, Roger Chafee, and Ed White — were killed shortly before the launch of the first moon rocket, NASA had to regroup and spent countless hours testing and planning for the moon program's ultimate goal.

There had been ten test flights of increasing duration and difficulty until astronauts had begun to circle the moon regularly in preparation for the first actual landing on the moon's surface. Calculations of orbit, thrust, gravitational pull and slingshot effects had all been perfected and were sketched out in special supplements to the Sunday paper published to illustrate for the public the program's careful and intricate science.

Photographs of the moon taken by the streaking lunar spacecrafts in earlier missions had allowed for careful selection of the landing site. Now with Americans learning the geography of a new world, including the names of giant craters and rivulets, the astronauts — Buzz Aldrin, Neil Armstrong, and Mike Collins — were visualizing their mission and spending the last few days practicing each step of it. There were elaborate simulators in which

The Apollo 11 spacecraft in all its quiet elegance (NASA).

they worked out the moment to moment realities they would encounter as they prepared for mankind's furthest reach in space and history.

The moon launch was pushing the less sanguine news to the sidelines. Americans were focused on the bright potential of the country's achievements in space, not the war still raging in Vietnam. Slightly more than 150 American soldiers died in the second week in July. A lull in fighting had brought the number down from 240 the week before, but American soldiers in Southeast Asia were still dying at a rate of ten thousand a year, and the great cargo planes that brought the caskets of the dead back home played on the news as a grim reminder of less lofty realities.

Americans went about their routines with the moon launch as emotional wallpaper, and the lowly Washington Senators continued their program to ascend to new heights as well. Washington fans were delirious with their new toy — a winning baseball team. There were fans dancing on top of the opposing team's dugout, carrying signs that read, "Yankees Go Home," and "The Nats Are For Real." The attendance for the Yankee series had Bob Short gushing to the press, "Now they are coming in the kind of numbers that will make us a success." Short was projecting attendance to hit the magic figure of one million, and indeed the team only needed to average 15,000 for the remaining games to hit that total. Attendance for the series against New York was the highest since 1946, and everyone laid the credit at the feet of Ted Williams.

George Susce said that Williams was the force behind it all, contending that in the close games it was Ted's encouragement and bench chatter that got them to play harder. He described Williams pacing in the dugout, talking to the players in an ongoing seminar on baseball, soliciting ideas and then teaching with the responses. Susce described a process that made Williams seem like a baseball Socrates.

Povich was no less admiring, saying that the Senators' relationship with Williams had entered a new phase. Gone was the outright fear that many had felt initially. It had been replaced with a "total commitment to the game and their daring, and it has been working, and Manager Williams now can behold the beauty of his work form somewhere near second place in the American League East." Povich compared Williams again to Billy Martin and found the latter clearly the inferior of the two rookie managers. Williams was gaining some of the fire of Martin, but brought with it more wisdom. He was winning the press over, even if they still could not get into the locker room until fifteen minutes after the game ended.

Like the press, Washington fans enthusiastically embraced a Senators team that was three games over .500 and had maintained its status as a winning team for weeks. Optimistic fans could look forward to eight games against the fabled Yankees and a chance to move up in the standings as the All-Star Game approached. The wonder of it all was that they could expect to win those games and prevail against the once-proud Yankees. And after that, anything was possible; even the moon.

The first four games against New York were in Washington, followed by four against the Detroit Tigers before a final four-game series in New

York that led up to the All-Star break. After the Opening Day loss against New York, Washington had split its early-season games with the Yankees three games apiece. But the Yankees had found no one else against which the old magic still worked and were six games under .500. Their lineup was particularly anemic, with only Joe Pepitone still remaining from the power hitters that had brought pennants home in the old tradition.

Many thought that Bobby Murcer was going to be a great ballplayer. Ted Williams was convinced of Murcer's star potential and had talked to Short about acquiring him, but there was little hope the Yankees would give him away. The Senators had no general manager, no shrewd baseball man paid purely to put together a winning combination on the field. Bob Short was not about putting a winning team on the field as much as he was putting a winning bottom line on a risky investment. The gem of his product line and the only baseball talent he had convinced to join the new Washington Senators was Ted Williams.

Murcer and Pepitone gave the Yankees all the punch they would need in the first game at RFK as Mel Stottlemyre held the Senators to only three runs while pitching another complete game. The Friday night game drew 22,000 fans. They saw Barry Moore pitch better than he had in weeks and Darold Knowles throw two perfect innings at the end, but the Yankees made four runs stand up as Washington went down by a 4–3 score. Washington hit Stottlemyre hard, but the New York ace was able to wriggle off the hook every time the Senators mounted a rally.

The Saturday game continued the frustration. Dick Bosman allowed only two runs into the seventh inning, but a little-known Yankee pitcher named Bill Burbach, who would never be heard from again, blanked Frank Howard and Mike Epstein and limited the Senators to a single run. Washington's record sank and the team slid that much closer to the Yankees in the standings. Suddenly Shirley Povich's estimations going into the series seemed hopelessly optimistic.

The final two games of the weekend were played on Sunday in a forgotten baseball bonanza: the double-header. Ken McMullen brought back the enthusiasm of newly hopeful fans by hitting a three-run home run in the first inning. His big fly highlighted a five-run rally to give the Senators breathing room for the first time in the series. But Jim Hannan could not hold the lead, and when Casey Cox came in for the fifth inning, the advantage had slimmed to 5–4. Cox was the real hero again as he shut down the Yankees in the last five innings to pick up his seventh win.

In the second game, Frank Howard gave the 32,000 fans at RFK Stadium even more reason to believe. In the fourth inning he hit a long, deep home run to left field that landed far into the upper deck and was measured at more than 500 feet. All of the power was generated by the Gentle Giant and his powerful swing rather than the slow, fluttering knuckleball thrown by Yankee pitcher Ken Johnson. Johnson's knuckleball danced more on the way out than on the way in.

Jim Shellenback continued to pitch as a starter and threw a complete game six-hitter as the Senators took the laugher at 10–1. The win put Washington comfortably ahead of the Yankees again in the standings and focused attention once more on two of the upper-tier teams — Detroit and Boston — staying just a few games beyond the reach of the Senators.

Detroit was in second place in the AL East, only four games ahead of Washington. The home series gave the Senators a chance to close that gap and spark additional interest in the new divisional race. When Joe Coleman began the series with a 3–0 complete-game shutout, anything seemed possible. Frank Howard, Mike Epstein, and Ken McMullen were all shut down by Detroit in the first game of the series, and Joe Coleman had to drive in two of the three runs himself. The gathered crowd of more than 23,000 gave Coleman a standing ovation in the eighth inning when he came to bat. The appreciation was for another fine performance on the mound, but also with the bat as he carried the Senators to new heights — just two games out of second place in the division.

The Senators now had two pitchers vying to be considered the ace of the staff. Dick Bosman and Joe Coleman both were tossing gems, and now the team was four games over .500, just inches behind Detroit in the race. With Barry Moore looking like he might regain his early-season form, Ted Williams' pitching staff looked better than anything Washington had seen in decades.

Joe Coleman had added a pitch to his arsenal despite his stubborn belief in his fastball, and it was the new forkball that was the key to his dominance. His forkball was a good one that dropped precipitously at the last moment to avoid the onrushing bat. It was still the big curve and fastball that were getting the strikeouts — Coleman had twenty whiffs over two consecutive games — but the forkball was getting the ground balls and keeping the hitters honest. Ted Williams was happy that his young pitcher was willing to grow into his role on the team.

Bob Short, meanwhile, was ecstatic because season attendance on July 14 exceeded the entire 1968 attendance by 11,000. Short's goal of one million fans seemed within reach. It was announced earlier in the day that Frank Howard would be in the starting lineup for the American League at the All-Star Game. Howard had been selected during the 1968 season when he was the home run king of the American League. His second selection may have been more important to the fans than to Howard, who said in an article that he had actually been looking forward to the three days at home with his family.

The second game of the Detroit series brought more than 16,000 to RFK on a Tuesday night, and President Nixon was in the crowd. He saw his first win as president, but may have had other things on his mind with the Apollo 11 launch scheduled for the next morning at just after 9 A.M. The Saturn, as spotlighted as a movie star on opening night, had been the toast of the nightly news before game time, and an anxious nation looked forward to the spectacle of the liftoff. The Tuesday night crowd was down from the levels reached during the long winning streak; many may have stayed home to watch the news programs highlighting the astronauts and the pre-launch activities.

Tim Cullen, sporting a .208 batting average as the game began, was the offensive spark for the win, which surprised President Nixon and everyone else. Cullen hit his first home run of the season and ended the evening with a double, going 3-for-4 and driving in three runs. Washington drubbed six Detroit pitchers in the 7–3 win. The win put the team at its highest pinnacle in seventeen years. Not since the 1952 season had a Washington team stood five games over .500 at the midpoint of the season.

The Detroit Tigers almost stole the show by turning a rare triple play, but still saw their lead trimmed to a single game over the Senators, who were only a game and a half back of second-place Boston. The 1968 world champion Tigers were threatened with slipping below lowly Washington in the standings, and they sent out none other than World Series hero Mickey Lolich to defend their honor.

The launch of Apollo 11 on the morning of July 16 was flawless and the entire nation was riveted to its progress throughout the day. The astronauts broadcast from space during the day, and they were pictured on the evening news making small talk.

The Tigers and the Senators squared off at RFK Stadium that evening for the important grudge match with the course of the season at stake. Mickey Lolich had beaten Bob Gibson in the crucial 1968 World Series game, and on Wednesday night he showed exactly how he had done so. Dick Bosman was hurt by a rare Eddie Brinkman error that led to all three Detroit runs, but it was Lolich's domination that was the story. He allowed only four hits over the course of the game and not a single run. He went the distance for the shutout, and struck out nine. The game drew over 21,000 to see what may have been one of the better matchups of the season, certainly the best at RFK.

Ted Williams sensed the importance of the moment. Despite the loss, he was proud of how far the Senators had come and said of his team, "They're heads up and hustling. They're alive. If we can hold this spirit, we might surprise somebody." The spirit in the dugout was a contagion passing from player to player. Eddie Brinkman needled Howard, and the smaller man delighted in keeping the Gentle Giant loose. Williams said, "The spirit is good, the spirit is good. Let's keep it that way."

In the last game of the Tiger series, with a chance to take the series and head to New York with real momentum, Williams was on the dugout steps in rapt attention to the action on the field, biting his nails as almost 25,000 happy fans watched their hometown team lay siege to the 1968 champions. Detroit scored three runs in the first inning, but the Senators battled back, scoring two runs in the bottom of the eighth inning to pull to within a single run, trailing, 4–3. In the ninth inning Washington continued to surge. The Senators had men on the corners with a single out and sent out their best, Frank Howard, to face Detroit journeyman reliever Don McMahon.

The crowd came to its feet and stayed there as Howard was announced. His 34th home run in the bottom of the sixth inning had put Washington on the board, and the crowd had gone wild for their slugging hero as he rounded the bases. Now the fans were looking for another big fly that would send everyone home behind a fairy tale ending.

Hondo was facing a 39-year-old has-been in McMahon, and suddenly the thin pitching of the Tigers was just waiting to topple them into the laps of the Senators. McMahon had faced five batters two nights earlier and had not retired a single one. All Hondo really needed was a fly ball to score the tying run. A hit would win it. McMahon threw only one pitch, however, and Howard — perhaps a bit over-anxious — hit a grounder to short that Tom Tresh took in and flipped to second. Tim Cullen's slide took out the second baseman as he made the relay throw, but the ball had enough on it to beat the slow-running Howard to the bag. It was a game-ending double play.

The headlines the next day underscored how close the Senators had come. Casey Cox had pitched well enough to win it, but Dennis Higgins was showing the effects of all the innings he had pitched early in the season before Darold Knowles came back from the air force. Higgins gave up what proved to be the winning run on a wild pitch in the top of the eighth inning, and Williams slammed around the dugout in a rare show of frustration.

Although the homestand did not catapult the Senators into contention for first-division money, it did demonstrate what winning could do to generate excitement among the baseball fans in the nation's capitol. The 11 games brought in 188,657 fans to see the reigning world champs, the Yankees and the lowly Indians. It was obvious to the scribes and fans alike that an exciting, winning team would draw more than the requisite one million fans Short demanded as ransom for keeping the team in Washington.

The sleepy southern town in the District of Columbia had as much baseball potential as western cities, but did Washington have the money? Morris Siegel pointed out in the *Washington Star* that owner Short had bounced out of his seat with a flashing grin when the attendance was announced at 23,000 for one game in the Tiger series. Yet the next day in the press, Short was still hedging his bets, still surprisingly equivocal about attendance when interviewed by the *Washington Star,* saying that with the Yankees in town the attendance should have been better.

After the disappointing back-to-back losses to the Tigers, Washington went to Yankee Stadium for a four-game series before the All-Star break. The fifth-place Yankees gave the Senators one last chance to turn the All-Star break into an opportunity for reflection on what the second half might bring. Winning the New York series would put the team record well over .500 and keep Washington within easy distance of the top three teams.

The Senators, however, could not get their All-Star rocket, Frank Howard, off the pad in New York. Howard was sick and weakened with a virus for the Yankees series and it showed. In the first two games, the Senators were shut out. Fritz Peterson gave up only six hits on Friday night to beat Washington, 5–0. The next day in the first game of the Saturday double-header, Mel Stottlemyre was even better, throwing a three-hitter to beat the Senators, 9–0.

In the second game on Saturday, Mike Epstein and Lee Maye finally brought the offense alive, but it was Joe Coleman who was the standout. Striking out eleven and yielding only two hits, the new forkball pitcher was no longer tilting at windmills, and even Ted Williams was smiling after a 4–0 win that assured the Senators of having a winning record at the All-Star break. The final game of the series saw a healthier Frank Howard back in the starting lineup, where he garnered two hits. Jim Hannan continued to search for his command of the sinker, and after the bullpen shut the door for five innings, Casey Cox gave up a ninth-inning run that allowed the Yanks a 3–2 win.

The weekend papers announced that Darold Knowles had been named to the American League pitching staff for the All-Star Game, the only reliever so honored. Yet there were other All-Stars on the minds of baseball fans and all Americans. Three American astronauts were orbiting the moon, readying for their descent to the cratered surface below that the world was seeing in such detail for the first time. There had been moon missions and pictures broadcast back to earth before, but even Bob Short would have been excited at the television ratings for Apollo 11.

The little spacecraft Eagle was detached from the orbiting command craft early on Sunday when the astronauts went out of communication on the dark side of the moon. Lonely astronaut Michael Collins remained on the command module — Columbia — while the Eagle was readied for Sunday. On Sunday afternoon, during Washington's final game with the Yankees, the Eagle began its descent to the surface and the world held its breath.

When the spacecraft successfully touched down on the surface of the moon with Neil Armstrong and Buzz Aldrin aboard, the Yankees interrupted the flow of the game and announced the moment to the crowd. "The Eagle has landed" was the fateful statement to the world from NASA. Richard Nixon, from the White House, stated, "For one priceless moment, all the people on the earth are truly one." Even the damn Yankees and the Senators stood together silently on the field, most with their heads bowed in respectful silence, totally in awe of the moment.

13

Build a Ladder to the Stars

The Apollo astronauts featured so prominently on the front pages of every American newspaper in the middle weeks of July 1969 were the straightest arrowed of American heroes. They showcased the buzz-cut look that Richard Nixon sought to contrast with that of protesters and counter-cultural icons. The Silent Majority upon whom Nixon based his appeal feasted on the astronaut persona, but in truth the astronauts were heroes to everyone. The World Series atmosphere of the Apollo 11 launch at Cape Kennedy brought out patriots as well as thrill seekers, Americans of every stripe. Young children began dreaming of becoming astronauts, and rocket travel and space exploration became part of their games of fancy and imagination.

The heroism of the Apollo 11 crew was front page news for weeks during the summer of 1969. Pictures of moon rocks and lunar landscapes, where the footprints of the astronauts were featured on front pages, displayed as proud evidence that Americans had regained supremacy in science from the Russians, whose unmanned mission to gather moon rocks had failed. America's jubilant space scientists were planning missions to Mars as the next step in a race to the stars.

Major league baseball was in its own race to recapture its place atop the world of sport. When the baseball All-Stars gathered in Washington for the mid-summer classic in 1969, they featured their own buzz-cut heroes like Frank Howard. But the baseball brain trust had grander schemes than Howard's home run race with Reggie Jackson to generate the visceral appeal that once held the nation in its thrall.

Major league baseball wanted the 1969 All-Star Game to be about much more than one year, one game. The celebrations that began in the early summer focused attention on baseball's century of rich history. Commissioner Kuhn and his office were seeking to remind Americans of the long tradition of which the game was a part. Football could make no such claims. In looking backwards at baseball's history, it was the more recent trends that were the cause for concern.

Baseball's huge popularity supported not one, but two All-Star Games each summer for a four-year period, from 1959 to 1962. Despite the extra games, the American League had won only one contest. During the decade of the sixties, the AL had a single win against ten defeats going into the 1969 All-Star contest, to be played in Washington at the stadium that would be renamed in honor of Robert F. Kennedy, Jr. The lone American League win had come in 1962 at Wrigley Field during the second All-Star game played that year. The second game tended to provide the marquee players a break, with secondary stars more prevalent in the starting lineups. The first game held at the new Washington, D.C., stadium in 1962 was lost by the AL, 3–1.

Not only was the AL losing consistently, but the games were losing appeal with fans. The All-Star Game was losing its draw for the same reasons baseball itself felt threatened. The games had become defensive masterpieces, and writers were derisively calling them snorers. The pitchers were dominating the All-Star Game as they were dominating everything else. The mid-year classic in 1969 would feature the new mound and the new strike zone and would present a serious test of the changes set in place by the rules committee.

No single event told the tale of baseball's offensive drought more thoroughly than the All-Star Game as it was played in the late 1960s. In the three years leading up to the 1969 All-Star Game, the laughable total of only seven runs had been scored. The contests had been settled by scores of 2–1, 2–1, and 1–0. The best players in the game, including Hall of Fame sluggers like Harmon Killebrew, Willie McCovey, Frank Robinson, Willie Mays, and Carl Yastrzemski, had failed to dent the scoreboard over a three-year stretch in which an amazing average of only two runs were scored per game. The 1968 game had been the worst. Almost totally devoid of offense, the AL managed only three hits during the interminable affair played at the new Houston Astrodome.

The National League had won the game on a manufactured run scored by Willie Mays. He singled to lead off the game, moved around to third on a walk and a wild pitch, and then scored on a double play that left the bases cleared, which is the way they remained throughout much of the game. Yet as boring as the game was, it pointed out one of the differences between the two leagues. The NL had brought in the best players from the Negro Leagues, where speed was used to add excitement as much as power.

The NL style of play included the speed and daring displayed by the best multi-dimensional African American players, who scored runs using not just power, but finesse. Speed was not only about stealing bases, but about always putting pressure on the defense by taking the extra base, going from first to third or laying down bunts to get on base. Speed forced the defense to play harder and make more mistakes. It kept the ball moving on the field.

The AL, by contrast, waited for one thing: the long ball. They played largely station to station, never chancing the possible out, which would limit the potential for a three-run homer. The problem with that approach was that in 1968, the home run was occurring with notably less frequency; the wait was longer and fans were growing weary of it. During the course of the sixties, the term "senior circuit" had come to mean not just the greater longevity of the National League, but a deeper talent pool, and it was not even close.

David Halberstam, in his book *October 1964*, raised the issue about the racial disparity that grew up between the National League teams and those in the American League during the era. He wrote, "Most astute observers believed now that the entire American League was inferior to the National League because it had lagged behind in signing black players." Halberstam's contention was about the '64 season, but he described a trend that had been long in the making and one that endured well past that single year.

During the second half of the 1960s, the AL began to close the gap. There was still a marked difference in the style of play and the color of the great players in the two leagues, even as late as 1969. That year the National League All-Stars featured Hall of Fame players of color like Willie Mays, Bob Gibson, Henry Aaron, Ernie Banks, Lou Brock, and Roberto Clemente. The American League Hall of Fame players included only Frank Robinson, Rod Carew, and first-timer Reggie Jackson, who served to help bridge the racial divide for the first time.

The Washington Senators had been stalwarts in maintaining the racial antipathy of the '50s and early '60s. Calvin Griffith expressed a prejudice as clearly as any owner, but he was not the trendsetter. The other owners in the AL did not look to him for direction. It was the deep racism of the Yankees management that Halberstam credited with setting the standard.

The Yankees stockpiled talent like Mickey Mantle from the Ozarks and other stars from the southern states. The idea that these players could play alongside blacks was anathema to Yankees management. It was the attitudes of George Weiss that were at the heart of it, not those of the players. Weiss and other AL owners, including Calvin Griffith, were determined to keep the middle-class white clientele they were drawing. They were looking for affluent whites who would pay higher ticket prices. In their minds such a demographic profile was incongruent with increased black attendance, which they saw scaring off the white middle class. Yet the experience of National League teams suggests these concerns said more about the owners than the fans.

In the National League the Brooklyn Dodgers, led by Branch Rickey, had set a different direction. Not that Rickey was an altruist. He refused to pay the Negro League teams a nickel when he signed their best talent and led the migration away from the historic black-only game. But he laid down the gauntlet to other teams in the National League. If they wanted to compete, they were going to have to follow his lead. When the Brooklyn Dodgers in the 1950s featured fine African American MVPs like Don Newcombe and Roy Campanella, their rivals had no choice except to come up with their own great players of color. The Giants, arch rivals to the Dodgers, signed Willie Mays, the Braves, Henry Aaron, and the Cubs, Ernie Banks.

On the day the 1969 All-Star Game celebrations kicked off, Shirley Povich's morning column noted the disparities. He said that the National League had made the most of the racial imbalance between the two leagues that started with Jackie Robinson's historic entry into white baseball, noting that before Robinson, the AL won twelve of the first sixteen All-Star contests. However, Povich noted that once the NL had made the most of its forays into the Negro Leagues, "Of the last 22, the AL has won only six."

Although the American League teams like Hank Greenberg's Cleveland Indians signed Larry Doby and Chicago signed the great black Cuban player, Minnie Minoso, most of the teams in the AL stood and watched from the sidelines, ignoring the depth of talent available in the Negro Leagues. The differential in the sixties between the National League and American League was a dramatic one, as Branch Rickey and others forced to compete with him siphoned off the best black players and added them to National League rosters. In 1965, a young Pete Rose and Joe Torre were the only white players in the National League's All-Star Game starting lineup that included Hank Aaron, Richie Allen, Ernie Banks, Willie Stargell, Willie Mays and Maury Wills. The starting pitcher was Juan Marichal. The AL's only African American players were Willie Horton and Earl Battey, two talented players but hardly of the caliber of the National League's black All-Stars.

Hall of Fame players like Maury Wills and Lou Brock were not simply speedsters on the bases who re-wrote the record books; they were talents that changed the offensive tenor of the game for a generation. The deeper reservoir of speedy outfielders available in the NL added a dimension to the defensive game in the senior circuit as well, especially important in the larger ballparks built in the period. Roberto Clemente and Curt Flood were defensive players of unmatched ability, except for Willie Mays, who needed a special league of his own.

The Washington Senators stood timidly on the shoreline along with other AL owners, afraid to venture into what they perceived as roiling waters of potential controversy. They decided against signing Negro League players and did not heavily scout young African American talent coming up. Chuck Hinton was the Senators' most talented black player of the era, and he was signed only after the Griffith family left town.

Calvin Griffith left as a legacy his concern that a team that was "too" black would draw too many black fans to the detriment of white patrons. It was a conventional wisdom largely undisputed by writers or community leaders who might have been concerned about the future of the team after Griffith left. The lack of any bold vision in Washington at a time when change was shaping every aspect of American life was like a millstone tied around the neck of the Senators as their expansion team tried to move forward.

A sharp and telling contrast can be drawn between the directions charted by the Washington Senators and the St. Louis Cardinals. Washington, D.C., was much like St. Louis, Missouri, in the late 1940s and early fifties. St. Louis was seen by players and management alike as a southern town heavily influenced by its proximity to southern states and white southern fans. The Cardinals always drew from areas into which KMOX broadcast. It was the powerful radio station that carried their games and beamed its signal purposely toward the Ozarks, to Mississippi, Texas, and Alabama. There was not a more hardcore southern team playing in either league than the Cardinals.

Yet by 1961, the Cardinals had changed completely and set a new direction. Within a single decade, they were the team whose standard for interracial cooperation among black and white players was being modeled by other National League teams who were forced to try to keep pace. The story of the transition by baseball's St. Louis Cardinals is made more poignant for its unlikely heroes.

The integration of the Cardinals' St. Petersburg, Florida, spring training facilities in 1961 has been documented in sports literature, but is told well by Halberstam. Influential white players like Stan Musial and Kenny Boyer supported black players like Bill White, who were challenging their segregated accommodations and together changed a difficult situation into a model of team togetherness. The team took the challenge of racial tension and turned it on its head. Rather than be undone by it, the Cardinal players — white and black — crafted a team spirit that defined the pacesetting Cardinal teams of the 1960s.

Even such disparate players as Tim McCarver and Bob Gibson became not only teammates whose talents meshed well, but friends whose respect for their different backgrounds made the bond stronger. The role of leaders like White, Musial, and Gibson was important. They were smart as well as talented, but they had to work through the personal perceptions of southerners like McCarver, as well as the steamy passions of players like Gibson. They did so at a time when teams like the Senators were not even trying.

Washington was still timidly putting one toe in the water and deciding that taking the plunge was for braver sorts. As the Senators moved forward towards 1969, there were fine African American players like Fred Valentine and Chuck Hinton, but the team never sought out a black star when many teams were signing talented young players from the Negro Leagues. They never sent scouts into the Deep South to search out and sign the best young black players.

The Washington attitude started working early and lasted into the final hours of the city's tenure in baseball. Although it is disputed, the Senators are alleged to have turned down a trade for Larry Doby in the early 1950s. Shirley Povich claimed that Dan Daniel, the New York sports columnist who claimed the trade discussions were real, was just creating rumors the way writers often do. But Daniel stuck to his guns, asserting that Hank Greenberg had offered Doby to Clark Griffith for the young Jackie Jensen.

At the time of the discussions, Doby still had many good years to play at the All-Star level he attained. Jensen was a star in the making who would be the AL MVP in 1958, but with Doby in the middle of a Washington lineup that already included Pete Runnels, Eddie Yost and Roy Sievers, the team would have been a powerhouse. Clark Griffith, who turned down the trade, kept his attitudes about race close to the vest, but Calvin Griffith's words about a city too black to support baseball were not born in a vacuum.

Washington's African American fan base was developed during the long tenure of the Homestead Grays at Griffith Stadium, and those fans supported the Senators as well. They would have added important paying patrons to a Senator fan base that was dwindling to extremely low levels in the late 1950s and even lower after the expansion Senators came to RFK. Dick Bosman believed that the ownership of the Senators prior to Bob Short's arrival was trying to hang on, hoping only to survive. The words certainly ring true. There was no one willing to shake the tree until Short came along. The shame of it was that while Bob Short was willing to set a different direction for the Washington Senators, it ultimately would be for Texas.

Shirley Povich said that prior to the arrival of Short and Ted Williams, African American players had been more or less banished from the Senators. Williams especially gave black players on the team a sense of having someone in their corner. During his speech before the gathered dignitaries in Cooperstown, Williams called for the induction of the famed Negro League players who had no opportunity to cross the color barrier. He used the singular opportunity of his own induction into the Baseball Hall of Fame to state his belief that players such as Satchel Paige and Josh Gibson should be given an equal chance for the honor he was receiving.

Jim Hannan recounted a story about Williams and Mudcat Grant. Before the end of segregation, Williams ran into Grant, the fine African American pitcher who was standing outside of the players hotel in Orlando during spring training. Grant was expecting his bags to be outside the hotel where he could pick them up and take them to a hotel in the black section of town — normal practice for black players at the time. When he arrived at the hotel, he asked the doorman to see if the bags had arrived, but was told that all of the bags had been taken inside. When Grant started into the hotel, the doorman informed him that blacks were not allowed in the hotel.

Ted Williams walked up just after those remarks from the doorman and asked Grant what he was waiting for. Grant told him about the incident and said he was hoping for a bellboy to bring him his bags so that he could carry them to the hotel in the Negro part of town where he was staying. Williams was incensed. He went into the hotel, found the doorman, brought him out to where Grant was waiting, and said, "I would like you to say hello to Mr. Grant. I want you to go get his bags for him and bring them out here. Then I want you to apologize to Mr. Grant."

Changes in the racial profile of the Washington Senators came too late. In 1969 Reggie Jackson was a one-man leveling influence for the American League. During his run as an All-Star player, he would help swing the competitive balance back toward the American League. For Jackson, 1969 was his first All-Star Game appearance, coming in his rookie year. It was the beginning of a long and wonderful time for Reggie and anyone who loved the game.

For baseball's brain trust, it was not the mismatch between the leagues, rooted as it was in baseball's racial politics, that mattered in 1969. It was the mismatch between pitcher and batter. The question plaguing baseball writers, the owners, and those who cared about the game was whether another All-Star Game would pass with the grand old game falling further behind football as the favorite sports pastime of American fans. Baseball was orchestrating a full frontal attack to overtake football before its exhibition season began in earnest in August.

Bowie Kuhn was the ringleader of the gang out to change the game. The Commissioner's Office was behind the centennial celebrations. The morning before the All-Star Game, Shirley Povich profiled Kuhn in his daily column. Povich wrote of Kuhn's childhood growing up in Washington, D.C., where he had tended the scoreboard at Griffith Stadium for a dollar a day. Now Kuhn was a successful lawyer who could walk away without any tears from the job of commissioner and its $100,000 salary. The working class kid who peered out at games from the scoreboard was now the well-heeled lawyer to the rich and powerful.

The owners needed Kuhn as the patrician spokesperson for the game, and the three-day festivities in 1969 for the game and its All-Stars demonstrated that Kuhn had been a very shrewd choice by the owners. Kuhn had from the beginning of the season encouraged President Nixon to take part, to give vent to the inner fan in Richard Nixon. Now, Nixon jumped into the action once again, hosting a White House dinner for all of the writers, the All-Star players — past and present — and the celebrities who were part of the game.

He spoke enthusiastically to the crowd at the White House about the game, but he focused much of what he said on the Senators and their manager, Ted Williams. Nixon spoke as if the weeks in June and July when the team had established its first winning record in decades were a settled claim to contender status. Bowie Kuhn may have helped orchestrate Nixon's participation, but another cog in the marketing of this historic All-Star Game was Bob Short. Short's friendship with Nixon dated to when Short was the owner of the Los Angeles Lakers. He had invited Nixon to the games then and shared his owners' seats with the former vice president.

Nixon's formal White House dinner for the baseball All-Stars brought together 500 of the game's greatest personalities. The president rubbed elbows with Casey Stengel, Joe DiMaggio and the widows of Babe Ruth and Lou Gehrig. It was in the receiving line talking to DiMaggio that Nixon said that if he were not the president his chosen field would be sportswriting. The White House banquet was just the first successful step in creating a gala atmosphere. The *New York Times* opined the next morning that the centennial celebrations and the Nixon dinner were a certain sign that baseball was once again the national pastime.

The next evening the Commissioner's Office hosted the centennial celebration marking the first 100 years of baseball. The event was held at the Shoreham Hotel and was attended by 2,200 dignitaries, most from the world of sport, including 35 members of the Baseball Hall of Fame. There were also six members of the Nixon cabinet, Broadway and Hollywood personalities, and an astronaut who had not yet flown into space.

The process of naming the greatest players of all-time had been moving across the country through every major league city in June and July, gathering momentum and fan attention like a circus train going through the outskirts of town. Now the circus was in town, and the show reached its conclusion as the greatest player and his court were named at the Omni Shoreham banquet. The results were based on fan voting, which proved problematic. Cities like Minneapolis/St. Paul had shortened histories, and other cities like Seattle had no history at all; their votes went solely for current players of note.

The consummate prize went to Babe Ruth in a proclamation from the Commissioner's Office naming him officially the greatest baseball player of all-time. He was joined by fellow Yankees Lou Gehrig and Joe DiMaggio. Walter Johnson represented the Washington Senators as the greatest right-handed pitcher, with Lefty Grove as the greatest left-hander. The other players included Mickey Cochrane as catcher, Rogers Hornsby at second base, Pie Traynor at third and Honus Wagner at shortstop. Joining Ruth and DiMaggio in the outfield was Ty Cobb, and the manager of the team of greatest players was John McGraw of the Giants.

Ruth was an easy choice as the greatest baseball player during the first 100 years. Cobb was reputed to have been second in the voting, although this was not officially announced. It was no mistake that the greatest home run hitter of all-time who had changed the course of the game was being celebrated in 1969. Babe Ruth and the advent of the home run had made baseball the popular game it became after the First World War.

Baseball, Inc. with Bowie Kuhn at the helm was charting a course back to that safe harbor of celebrity hitters. The other irony — noted by Shirley Povich in his daily column — was the attention paid to great American League heroes such as Ruth and Cobb at a time when the league was being totally overshadowed by the NL. In its heyday, the AL had both speed and power.

Cobb's rumored selection as number two started a series of squabbles about the voting and the results. He was a man liked neither on nor off the field despite his accomplishments. There were notable players who were left off the final all-time great rosters, creating local squabbling about it. There were racial issues about African American players who were not included that would have been raised to a different level had there been prominent African American writers to give them voice.

Willie Mays was considered by many to be the greatest center fielder of all-time, and his numbers warranted consideration as his career neared its end. Shirley Povich noted the absence of Willie Mays in his morning column on the day after the posh banquet at the Shoreham Hotel. Joe DiMaggio had been voted the greatest center fielder, and the celebration of the great Yankee teams, of Ruth, Gehrig and the great Yankee players of the pre–World War II era, pushed any debate right off the page. The writers and fans tended to see the era of Yankee greatness as the embodiment of baseball's greatness.

Yet the comparison between DiMaggio and Mays was a stark one. In 1969 Mays' career was drawing to an amazing close. He had almost 600 career home runs, a career batting average over .300, almost 300 stolen bases, and was widely considered the best defensive center fielder ever to play the game. His over-the-shoulder running catch of a Vic Wertz fly ball in the 1954 World Series is thought to be one of the greatest defensive plays of all-time. He had hit more than 50 home runs twice in a single season. He starred for the world champion Giants in 1954 and went on to captain the 1962 Giants team that won the National League pennant. Mays was a lock to reach the 3,000-hit mark as well.

The popularity of Joe DiMaggio as a spokesman for the game made his choice seem obvious to everyone making the selections, but at second glance it may have been unfounded. The Yankee Clipper had fewer than 400 home runs, fewer than 3,000 hits, and while a great fielder, was arguably the inferior of Mays with the glove. Although the war years robbed him of some statistical advantage, Mays was likewise robbed of time during the Korean War. However, it is unlikely that the three years DiMaggio lost to service would have put him above the landmark milestones of others with his reputation. Whether it was his celebrity status, cemented by his marriage to Marilyn Monroe, or his importance to the great Yankee teams of an era, DiMaggio's appeal to the writers and the fans exceeded an objective statistical analysis of his contributions as a player. Holding the DiMaggio mystique in abeyance, it was debatable whether he belonged among the very select few to play the game.

Ted Williams was not quibbling over who was the best center fielder. Baseball, Inc. wasn't just naming DiMaggio the best center fielder of all-time; they were giving him the award as the "Greatest Living Player." So whether he was the best center fielder of all-time hardly mattered. The affront to Mays was a small thing in relation to the affront to Williams. The Senators manager was so steamed the writers had selected DiMaggio as a better player than Teddy Ballgame that he refused to attend the All-Star banquet dinner. His award as the "Greatest Living Hitter"—what he considered a throw-away sop since he failed to make even the greatest outfield list—had to be picked up by his wife, who came down from their residential apartment in the hotel to accept for her husband.

"He is not ill," she said. "He just does not go to these functions." Indeed he did not go to functions that gave his long-time rival the award that he realistically should have received. Ted Williams attended the White House dinner the night before hosted by President Nixon and was charming, congratulated the trophy winners, and clearly enjoyed the evening's festivities. But nothing could persuade Williams to watch Joe DiMaggio—whom Williams led in every offensive category by large margins—walk off with the award as the greatest living ballplayer.

TABLE 13-1. COMPARISON OF GREATEST LIVING PLAYERS, 1969

Hitting Statistics

Player	AB	R	H	HR	RBI	BB	SO	AVG	SB
Joe DiMaggio	6821	1390	2214	361	1537	790	369	.325	30
Willie Mays	10801	2062	3283	660	1903	1464	1526	.302	338
Ted Williams	7706	1798	1654	521	1839	2019	709	.344	24

Fielding Statistics

Player	G	PO	A	E	DP	Field Pct	PO/G
Willie Mays	2929	7752	233	156	121	.981	2.65
Joe DiMaggio	1722	4529	153	105	30	.978	2.63
Ted Williams	2152	4158	142	113	30	.974	1.92

Williams made 18 appearances in the All-Star Games held during his career, more than any other American League player. The only year he failed to make the team was his rookie year, when he was hitting only .265 when the votes were cast. He wound up hitting .327 that year and led the league in RBIs with 142. He shared his favorite memories of those games with the press despite his boycott of certain events. In 1941, when the All-Star Game was still a new event, the contest was held at Briggs Stadium in Detroit. Williams' mammoth home run off the facing of the upper deck in the ninth inning had given the AL a come-from-behind win. In the '46 All-Star Game held in Boston, he hit another memorable homer along with five RBIs and four runs scored during the post-war era when the stars played the duration of the game.

Williams' play in the 1958 All-Star Game raises questions about the claims made during his lifetime that he did not play hard-nosed defense in the outfield. Williams was injured seriously during that All-Star contest while chasing a fly ball off the bat of Bill Virdon. He crashed into the wall and injured his elbow. Williams did not leave the game, but the injury was serious enough to put Williams out of action for much of the rest of the season and affected the last years of his career.

Unbowed by the effects of the game on his career, Williams said of the All-Star Games in which he played, "I enjoyed the challenge of facing the best pitching in the National League. Every player should take pride in the All-Star Game."

Williams' failure to appear was disappointing but not unprecedented. There was a more rancorous note sounded after the centennial festivities. When Jackie Robinson spoke at the celebration, he issued a call for more participation at higher levels by African Americans. He called for the hiring of coaches and managers from among the ranks of his black peers — those who had integrated the game and knew it as well as anyone. It raised the ire of Cleveland's Hall of Fame pitcher Bob Feller, who questioned the notion in the press the following day. He and Robinson sparred in the papers for several days before the debate was forgotten.

Reggie Jackson was taking the opportunity Jackie Robinson had given him for all it was worth. Jackson looked in his second full season like he might be the greatest black player of all-time, waiting to be crowned at the next centennial. Jackson was selected to the starting lineup in his second full season in the major leagues. His amazing career launched as quickly as Ted Williams had twenty years before, and he pushed other more notable players to the sidelines when he was chosen as a starter.

Ted Williams' history as an All-Star included the years when the AL dominated the NL; he would be back in the dugout with the 1969 AL All-Stars, hoping to restore the league's reputation. There was plenty of power on the side of the AL as Harmon Killebrew and Carl Yastrzemski were named as reserve players. The home run race between Reggie Jackson and Frank Howard garnered them more votes than several long-time all-stars. Brooks Robinson, who would play in his 13th All-Star Game in 1969, the most of anyone in the '69 contest, did not crack the AL starting lineup either. The players chose the starting lineups — the last year they would do so — and they went with the following:

TABLE 13-2. STARTING LINEUPS, 1969 ALL-STAR GAME

American League

Catcher:	Bill Freehan, Detroit Tigers
First Base:	Boog Powell, Baltimore Orioles
Second Base:	Rod Carew, Minnesota Twins
Third Base:	Sal Bando, Oakland Athletics
Shortstop:	Rico Petrocelli, Boston Red Sox
Outfield:	Reggie Jackson, Oakland Athletics
	Frank Howard, Washington Senators
	Frank Robinson, Baltimore Orioles

National League

Catcher:	Johnny Bench, Cincinnati Reds
First Base:	Willie McCovey, San Francisco Giants
Second Base:	Felix Milan, Atlanta Braves
Third Base:	Ron Santo, Chicago Cubs
Shortstop:	Don Kessinger, Chicago Cubs
Outfield:	Hank Aaron, Atlanta Braves
	Matty Alou, San Francisco Giants
	Cleon Jones, New York Mets

Mayo Smith was the manager of the champion Detroit Tigers and therefore the helmsman for the AL team. Smith chose 20 of the 28 players who would represent the American League, as well as the coaches. One of his last choices to help with the coaching was Ted Williams. When told of the decision during the Tiger series in Washington in mid–July, Williams told Smith that he would be there whether he was paid or not. It was Williams' coaching prowess that was needed, however, and Mayo Smith knew the AL needed the kind of surge in offensive production that Williams had brought to the Washington Senators.

Bob Short was a big part of the All-Star celebrations in Washington in 1969 and was happy to shine the limelight as brightly as possible on his star performer, manager Ted Williams. But the city of Washington, D.C., was the host, and some in the press tried to shift the spotlight to the historic nature of the game in the nation's capital. Merrell Whittlesey pointed out that Washington had hosted four previous All-Star Games, more than any other city. Clark Griffith hosted the first in 1937 and Franklin D. Roosevelt was in attendance, notably standing to throw out the first pitch.

Calvin Griffith's Senators hosted the game in 1956, and the expansion Senators brought the All-Star Game to their new stadium that would become Robert F. Kennedy Memorial Stadium. Robert Kennedy's brother, President John F. Kennedy, threw out the first pitch in '62 before a full house of 45,480 fans. Whittlesey in the *Sporting News* remarked that the game in '37 had a very sad highlight, the end of the playing career for Dizzy Dean. Dean was the dominant pitcher of his day until a liner off the bat of Earl Averill broke his toe in that All-Star contest. He failed to care for it properly and it never healed correctly, rendering the rest of his career an afterthought to what had gone before.

On the day the game was to be played, nature dealt a blow to the careful planning of Commissioner Bowie Kuhn. The gala setting for the centennial show had been moved to majestic looking tents with medieval bunting outside RFK. Three massive tents were set up for the dignitaries on the lawn outside the stadium, but before the first martini was stirred, the first champagne uncorked, a freak thunderstorm of rare savagery struck. The tents were the first to go as young men looking like lawn boys at a tennis match dashed about trying to stabilize the tent poles in the heavy wind and rain. The dugouts and the stadium were pictured with torrents of water washing through them at knee-high depth.

There was no choice but to cancel the game. Bob Addie may have caught the tenor of the deluge as well as anyone with the title to his morning column the next day, "100 Years of Rainfall." He said the field flooded alongside both foul lines appeared to be celebrating the centennial with "100 years of rain." The torrential rainfall in Washington resulted in other cancellations as well. Fans of every ilk — whether celebrities from another era or simply Washington's loyalist fans — were forced to regroup. Many fans that had carefully planned and put aside time for the game found themselves left high and dry.

President Nixon was the first to bow out. His schedule had been tight for the game as originally scheduled. He left for Hawaii to greet the astronauts who were touching down in the Pacific. He dispatched his daughter Tricia, who had attended games with him several times, to represent the family the next night and Vice President Agnew to represent the administration. Many just could not attend and the sold-out game drew barely twenty thousand fans, although the paid attendance was 42,259, a sellout. The newspaper the next day cataloged the disappointment of the fans. There were no refunds for the inflated ticket prices, but as one fan with his son standing glumly at his side said, "The money really isn't what's important. It would have been our first All-Star Game."

The players were forced to spend another night in the city. The bus driver who had been hired to drive to the airport was unprepared and could not find the hotel where the players were staying. The trip took so long that Mickey Lolich asked the driver for a note for his wife, who would never believe he had been on a bus the entire evening. For all the confusion, plans were changed and, not quite like a Broadway show, the game went on.

The next day the game was set for early afternoon so the players could return to their teams that night for regular-season action set to begin again the next day. The pitching lineup for the National League was no less daunting than it had been in 1968. Bob Gibson, Steve Carlton, Tom Seaver and Jerry Koosman were set to go and would present a severe test even for the starting lineup with as many home runs as Jackson, Howard and Petrocelli could boast. Carlton would start for the NL and Denny McLain was scheduled to start for the AL.

McLain and his private jet failed to show. He claimed a dental appointment. Displays of arrogant disregard would become a calling card for McLain as his short career reached amazing heights, but flamed out quickly and crashed with horrible consequences. What was puzzling to many was why Mayo Smith approved McLain's decision. It denied the ability to throw another top pitcher at the National League lineup since Smith had used Mickey Lolich just before the break. Whatever McLain was up to, Mayo Smith was not chancing Lolich on short rest. It left the ball in the hands of Mel Stottlemyre, who was having a great season, but was not the equal of Lolich.

The game started out as if scripted by the commissioner. Two innings into the game, with the National League up, 3–1, there were as many runs on the board as the two previous All-Star Games combined. Frank Howard's home run in the bottom of the second had put the American League back into the game, although his error in the top of the inning had led to an unearned run.

In the third inning, Mayo Smith pulled the wrong lever again. Stottlemyre had been ineffective, allowing three runs, so Smith made a pitching change. He had "Sudden Sam" McDowell in the bullpen who was chasing Lolich for the strikeout lead in the AL. He had Dave McNally, arguably one of the best arms in the league, as well, but he went with the young, first-time All-Star "Blue Moon" Odom instead.

Odom set a torch to the AL's chances of getting a win, recording only a single out and giving up five runs, including Willie McCovey's first home run with Hank Aaron on base. Frank Howard's home run was long and deep, but McCovey's was a rifle shot that appeared to still be rising when it hit the wall above the scoreboard. Rico Petrocelli, booed by the Washington faithful who believed Eddie Brinkman belonged at shortstop, made an error to prolong the third inning. Manager Smith finally brought in Darold Knowles, and the ace fireman closed down the National Leaguers. The damage, however, had been done.

The score was 8–1, and Tricia Nixon had seen enough. She departed along with the chances for the American League. Frank Howard played another inning before giving way to Reggie Smith. Boog Powell, Reggie Jackson, Frank Robinson, Rod Carew, and Carl Yastrzemski were all handled easily by the National League's better pitching. Only Howard and Bill Freehan tallied for the AL, and it was not close. The final score of 9–3 provided plenty of offensive fireworks, but the contest was one-sided from the beginning.

Willie McCovey was named the Most Valuable Player in the game after he hit a second home run. But Frank Howard was awarded the longest and loudest ovation of the day when the home crowd cheered him. "Howard's was the daddy of them all," Shirley Povich wrote about Howard's homer the next day. He drew the adoration of his fans first when he was announced along the foul lines and even longer when he hit his home run. The effectiveness of Darold Knowles and Howard's offense left the blame for the loss on the failures of others. The Senators had shown up to play. When the writers second-guessed Mayo Smith's choices of pitchers and his decision to pinch-hit with Don Mincher instead of Carl Yastrzemski, Senators manager Ted Williams said, "I just watched the game, kept score, and called the bullpen."

Johnny Bench added a late home run to put the game total at five. It had been four years since an All-Star contest saw such fireworks, in 1965. So with the aura of Babe Ruth hanging over the game, the home run had returned. Bowie Kuhn had pulled off a stunner only dimmed by the weather. Yet the reach of the celebrations may not have been as deep among fans as it was among the attending press and dignitaries. There was not a paying fan anywhere near Bowie Kuhn's gala events.

It may have been the baseball writers like Red Smith, Pete Axthelm, Shirley Povich and Red Barber who were writing the story of baseball's demise. It was natural to gather the faithful for the All-Star Game to preach the message of rebirth. The sports editor of the *Chicago Tribune*, Arch Ward, had conceived of the All-Star Game as a way to sell more newspapers, so it was a natural for the press to gather and assess the progress made in the first half-year of repackaging the tired old game. The *New York Times* had issued its positive verdict early in the week. *Newsweek* magazine declared the All-Star Game a success in the most important way possible — it was more fun, more alive than it had been in many seasons.

Now it was left to the players and teams to see if they could create in the second half of the season the same kind of drama. And ultimately it would be the fans who decided whether the game was too boring for the modern generation of sports enthusiasts. Whether the writers could be won over rubbing shoulders with 100 years of history or not, fans were watching the game as it was played in 1969 to see if it was changing.

14

In for Nasty Weather

After the All-Star break, there were only 61 games remaining, but it was the toughest part of the baseball season. Late July heat put temperatures into the 90s in every baseball venue across the country. In Washington, perhaps more than anywhere else, baseball fans scheduled vacations and spent the hot August weather at the beach. For the players, the next two months were the time when baseball fortunes were put to the test, when young players like Reggie Jackson, who had prospered in the early months, might wilt in the pressure of the long dog days of August.

President Nixon may have declared the Senators a winning franchise at the White House dinner, but he had left to bask in astronaut glory in Hawaii. The president traveled onward from Hawaii to Southeast Asia. He would need sharper insights into the war there than he had shown into baseball in Washington, D.C. The Senators were following Nixon on a westward tour, landing first in Oakland. They would visit four cities and play twelve games before returning to RFK in early August.

Washington's baseball fortunes had taken a nose dive in the week before the All-Star break. Just when the team seemed to have secured the beach and a winning season, they were knocked back. Washington lost five of its last six games before the break, and Frank Howard's injury during that losing streak demonstrated the tenuous nature of the new offense Ted Williams had created. Without Howard in the lineup, there was no depth to the Senators' attack.

In late July both Howard and Reggie Jackson were on a pace to better Ruth and Maris' single-season mark. Despite the wear and tear of the second half, Howard was a workhorse of a man and stood as good a chance as any. He had won the home run crown the year before with 44, and with Williams behind him, there were many hoping he could make the rest of the season interesting.

The Washington Senators' most well-known All-Star did not like to talk about his home runs, however. He was concentrating on his batting average. His average still stood among the league leaders and had been above .300 for much of the season. That was Frank Howard's passion, to hit .300 for the 1969 season. After the years of platooning in Los Angeles and being labeled a one-dimensional player, nothing would give him more satisfaction than to look back on a season with a batting title. Five hundred-foot home runs like the one he hit on July 13 for his 33rd of the season were great. They got him new painted seats in the RFK upper deck, but Hondo was more interested in the .313 batting average with which he finished that July evening after going 4-for-5.

In his third season, the best he had with the Dodgers, Howard hit .296, and it had been the year he convinced both Buzzie Bavasi and Walter Alston to let him play full-time. The next season had been his undoing, however, and he slid backwards until in his last year in Los Angeles, the year after which he was traded to Washington, he hit only .226. In an era when the batting title was won with averages dipping almost below .300, Howard's numbers in previous seasons had been respectable for a power hitter. His .300 batting average in 1969 and the additional bases on balls were what he wanted to talk about when he sat down with a cigar after another long night at the ballpark.

Howard was healthy and back in the lineup for the first games after the All-Star Game. The rain-delayed All-Star Game had left players like Howard and Darold Knowles with almost no time off. As soon as they returned, the team left the friendly confines of RFK for a long flight across the country to Oakland. The Athletics were locked in a tight race with the Minnesota Twins for first place in the new AL West. The Oakland team featured many of the players who would go on to win the AL championship and three consecutive World Series titles in the 1970s.

Joe Coleman started the first game of the Oakland series for the Senators, and was coming off three shutout performances in a row. The record of four straight shutouts was held by none other than Walter Johnson, set in 1913. Coleman was treading on his own lunar landscape, but also attempting to stake his claim as ace of the rotation, just as Barry Moore and Dick Bosman had before. In the first game, he was up against one of the best in Jim "Catfish" Hunter. Hunter would anchor the Oakland rotation during its dynasty years in the early '70s.

The game was a well-played and tightly contested match-up of two excellent pitchers. Washington held the lead after the first inning on a Lee Maye homer, but Coleman lost the shutout in the fourth on a single run and then gave up the go-ahead run in the eighth on a Sal Bando single that scored Reggie Jackson. Both pitchers closed out the game, but Washington

Joe Coleman was treading on his own lunar landscape. National Baseball Hall of Fame Library, Cooperstown, N.Y.

could not counter against Hunter and lost by a 2–1 margin. The loss pushed Washington back to the .500 mark with eleven more games on the long road trip to go.

Reggie Jackson continued to get the best of the head-to-head match with Frank Howard in the second game. There was a point of pride involved that extended beyond the home run race between the two sluggers. Joe DiMaggio, who hailed from the Bay Area, had joined the Athletics as a hitting coach in the spring. He had made Jackson his personal pupil to such an extent that Jackson seldom agreed to an interview without approval from the Yankee Clipper.

Ted Williams' star pupil, Frank Howard, was 0-for-4 in the first game, and in the second Jackson's 38th home run, off Darold Knowles in the seventh inning, sparked Oakland to a 4–3 win against Barry Moore. The Senators were back below .500 for the first time in almost a month, and Reggie was increasing his lead over Howard, who was 1-for-3 to keep his average at .309.

"Blue Moon" Odom returned to the mound for the first time since the All-Star Game. Odom was able to right himself after the disastrous outing at RFK, and he pitched a complete-game six-hitter against the Senators. Yet there was no forgiveness for Odom. He also walked six batters and gave up three runs in the game. In the tenth inning, Del Unser's fly ball scored the go-ahead run that gave the Senators a 3–1 win. The hero for Washington was once again Jim Shellenback, who limited the Athletics hitters to only a single run over nine innings and struck out ten.

An important moment in Senators history was on display back on the East Coast. Stan Coveleski was inducted into the Baseball Hall of Fame in Cooperstown, New York, along with Stan Musial, Roy Campanella, and Waite Hoyt. Coveleski was the missing piece that Clark Griffith had added to the Senators starting rotation that allowed them to repeat as American League champs in 1925. The right-handed pitcher had great seasons with the Cleveland Indians from 1916 to 1924. When he joined the Washington rotation in '25, he gave Walter Johnson enough help to beat the Athletics down the wire. He went 20–5 for Washington in 1925 with a 2.85 ERA.

In the '25 World Series, when Washington was looking for its second straight world championship, Coveleski was a hard-luck pitcher. Coveleski pitched well, but lost both games he started in the Series. The team did not have enough firepower to beat Pie Traynor and the Pittsburgh Pirates.

The occasion gave Shirley Povich a chance to tell the story of Sam Rice's controversial catch in that Series when he tumbled over the low center-field wall at Griffith Stadium, ostensibly with the ball in his grasp. No one ever knew if he held onto the last out of the game when he fell into the bleachers, and Povich said the secret would only be revealed after Rice's death. The story and other pieces of Washington lore were in the book Povich had published just before the All-Star break, *All These Mornings*. It became cherished reading for sports fans in D.C. Povich went on tour promoting his book and left Bob Addie to cover the team on the long West Coast road trip.

Povich's stories made for better drama than the Senators, who were playing late games on the West Coast that were not reported back home until the afternoon papers arrived at dinner time. Bob Short may have been reading the stories, but the man who insisted he was smart enough to be his own general manager was doing nothing to make his team better. He could find no Coveleski or a Roger Peckinpaugh to add to his team like Clark Griffith had done. Peckinpaugh was the shortstop Griffith brought in to cement the infield of his '24 team that went on to win the World Series.

Short did bow to pressure from Williams to provide some help, but as usual it was of the bargain basement variety. Short picked up shortstop Zoilo Versalles on waivers from the Cleveland Indians. Versalles had left Washington with the old Senators for Minnesota in 1960. Officially only 30 years of age, Versalles' career had begun when he was 20. He had become the starting shortstop for the very good Minnesota teams in the mid–60s that had won the AL championship in 1965. Whatever his age, Versalles' best playing days were behind him, and he only muddied the situation for the much-improved Eddie Brinkman.

Brinkman, who had been the favorite of Senators fans to start the All-Star Game, was having his best season in professional baseball. He had more hits, runs, extra-base hits and RBIs than in the prior two seasons combined. It wasn't a waiver-wire shortstop the Senators needed as much as another starting pitcher like Coveleski. As Mike Epstein would say years later, with one more quality pitcher, the Senators would have been in contention all year. Short, however, was either too cheap to spend money on quality players or did not have the expertise to pull it off. He put in another waiver-wire claim, this time on George Brunet of the California Angels. But Seattle put in a prior claim that left Short empty-handed. The Pilots acquired Brunet, who earlier in the summer had been named the Angels' greatest left-hander in team history, another anomaly of the all-time All-Star balloting for expansion franchises with no prior baseball history.

The Senators' best pitcher in 1969, Dick Bosman, had been leading the league in ERA at the All-Star break, but he and Dennis Higgins gave up seven runs in another loss to the Athletics in the last game of the series in Oakland. The defeat put the Senators back below .500 as the team headed toward Seattle for a series with the Pilots who, like the other expansion team in Kansas City, had been a relentless source of misery for Washington. It was almost as if the expansion teams waited to play their best baseball against Washington on the assumption that the Senators were their best chance to win.

Seattle played in a ballpark that had been designed for minor league crowds. Not only was it too small, but it was badly outdated. Seating behind the reserved field level sections was on bench seats with no backs, and the old stadium held a capacity crowd of only 23,000. If Bob Short thought things were tough in RFK, Seattle was an object lesson in baseball poverty.

Short received good news from an unexpected source. Charlie Finley announced that his sale price for the Athletics after the season would be $12 million. The figure was enough to warm Short's cold, cold heart. Oakland was in a tight pennant race with the Twins under the new divisional concept, and with a young player like Reggie Jackson, the market for the team was bullish. The price was $3 million more than what Short had paid for the Senators, and was evidence that small market teams could be sold for a profit. All Short had to do was pump up the value of the Washington team a little more.

Short's primary commodity, Ted Williams, was equivocating to the press about his commitment to managing. On the team's West Coast swing, Williams' publisher for his book, *My Turn at Bat*, arranged a promotional tour that featured the star author signing copies in all of the cities where the team played. The book was at number seven on the *New York Times* "Best Seller List." Teddy Ballgame was talking about how much he missed fishing with his friends in the Canadian wilds, but no sooner had he waxed nostalgic for his days of retirement than he was back on the topic of hitting, the woes of his players, and how if they could just get a good pitch to hit, they might be better at the plate.

The owners of the new Seattle Pilots were more focused on the task at hand and were busy with plans to build a new stadium. Like almost all of the stadiums built in the 1960s, it was to be a "multi-purpose" facility to house both football and baseball. The design compromise was necessary during an era of cost conscious municipalities using Urban Renewal land and other programs to underwrite the expenses. The deal resulted in stadiums that were not especially conducive to either football or baseball.

At the end of July, the Senators had far greater success in the little Seattle stadium than had been the case on the previous road trip. Coleman and Shellenback pitched the team to two wins against the Pilots to give the Senators their first series win since taking two of three against the Cleveland Indians in early July. Shellenback was making increasingly important contributions to the staff and gave the team another left-handed starter behind the fading Barry Moore.

Shellenback's ties to Ted Williams surfaced in the press after the win against Seattle. Merrell Whittlesey wrote about Shellenback's uncle Frank, who had been Ted Williams' first manager in professional baseball when Ted played in the minors in San Diego. It was another Red Sox connection, this time to Johnny Pesky — Shellenback's former manager — that had returned him to form. Pesky had managed Shellenback in the minors and noticed something off in his delivery. Pesky had mentioned the difference in the pitcher's motion to Sid Hudson in Boston. Hudson put the tip to good use, helping Shellenback go from bullpen filler to one of the better starters the team had during the month of July.

More important was the thunder back in Frank Howard's bat. He went 3-for-5 in the get-away game in Seattle. The three hits raised his batting average, and he hit his 35th home run to provide the margin for victory in a 7–5 win. Mike Epstein and Ken McMullen hit a long home runs in the second game as the bats in the middle of the lineup showed renewed signs of life.

The team was see-sawing back and forth along the .500 mark and the West Coast road trip was half over. The Yankees were playing better baseball, as the last series against Washington demonstrated. They were pushing the Senators for fourth place in the division with the long, hot month of August looming ahead. Immediately in front of the Senators were the California Angels. The Angels were mired in last place in the AL West. The Angels were a team of defense — with Jim Fregosi at shortstop — and pitching with Andy Messersmith and Jim McGlothlin, but they had no offense to speak of.

Against the Angels, the Senators were able to take their second series in a row, winning the first two games. The offense banged out 14 hits in the second game as the lower part of the order — Brinkman, the Allens and Jim French — continued to hit. Dick Bosman won the first game, but in the get-away game, Joe Coleman lost a heartbreaker to Messersmith in a 3–2 pitchers duel.

Washington's record stood at 56 wins and 55 losses when the Senators left the West Coast for the last time. They had a short two-game series in Chicago, and then headed home to D.C. It was in Chicago that Mike Epstein had come alive early in the year with three home runs in a single game. Epstein had two home runs in front of the hometown California crowds in Oakland and Los Angeles. Epstein's father came to see his son play for the first time. Wanting his son to pursue a legal career, Epstein's father had refused to attend any of his son's football or baseball games at Cal, but was now proud to be in the stands for Epstein's 22nd homer.

Epstein continued to hit in the first Chicago game, going 2-for-3. The rest of the team was ailing. Eddie Brinkman had a sprained ankle, and Ken McMullen continued to encounter problems that required Williams to rest him periodically. Bernie Allen was playing hurt as well, but it was the pitching staff that looked bruised in the first game against the White Sox in Chicago. Jim Shellenback could not duplicate his fine outings as he gave up four runs in the first two innings in Chicago, and then the bullpen gave up seven more for a 11–4 rout.

Dick Bosman salvaged the team's pride with a win in the final game of the road trip with a respectable outing that gave the offense a chance to win the game. Frank Howard connected for his 36th home run, but the hero was Paul Casanova, whose dramatic ninth-inning homer won the game, 4–3, to keep Washington over .500 upon heading home.

Back home at RFK, the Redskins had started their exhibition season under new coach Vince Lombardi. The legendary Green Bay coach would become fast friends with Ted Williams in the weeks ahead as the two sports icons shared adjoining dressing rooms at RFK Stadium — another of the venues built to accommodate both sports.

Williams is reputed to have said to Lombard at their first meeting, "I hear that you can walk on water," to which Lombardi replied, "I understand that you can too." Lombardi was off to a good start. His team won, 13–7, against the Bears in the first exhibition game, but local football fans were hoping he could pull off a miracle of the magnitude that Williams had done with the Senators. Washington's baseball players came to love the Lombardi locker room talks they could hear sometimes through the walls at RFK from their own lockers and facilities beneath the stands.

Whether the players approved of the Redskins' presence or not did nothing to put to rest the serious problem of shared ownership of the stadium between football and baseball. The primary issue was the wear and tear on the field caused by football games — especially in the summer heat when the grass was dry and susceptible to damage. The Redskins' game against the Bears on August 2 was a case in point. The game had done significant harm to the Senators' infield grass, and groundskeeper Joe Mooney had seen the damage immediately after the Redskins' contest. Mooney declared in the Washington papers that the field was a disaster.

Bob Short's solution was to install artificial turf, as long as someone else was going to pay for it. When the Senators returned to RFK and Short saw the field, he was apoplectic. Saying that he paid $200,000 for maintenance to the D.C. Armory Board that oversaw the stadium, Short ranted that he wanted the money back. There was hardly a blade of grass left in the infield.

The football game had been played in the same kind of nasty weather that had visited RFK for the All-Star Game. The driving rainstorm that struck RFK soaked the field and left football players sliding all over it, their cleats pulling up sod as they went. The areas along the sidelines where the football benches had been positioned were stripped bare and much of the field was still a sodden mess. Joe Mooney had been right. It was a disaster.

Mooney had gotten the field ready after the downpour that cancelled the All-Star Game when many were skeptical it could be done. Now, bringing in new calcified clay with wheelbarrows, Mooney pulled the field back together. Short brought in a helicopter to blow-dry the field, but the teams who came in for the eleven-game homestand remarked that the infield conditions were among the worst they had seen in the majors.

Mooney was a gifted groundskeeper; after working for the Senators, he would be asked to maintain one of baseball's great legacy ballyards, Fenway Park in Boston. Yet nothing he nor Short could do changed the fact that it was football season in Washington, D.C. The actions of the D.C. Armory Board and the newspaper headlines told the story — Washington was a football town. The *Washington Post's* football columnist, William Gildea, was already getting top billing in the pre-season, and stories about the games were headline news above that of the Senators.

The baseball homestand started with the Seattle Pilots and continued with other AL West teams Kansas City, Minnesota, and Chicago. The joy of return was evident in the Senators' play. The Pilots sent out newly acquired waiver-wire pitcher Bob Brunet, and he shut Washington down until the sixth inning when the lineup's peskiest hitters — Brinkman, Unser, and Bernie and Hank Allen — bunched a series of hits to chase Brunet. Joe Coleman continued to pitch well and won his ninth game in a 10–3 rout. Seattle lost shortstop Ray Oyler during the game when he fell into a depression in the outfield while chasing a pop fly.

The second Seattle game went to the Pilots after the Senators built a 5–0 lead in the first inning and a 6–3 advantage in the second on Frank Howard's 37th home run. But Jim Shellenback and Jim Hannan pitching in relief were unable to hold the lead. The 8–6 loss clinched a win for Seattle in the season series. The Sunday game ended almost as badly, but Washington rallied in the eighth inning to win, 7–5.

Although the Senators had won the home series and saw their record climb to 59–57, the attendance for the weekend set was discouraging. None of the three games drew more than 10,000 fans. Whether it was the hot weather, the shift of attention to the Redskin, or the lack of an exciting opponent, Washington baseball was not attracting fans.

If the problem for baseball as a marketable commodity was a lack of excitement, then Billy Martin was doing what he could to spice up the game in Minneapolis. When the Twins took a swing along the East Coast, they landed in Baltimore where a fistfight erupted in the visiting Twins clubhouse. Dave Boswell started the mess by physically confronting Bobby Allison after the latter called Boswell out for not running his required laps after the game. Martin then sought out Boswell at a Baltimore restaurant in a secondary fight.

Martin had twelve stitches taken in his badly bruised hand after he confronted Boswell outside the restaurant. The damage to Martin's hand came when he knocked Boswell unconscious with two powerful punches. Bob

Short expected Ted Williams to generate excitement among Washington fans, but there was nothing either of them could do to compete with Billy Martin.

The Senators' one-two punch of Joe Coleman and Dick Bosman continued to show results when the Kansas City Royals came to town. Bosman won his eighth game and scored the winning run in the eighth inning as he pitched a complete-game gem, winning, 2–1. Attendance was sliding even further, for the Monday night game drew only slightly more than 4,000 fans.

The Senators lost the final two games of the series to the Royals, increasing the likelihood they would lose another season series to an expansion team. Washington had an enviable record against Ted Williams' old club, the Boston Red Sox. Were it not for the Red Sox and the Cleveland Indians, Washington's record would be well below the 60 wins and 59 losses, which is where it stood on August 13 at the end of the Kansas City series.

After the Royals left town, there was an off-day for Joe Mooney to work on the field before the brawling Minnesota Twins came to town. Washington had a winning record against the Twins. It was as if the Twins — the old Senators — and Ted Williams' old team, the Red Sox, provided a winning motivation for Washington that they could not find against the expansion teams.

15

We Are Stardust,
We Are Golden

In mid–August the astronauts were celebrated with ticker tape parades through the canyons of New York City skyscrapers and those in Chicago as well. The tributes ended with a formal dinner hosted by President Nixon, his family and White House dignitaries in Los Angeles, where the astronauts and their extended families were in attendance. The host and his guests were dressed elegantly, featuring long flowing shiny gowns for the women and tuxedoes for the men. The newspapers covered the event as though it were the royal family dining in the winter palace.

Far away, in a cow pasture in Bethel, New York, 500,000 rock-and-roll fans — some of whom were pictured wearing nothing at all — had gathered for what was perhaps the climax of the sixties counter culture, a three-day festival of "peace and music" that came to be known simply as Woodstock. Woodstock brought together every great rock-and-roll band of the sixties. The list was as mind-boggling as everything else about the festival, and included headliners like the Grateful Dead, the Who, Crosby, Stills, and Nash, the Jefferson Airplane, and the Band.

In the festival planners' most ambitious dreams, they had hoped for sales of over 100,000 tickets. The site and its amenities were scaled to a maximum crowd of approximately 150,000 persons. Planning went out the window during the first afternoon of the concert. The exact number of tickets sold was lost when the gates that held the huge crowds at bay collapsed before the festival began. Suddenly there was free access for the multitudes, many of whom had waited in long lines of cars stalled for dozens of miles surrounding the 600-acre dairy farm of Max Yasgur, where the concert was held.

The crowd was the story. Estimated at "half a million strong," the impact of the festival was calculated not so much in terms of the great music that everyone had come for, but by the sheer magnitude of the people assembled for it. The ripple effect of Woodstock spread through an entire generation of youth, many of whom felt a growing emotional kinship with those at the concert. Like the song "Woodstock" by Joni Mitchell, much of the historic import of the concert — the site now has a historic marker — came from those who were not there.

Mitchell did not attend the festival, but she had close ties to David Crosby, and his recounting of the event served as the inspiration for the song. The promoters of the festival advertised "peace and music," but the American generation that had reached its adolescence in the unparalleled affluence of the 1960s read the festival theme as "drugs, sex, and rock and roll."

The buzz-cut crowd at President Nixon's formal Los Angeles dinner was unaware of the changes afoot on the other side of the country. Yet the historic swell of Woodstock may have matched that of the astronauts in the longer term. In several short years, even major league ballplayers would discard their conservative attire and adopt the trappings of the Woodstock generation, experimenting with all the more notable aspects of the lifestyle featured in the bucolic surrounds of rural New York.

There was nothing lovable or peaceful about Billy Martin in 1969, and he would never mellow or change with the times. On Friday morning before the game, Martin was called a "trigger-happy frontier marshall" in the press, a John Wayne caricature that Ted Williams and Richard Nixon could appreciate. Martin was not shy in providing the press a colorful depiction of his confrontation with pitcher Dave Boswell outside the Baltimore restaurant.

"He hit me in the chest and on the head and I hit him five or six times in the stomach," Martin said. "Then I hit him in the head, and when he came off the wall, I hit him again. He was out before he hit the ground." The accounts listed Martin's altercations like that of a prize fighter, ticking off his wins against Jimmy Piersall, Gene Conley, Clint Courtney and the bouncers of famous restaurants and nightclubs.

The brawling rookie manager of the Minnesota Twins brought his team of scrappers to Washington for the second time in the 1969 season on the same weekend that Woodstock opened its gates to the "peace and love" generation. Martin's profile was compared to that of Mayo Smith in Detroit, who could not keep Denny McLain, the ace of his pitching staff, in line.

Martin had sparred with Ted Williams in the papers earlier in the season, but now had more serious questions about his conduct to answer than when he had been forced to backtrack over his remarks about Williams' playing career. The first game of the series on Friday night was a quiet affair with Jim Perry shutting out the Senators for seven innings and Ron Perranoski closing the game out. In contrast to the weekend series with Seattle a week before, the attendance jumped to 14,000 to see Billy Martin's team and its ties to the old Senators.

In danger of sliding below the .500 mark again on Saturday, Washington sent Dick Bosman out against another veteran Minnesota pitcher, Jim Kaat. Like Perry, Kaat had logged ten years of service in the majors and threw much slower than in his rookie campaign. He resorted to finesse and may have learned a thing or two from Perry, as both of the Perry brothers — Gaylord and Jim — were accused of doctoring the baseball to achieve remarkable movement on their pitches.

Neither Kaat nor Bosman had his best stuff in the Saturday game. Frank Howard got to Kaat for a three-run homer in the fifth inning, but it was Ed Stoud's three-run triple in the eighth inning that gave Washington the winning edge in the 6–5 victory.

Ken McMullen's outstanding double play preserved the win in the ninth inning when he took a hard-hit line drive off the bat of Bobby Allison reflexively and turned it into two game-ending outs that impressed even Billy Martin. "McMullen makes great plays, like the one he made Friday night," commented Martin after the game.

The rubber match on Sunday was another hard-fought contest. Joe Coleman pitched eleven innings of masterful baseball only to surrender two runs in the top of the eleventh and give the Twins a 3-1 lead. Eddie Brinkman's RBI single and Zoilo Versalles' sacrifice fly tied the score in the bottom of the eleventh inning and kept the game going until the thirteenth, when Minnesota scored a run against Dennis Higgins for the win. The loss leveled the Senators' record again at 61 wins and 61 losses with the Chicago White Sox coming to town.

There was talk that Chicago could not support its two teams and that the White Sox might be moving to Milwaukee during the off-season. Everywhere in the American League, the drop in attendance had home fans worried and ownership looking for greener pastures. The White Sox had promising young players but little else, and the city was not supporting the struggling team. Only a decade earlier, Chicago had been led to the World Series by Senators coach Nellie Fox.

Casey Cox had no trouble with the weak Chicago lineup in the opener, needing only ninth-inning help from Darold Knowles to preserve a 3-1 win. Frank Howard's 39th home run kept him just behind Reggie Jackson, who hit his 42nd homer elsewhere, but it was Ken McMullen's three hits and two RBIs that won the game. McMullen's batting average had slumped to .255 as he fought through injuries, so a productive game from him was a sign that the team might finish strong and healthy down the stretch.

In the second game Dick Bosman continued to provide a bookend to the nice outings by Joe Coleman. Bosman pitched into the eighth inning only allowing six hits and a single run. The Senators bunched their hits in the second and sixth as Del Unser got three hits and Paul Casanova, hitting behind him, had three to knock in three runs in the 4–1 win. The Senators moved back out in front of the Yankees with a 63–61 record and were still a scant three games behind the Red Sox, who were in third place in the AL East.

The only exciting pennant contest in the AL was between Minnesota and Oakland in the Western Division. The divisional concept was theoretically providing the only boon to fan interest since the Orioles were well ahead of everyone in the AL East. Without the divisional structure, the Orioles would have still had a hefty lead. Baltimore had a winning percentage of .705 and was a lock to win more than 100 games.

In prior years Oakland and Minnesota would have been relegated to fighting for second place and there would have been no exciting pennant contest to garner fan interest. Now fans in Oakland and Minnesota should have been turning out to watch their teams compete for a chance to take on the mighty Orioles in the playoffs. Purists might scoff that Baltimore had won the right to be in the World Series without a playoff, but the new rules would govern.

The purists might have found other support for their arguments. The proponents of divisional play had foreseen significant boosts in attendance and interest. Yet so far Minnesota attendance was down from the prior year's level by 100,000. Minnesota was coming off a bad year in 1968. That year marked the first time since the move from Washington that the team was completely out of contention. The Twins had won the American League in '65 and finished second to the Orioles in '66 and to the Red Sox in '67. In 1968 the team had slipped badly to finish seventh in the 10-team American League.

But Minnesota was not the only AL team whose attendance was down. Only four AL teams were showing increases in attendance: Baltimore (the runaway Eastern Division winner), Oakland, New York, and Washington. Baltimore, however, had added only 90,000 additional fans, and of those teams with better attendance, only the Senators could show a significant increase — almost 300,000, which only brought them up to the AL average.

The contrast in the National League was a dramatic one. Average attendance in the NL was up by more than 100,000 fans per team. It was back above the AL average and climbing again as it had for much of the 1960s.

CHART 15-1. AMERICAN LEAGUE ATTENDANCE, 1961–1970

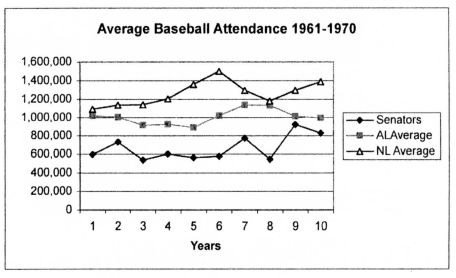

TABLE 15-1. AVERAGE ATTENDANCE COMPARISONS SENATORS, AMERICAN AND NATIONAL LEAGUE, 1961–1970

	1961	*1962*	*1963*	*1964*	*1965*
Senators	597,287	729,775	535,604	600,106	560,083
AL Avg	1,016,302	1,001,506	909,485	923,515	886,076
NL Avg	1,091,438	1,136,016	1,138,223	1,204,519	1,358,114
	1966	*1967*	*1968*	*1969*	*1970*
Senators	576,260	770,868	546,661	918,106	824,789
AL Avg	1,016,674	1,133,692	1,131,739	1,011,227	989,047
NL Avg	1,501,547	1,297,143	1,178,536	1,297,143	1,388,517

Source: *Baseball Almanac*

In the AL, the two new expansion teams had brought in 1.5 million new fans overall, but total league attendance was up less than a million, which meant attendance was falling at non-expansion parks from prior year totals. The baseball brain trust had concluded that the game needed to be more exciting. The excitement was alive and well in the National League as attendance would attest, but not so much in the American League.

In the AL, where the three-run homer ruled the roost, sluggers like Frank Howard and Reggie Jackson were on a pace to outslug the National League's great hitters like Johnny Bench and Willie McCovey by more than

200 total homers. Analysts like Halberstam looked back and found the NL's more exciting game part of the attraction, but other issues would come into play as well.

Even in Montreal, where the team was playing in a poorly configured stadium not much better than Seattle's, the draw of watching the Dodgers, Giants and Mets was bringing in more than a million fans in the team's first year. Neither Kansas City nor Seattle would draw close to a million fans to watch Harmon Killebrew, Frank Howard, and Rico Petrocelli hit the ball into the stratosphere.

Bob Short seemingly had more interest in league attendance than in his midwestern trucking empire. He went public again at the end of August, saying it was up to the press and fans to prove that Washington could support professional baseball by drawing one million fans for the year. "I think every city in the major leagues should draw at least one million people or it's no city for a major league franchise." Short claimed in the *Washington Post* on August 30 that if the team missed that mark by 100,000 fans, he would lose a quarter million dollars.

The claims seemed fatuous on their face. Given the sharp increase in ticket prices and the sharp increase in attendance, it was hard for fans to understand how the team was not making money. Although there were rumors of other teams like the White Sox seeking to relocate, Washington was among the more likely venues to be reaping profits in 1969. Only three teams in the AL had reached the million mark in attendance in 1968. The world champion Detroit Tigers had drawn almost two million, and the only other city even close had been the contending Boston Red Sox with 1.7 million. Winning baseball brought out fans.

The correlation to winning was almost absolute. For all the failures of the team in prior years, Washington attendance in 1969 stood at fifth in the league — almost exactly where its won-lost percentage put the Senators in a combined American League of twelve teams. Short's requests for one million fans might have been seen as ransom demands, but whatever they were, they were overly ambitious. The only AL cities drawing at that level were contending teams. Washington's team was imminently more exciting that in 1968, but it was not in contention for anything other than third place in the AL East.

Shirley Povich in a September column in the *Washington Post* provided the most compelling explanation of the disparities in attendance, especially for the American League's disappointing attendance and the rise in figures for the National League. He restated in the column the Opening Day goals established by major league baseball and Commissioner Bowie Kuhn to draw larger crowds in September with more competitive races. Povich noted that the American League was running almost two million fans behind the National League in overall attendance. He attributed this in small ways to Baltimore's early and total dominance.

Povich asserted, however, that the failure to provide a competitive race in the AL East was not the crucial element. Povich believed that AL owners had been beaten out by the NL on yet another major issue — the acquisition of expansion sites. The first expansion move had come in 1953 when the NL moved its struggling Boston Braves franchise that had never been able to compete with the Red Sox. Relocated to Milwaukee in the first westward move, the new Braves outdrew their Boston location by considerable margins. This initial success bred others, but it was not until Walter O'Malley moved the Brooklyn Dodgers that the race was truly on. He staked the first claim to the virgin land of California and was quickly joined by Horace Stoneham, who moved the New York Giants to San Francisco.

The move to Los Angeles made O'Malley a hated name in New York City — or Brooklyn, to be specific — but Povich accorded him visionary status. In Povich's assessment, the two owners, working in concert with one another, "stole the lush California territory, Los Angeles and San Francisco." The Dodgers owner had opened the National League to black players and had been one of the most active to plunder the best players from the Negro Leagues. He then moved his talented club to the richest untapped region in the country: the state of California.

Povich's assessment was correct. Walter O'Malley's impact on the game was immense, and he had been at the heart of creating the National League's competitive advantage that was so obvious in 1969. It was another three years before the American League put its first expansion team into California, the California Angels. By then O'Malley had the Dodgers operating in Los Angeles, fielding competitive teams and creating loyal fans. The original Angels did not draw well until they moved out of Los Angeles to Anaheim. There they found a fan base removed from the Dodgers.

Povich saw the move of the Washington Senators in 1960 to Minnesota as further proof of the lack of insight by AL owners. Minneapolis had been the first target of O'Malley, and he had been courted by the Twin Cities' investment class, but he chose California instead. After O'Malley and Stoneham had taken the richest vein of California gold, the American League had been left with the remainders.

With only a single team in the country's largest city and a fan base that had once supported three successful teams, the creation of the New York Mets was another coup for the National League. It was the "Amazing" Mets that were fueling the surge in attendance in the NL, and Povich was astute in seeing the unique disadvantage that American League teams were up against.

The Mets were establishing a second New York City franchise with a winning tradition of its own.

Povich was no less enamored of the Atlanta Braves, who were in a tight pennant race in the NL West. In Atlanta, the National League had created the first southern franchise. Atlanta could draw on the entire southeastern United States for its fan base. In their inaugural year, in 1966, the relocated Braves drew 1.5 million fans. The American League expansion franchises Kansas City and Seattle were both drawing well under one million fans, and the Seattle Pilots, whose attendance came in at a lowly 680,000 fans, was already being considered for a move back to Milwaukee, from whence the Braves had come.

So while the National League added successful teams in California, New York City and Atlanta, the American League took a second franchise in Los Angeles, one in Minneapolis that would share the north central region with Milwaukee, one in Oakland that would compete with the previously proven San Francisco Giants, and another in Kansas City that would compete for regional loyalties with the St. Louis Cardinals.

Povich used Washington's road attendance as proof that declining attendance was a problem of the smaller markets concentrated in the American League. While fans were coming to RFK at a rate 40 percent higher than in 1968, Washington's road attendance was off noticeably. That drop was part of an overall decline in attendance in 1969 that saw average attendance fall by more than 100,000 fans in every American League park. In 1970, average attendance in the AL would dip below one million while average attendance was expanding in the NL. There was nothing a lower mound or more home runs could do to offset the shortcomings that had been at play for almost two decades in the American League.

Whatever the reason — whether it was the exciting style of play or the deeper pool of baseball-starved fans into which the National League was expanding — the Senators were in the wrong league to look for dramatic fan increases in 1969.

The implications for Bob Short were troubling. His vision — whatever it may have been — was a flawed one. He was investing in the wrong market. Like O'Malley, he had moved his Minneapolis Lakers to California when it was virgin territory. He made a killing doing so. But according to Povich, there was no pot of gold to be found in baseball for Short. It was already the property of the National League.

If Short was aware of the problem, he made no mention of it. He continued to lament the lack of attendance in D.C., but was neither amenable philosophically nor financially positioned to drive up attendance the only way available in the American League, which was to invest in the team, add talent, and create a winner. Ted Williams had increased fan interest as had a winning team, raising attendance to levels that were in line with other teams in the American League.

Short did have one unique understanding of the Washington, D.C., market. As he had stated in July, trading Frank Howard for Reggie Jackson might have been to the immediate dismay of many loyal fans in D.C., but he was willing to gamble that it would bring in the black fans who were an important part of the local demographic profile. Short was the first sports entrepreneur in the Washington, D.C., area to understand how a successful sports franchise in the area might be built.

Short's call for better press coverage of his Senators was also perceptive. The *Washington Post* and to a lesser extent the *Washington Star* had shifted their focus as August wore on toward the Redskins' upcoming season. Vince Lombardi was doing for the Redskins what Ted Williams had done in the spring for the Senators, and baseball attendance in August dropped off noticeably. Whether it was the heat, vacations, or football, a total of only 15,000 fans had been in attendance for the Senator's first two games of the mid-week Chicago series and was lagging demonstrably over the course of the entire month of August.

The summer sun beating down on RFK could wilt the enthusiasm of the most dedicated fan and seemed to be doing just that. While total attendance had been well over 300,000 ahead of '68 figures when Washington was playing the Yankees and Red Sox earlier in the summer, that figure had diminished to just 278,000 over the prior year, through September 7. The August doldrums were taking a toll and the additional interest in the Redskins sparked by Lombardi was cutting into more than just press coverage. Crowds were dropping below 10,000 for many games.

While attendance was disappointing, the team's performance, as measured statistically, was remaining bullish. The team was fourth overall in team batting average, although sixth in runs scored. That was an improvement over '68, but team pitching was a total makeover that would have made Cinderella's fairy godmother proud. The Senators' team ERA was sixth best at 3.45, which made it more difficult to understand why Washington could not beat the Seattle Pilots, whose team ERA was more than a run per game worse at 4.61— worst in the league.

Dick Bosman was leading the league in ERA among all pitchers. Only Jim Palmer of the Orioles was in the running for the ERA crown, and the race was much the same as that of Frank Howard and Reggie Jackson for the home run title. The *Sporting News* called the Senators staff at the end of August one of the best balanced in the American League, recognition that the bullpen was strong and featured pitchers like Shellenback and Casey Cox

Dick Bosman was leading the league in ERA. National Baseball Hall of Fame Library, Cooperstown, N.Y.

who could start or relieve. Five Senators pitchers were projected to have double-digit win totals, including Bosman, Coleman, Cox, Higgins and Moore, and four pitchers had ERA under 3.00.

Ted Williams got into the act of establishing season goals. Teddy Ballgame wanted to win 87 games and said to the press that his team was capable of accomplishing the feat. Moreover, he stated that with a few off-season moves, Washington could easily be in competition for the league championship in 1970. "I am proud of how our team has performed," said Williams, "and yet they can get better." Williams announced that he would be back for the next season, which was welcome news. He said he would be active in evaluating the minor leaguers who might contribute the next year, although he was going on safari in Africa after the end of the season.

Although the fans were not showing up in the same numbers as in June, the level of excitement at RFK was still palpable, and the players commented on it to the press, saying they performed better in front of supportive home fans. With excited fans at the ballpark and high expectations playing in the local press, the team headed into the American heartland for three games with the Kansas City Royals and three in Minneapolis with the Twins.

Another group was hitting the road on the same weekend. Peter Fonda and Jack Nicholson were heading out to motorcycle across the silver screen. The film *Easy Rider* was debuting in theatres, and like the music festival in Bethel, New York, it would do much to change American culture in years to come. One lasting impact was establishing Jack Nicholson as a cinema icon whose fame would rival that of Reggie Jackson or maybe even Ted Williams.

16

Homeward Bound

Divisional play was having its greatest success in the National League where two exciting pennant races were shaping up in late August as teams steered for home. In the NL East, the New York Mets were closing the gap on the division-leading Chicago Cubs, while in the NL West, five teams were chasing the San Francisco Giants, with Cincinnati and Atlanta only a half-game back. Only the expansion San Diego Padres were out of the race in the West.

The Amazing Mets had been the laughingstock as an expansion team whose only draw was the witticisms of Casey Stengel. They joined the league at the same time as the expansion Senators, and it was a time when baseball was still the unrivaled sports story for the press and the fans.

In 1969, obscure players like Ron Swoboda were pushing for recognition during the Mets' pennant drive. The former University of Maryland baseball star had gone on a hitting spree in late August that helped fuel a six-game winning streak and pushed the Mets within five games of the Cubs. The Mets were not an offensive-minded team, rather one built around pitching and defense. Their youthful pitching staff featured 24-year-old Tom Seaver, 26-year-old Jerry Koosman, and 24-year-old bullpen ace Tug McGraw. Players like Bud Harrelson and Tommie Agee backed them with gloves that proved golden.

Swoboda was a working-class hitter who, like others on the team, was platooned by manager Gil Hodges to get the most out of what were modest talents to complement outfielder Agee, the offensive engine of the team. The Mets had traded in midseason for Donn Clendenon to add offense, and he was proving to be exactly the spark the team needed.

In 1968 the pennant races in September had failed to hold fan interest; the fans had tuned out baseball in September and tuned in football. That was the perception of the baseball brain trust that hoped to halt the loss of fan loyalty with a switch to divisional play. From the perspective of creating new interest and new fans, the Mets were good for baseball.

Not only were the September pennant races looking tighter and more exciting every day, but the universe of fans who felt ownership of those races were new. In addition to the Mets, NL West teams like the Atlanta Braves, Houston Astros, and Cincinnati Reds were in contention. Teams from these cites were either brand new to pennant fever or, in Cincinnati's case, had not known it in so long that for all intents and purposes, it was brand new all over again — as Yogi might have opined.

The Chicago Cubs had been contenders but were the perennial underdog team in the National League. It was shaping up as a season for underdogs, and it could not have been scripted better to have fledgling teams running down the stretch neck-and-neck against the Dodgers and Giants, whose presence in the thick of things was another ho-hum event.

The Senators were a similar feel-good story, and American hero Ted Williams orchestrating the resurgence of the old Senators added to the press appeal. On August 22, the team started a short six-game road trip to Kansas City and Minnesota. The team was without its defensive anchor Eddie Brinkman, whose badly sprained ankle put him on the shelf. The team called up Dick Smith from the minors, a capable fill-in, but a player who had not been schooled in all of Williams' hitting theories.

The Royals had bedeviled Williams' team all season and continued to do so in the first game. Kansas City threw a rookie pitcher at Washington's hitters who had no right to dominate them, but managed it nevertheless. Jim Rooker was a player making the most of his opportunities with the expansion Royals. Like Rooker, Ed Kirkpatrick was a young outfielder who might never have escaped journeyman status, but used expansion to carve out a regular role on the Royals. Kirkpatrick seemed to live for a chance to hit against Washington's pitching staff, and in the first game of the series, his eighth-inning home run scored two runs off Joe Coleman and gave the Royals a 3–2 win. The loss made Coleman a loser with a 9–10 record despite his 3.29 ERA and his status at the front of the Washington rotation.

Washington came back to win the series behind Jim Hannan and Casey Cox. Hannan was back in the rotation and was putting the lessons from Sid Hudson into practice. He gave Williams six strong innings. Dennis Higgins had been struggling in July and August, but pitched three strong innings of relief to save the win for Hannan. Cox pitched a complete game in the rubber match, but it was Zoilo Versalles, filling in for Eddie Brinkman, who supplied the offensive punch by going 3-for-5 and driving in three runs in the lopsided 10–3 win against the suddenly hapless Royals. Versalles' stellar defense did not hurt, either.

Washington's 65th win against 62 losses on August 23 made it certain the team would exceed the victory total for the entire 1968 season (65–96).

The winning percentage was again creeping toward the record levels the team had achieved in July before the All-Star break, and it continued in the first game against Billy Martin's Twins. Dick Bosman pitched well enough to win and Frank Howard's 40th home run and his 4-for-5 night carried the day for a 7–3 victory. The big night pushed Howard back over the .300 mark to .304 for the season.

Howard's home run came a day after Reggie Jackson hit his 44th and 45th; Hondo's homers seemed to come in succession to Jackson's. Reggie was keeping the pressure on the Twins as Oakland continued to keep pace in the AL East, only two games back. But the Twins were able to put some space between themselves and the Athletics as they won the next two games against the Senators. Dave Boswell, back from his run-in with Billy Martin, pitched well for his 14th win, against Barry Moore, who continued to pitch poorly lasting only two innings. Joe Coleman was chased in the fourth inning the next night, and Jim Perry was at the top of his game while getting a complete-game win, his 16th of the season.

Washington returned to RFK to end the month of August with a head-to-head matchup of Frank Howard and Reggie Jackson. The home run contest sparked interest in the Oakland series and 16,780 showed up for the Friday night opener. The attendance level exceeded the average of 15,000 needed to reach Bob Short's golden mean of one million. But the 5–0 loss to Oakland provided no fireworks, no home runs, and attendance dropped off for the Saturday game, which was barely over 10,000.

The next day, however, Frank Howard gave the fans in attendance all they could have hoped for. It was Ted Williams' 51st birthday and his Senators offense celebrated with seventeen hits and eleven runs. After the game, Williams said, "Please continue to celebrate my birthday ... keep celebrating until the end of the season." Dick Bosman shut down Reggie Jackson and the Oakland offense for six innings to get his team-leading 11th win. Frank Howard was 4-for-5 for the game and drove in five runs. He even stole a base, his first and only one of the season. Ken McMullen hit his 12th home run in the game and his 4-for-4 performance accounted for three more runs as the Senators pounded Lew Krausse and Vida Blue in the 11–3 romp.

The barrage of hits continued on Sunday afternoon as both McMullen and Howard homered again. This time were joined by Mike Epstein, who hit his 23rd homer. The offensive fireworks were in support of Casey Cox, who won for the 10th time. Reggie Jackson went 2-for-3, but Howard's 42nd home run edged him closer to Jackson's total of 45. The shot went out in right field, with Jackson watching, and served notice not only on Reggie, but on the Athletics dugout that had been needling Hondo during the contest. As important as the home run was to Frank Howard, the seventh-inning shot helped cement an important series win against the contending Athletics, and it pushed the Senators a little closer to third-place Boston.

Washington had never breached the first division in the AL East and had only been close once, but as Williams was articulating his goal of winning 87 games for the season, he was calculating exactly what it would take for Washington to climb past the Red Sox. There was no one in the Washington dugout more motivated to make the climb than Ted Williams. Of all the milestones that his team was reaching late in August, nothing could provide more sweetness for the manager than revenge: the chance to look down on the Boston Red Sox, who never seriously considered him managerial material. It was a long shot, but the wins over Oakland led to his dreaming once again.

September was a return to normalcy in Washington. The workforce was back commuting in from Virginia on the highways, the children were back in school, and the summer heat was slowly subsiding. Shirley Povich was back from vacation and back on the *Washington Post* sports page where he belonged. Oddly enough, though, Povich was covering only the Redskins, or maybe an occasional golf tournament; there was almost nothing on the Senators from the most prominent columnist in town. The message of the All-Star Game, "Baseball Is Back," was fading into the recesses of football madness.

September's arrival was celebrated with back-to-back double-headers against the California Angels. The first two games were on Labor Day, and after beating the Athletics two in a row, the team was upbeat. There was more good news from Eddie Brinkman, who was ready to play again. Joe Coleman got the four-game series off to a good start. He regained his winning form with another complete-game shutout. Mike Epstein always played well against California teams, and he hit his 24th home run to provide all the scoring that Coleman needed for his 10th win. Epstein was 4-for-4 in the game, driving in three of the team's four runs.

In the Labor Day nightcap, Ken McMullen hit two home runs, but Barry Moore's long slide into total ineffectiveness continued. The Angels won, 8–7, aided by errors and a failure of the bullpen. A robust crowd of almost 20,000 fans was in attendance for the Labor Day games in Washington.

The next day the Senators celebrated Eddie Brinkman's return to the field at RFK with a double-header sweep. Not only was Brinkman back, but Jim Hannan — or at least the Jim Hannan who had pitched so well in '68 — was back as well. Over the course of the summer, Hannan had refined his motion under the direction of Sid Hudson until he regained his form and rhythm. In the first game in September, Hannan had his sinker working perfectly again, always low and at the knees, always moving downward through the lower part of the strike zone.

Hannan faced only 29 batters in the game, two more than the minimum of 27. The two-hitter was only his fifth win of the season, but with Barry Moore struggling in every outing, Hannan gave Ted Williams a new option for the rotation. The other new option pitched in the second game against the Angels. Cisco Carlos was another waiver-wire bargain Ted Williams had urged on his skinflint boss, Bob Short. Carlos was a young right-hander who had floundered for the White Sox, but Sid Hudson had seem something he liked about the young man. It paid off as Carlos went five innings for the win in a rain-shortened game.

As usual Frank Howard was taking the words of Ted Williams seriously, and he was determined to celebrate his boss's birthday as deeply into September as he could. Howard was hitting .313, and in the second doubleheader against California, he hit his 43rd home run. Lee Maye was providing timely hitting as well and making the miserly acquisitions of Short and Williams look like genius at work. Maye was being platooned, but had appeared in each of the California games and recorded several key hits.

Winning three of four games from the Angels put the Senators only two games behind the Red Sox and placed the team five games over .500 for the second time in the 1969 season. With Brinkman back, McMullen, Howard and Epstein all hot in the middle of the order, and a pitching staff that was rounding into excellent shape, Washington was anxious for the head-to-head matchup against the Red Sox in Boston. McMullen, Howard and Epstein had hit eleven homers over the course of the most recent six games. Brinkman and Unser were getting on base and playing great defense, so Jim Hannan's return to form might be all it took to push the team forward into the first division.

The schedule gave Washington two days off to prepare for the series against Boston. Washington had won nine of twelve games so far against Boston, and with the rest days, Williams could shuffle his starting rotation and put up his best against the Red Sox hitters. Bosman would start game one, Coleman the second game, and Hannan would pitch the last, taking Barry Moore's spot as third in the rotation. A sweep of the series meant the Senators would move into third place, as high as any Washington team had been at this point in the season in decades.

Hope had been high in July before the All-Star break when Washington had the Tigers squarely in their sights, but a Frank Howard double-play ball had sent the team into a nose dive. Now hope had retaken the high ground and a big finish might even sweep Bob Short off his short-legged feet. But there was an ill-omened footnote. Only 6,000 fans had attended the Tuesday double-header. The goal of one million fans was slipping from sight.

By contrast, the Redskins' upcoming exhibition contest against the Browns at RFK on Saturday night was a sellout. The results of the game were a worry to groundskeeper Joe Mooney, who was hoping that the rain in the forecast would miss the area. After the away games in Boston and Baltimore, the team would return for a week-long homestand. It gave Mooney only four days between the Redskins game and the first Senators game to get the field at RFK back in shape.

Formal discussions were being held about a turf field for RFK. The Redskins and the D.C. Armory Board had both agreed to pay one-third shares of the cost of the new turf. The ball was in Bob Short's court, and with teams like the White Sox and the Seattle Pilots talking about moving to Dallas for the 1970 season, Short's options might be foreclosed by events. What Short was doing behind the scenes was unknown, but he was not talking about spending money for turf at RFK. On that subject he was notably silent.

With the season at an obvious fulcrum, Ted Williams was taking the days off to visit with his personal inspiration and favorite manager from his playing days, Joe McCarthy. McCarthy was spending his retirement years in Buffalo. Both Williams and Ed Doherty spent the day in the backyard with the Hall of Fame manager, reminiscing about old times. Doherty had his history with McCarthy as well. He knew McCarthy from Doherty's days as a batboy for Buffalo's minor league team when McCarthy had been a second baseman trying to make it to the big leagues.

Williams was still mulling over his fitness to manage in the majors as he made the trip. McCarthy gave him much-needed words of encouragement. Reminding Williams of the last game of their first season together, McCarthy said to Williams, "Do you remember what I said to you that day?" Williams said that the words had stuck with him all the many years since 1948, admitting, "They were the kindest words ever spoken to me in baseball."

McCarthy had told Williams after the season, "We did get along, didn't we? We surprised a lot of people who said we couldn't." Many of those same writers and experts had also said Ted Williams was not fit to manage a baseball team since he could hardly manage himself. Remembering how he had overcome so many who doubted him over the years could only have been inspiring to Williams as he considered his chances going into Boston.

The words of McCarthy on other subjects proved portentous. Williams asked McCarthy how he had dealt with the many hard cases he managed over the years. McCarthy's response was that he never criticized his players after a game or in public; he always waited and talked to them in his office. He told Williams a story about dealing with Hack Wilson, the great hitter who loved to take in the night life during the season. He did not criticize Wilson directly but in the quiet of his office, like dealing with a school boy after hours. McCarthy pointed out the damage Wilson was doing to his own reputation and to his teammates. Wilson responded by having the best season of his career — which was a great one.

Williams asked McCarthy about how Billy Martin set up his infield in a key situation against the Senators. McCarthy said that by playing the infield at double-play depth with the bases loaded, Martin had shown the team that even if a run scored, the manager had confidence his team could score and regain the lead. Building confidence was much of what the two men talked about, and McCarthy built quite a bit for the rookie manager. In the end McCarthy — a devout Catholic — promised to light a candle for the Senators, and Williams' response was, "How can you miss with a man like McCarthy praying for me?"

At first the effect seemed lost. Washington went into Boston for the all-important series and Williams sent out Dick Bosman in the first game. Bosman was arguably the best pitcher in the league over the course of the season, no mean statement with Jim Palmer as the competition. Palmer had won eleven games in a row and owned a slightly better ERA, but neither man would get the Cy Young Award that year. It would go to Mike Cuellar and Denny McClain, both of whom ended the year with more than twenty wins. Bosman and Palmer were still neck-and-neck in the race for the American League ERA crown. Had Bosman not missed six starts with a muscle strain in May, he might have had as many wins as Palmer, who was stuck on 13.

Bosman was especially tough on right-handed hitters with his sinker, but had trouble with left-handed swingers until the 1969 season. The shortcoming had kept him in the bullpen, but in the spring Bosman had added an overhand fastball that he cut to run in on lefties; his season was testimony to the effectiveness of the new pitch. He was also using the ideas Ted Williams had provided on how to set up hitters, how to approach the hitters, and how to gain greater concentration on the mound. It was all working, and the confidence that Williams had in Bosman was reflected in his choice as the starting pitcher for the first game in the crucial Boston series.

Bosman took the mound in Boston in front of 25,000 Fenway Park faithful for the Friday night game. Everything looked very promising through the first five innings. The Senators jumped on Vicente Romo for seven runs, only four of which were earned, as Boston committed two costly errors. Del

Unser got on base and Ken McMullen's hot bat drove him home. That combination accounted for two runs, and Epstein, Casanova and Brinkman accounted for the rest.

In the bottom of the fifth inning with the Senators ahead, 7–0, Carl Yastrzemski made up for his error in the field with a run-scoring double and Tony Conigliaro added another as the Red Sox cut the margin to 7–4 going into the sixth inning. Bosman righted himself and retired the side in the sixth without giving up a run. But in the seventh, Bosman ran out of gas. He gave up a run and trudged to the dugout with runners at first and third and two out.

Ted Williams was taking no chances. He had a rested bullpen, and in Casey Cox, he had one of his best pitchers waiting. He brought in Cox to pitch to Rico Petrocelli, who was having a career year. He was just behind Howard and Jackson in the home run race and for the only time in his career would hit 40. He greeted Cox with a towering home run into the left field netting above the Green Monster. The ball might have been caught at RFK, but in Boston it was a three-run homer that put Boston in front, 8–7.

Washington battled back, and on successive hits by McMullen, Brinkman and pinch-hitter Zoilo Versalles, scored a run to tie the game in the ninth. Then second baseman Tim Cullen booted a routine grounder in the bottom of the ninth and threw it all away. Cullen had help. Steady Eddie Brinkman made a rare error and Darold Knowles walked two batters — only one intentionally — to set up the game-winning situation. Ted Williams had pinch-hit his regular second baseman, Bernie Allen, with Zoilo Versalles, who had delivered the key hit in the rally to tie the score.

Williams may have over-managed when he sent in a pinch-runner for Ken McMullen after his hit to start the ninth inning rally. That is what got Cullen into the game and gave one of the weakest links on the team a chance to lose it. But Williams had put the best players he had into the right situations to win the game, and it had not been enough. He did everything he could to win, gave his team every chance to pull the game out, but it ended a lot like the game in July against Detroit. The team had no confidence they could deliver in clutch games and little experience doing so.

The Saturday afternoon game — the second in the series — matched Joe Coleman against Lee Stange. As important as the game was to baseball in Washington, D.C., the *Washington Post* headlines were all about the Redskins' loss to the Cleveland Browns, about Sonny Jurgensen and Jerry Smith's futile attempts to derail the Browns' running game. Shirley Povich was still covering football exclusively in his morning column. Bob Addie was left to tie up the loose ends of the baseball season.

Joe Coleman was not reading the Washington papers in Boston. He was a Boston area native who had pitched a shutout in his previous outing and had looked like a blossoming ace. When Coleman took the mound for the Saturday game at Fenway, he could not find inspiration to bring his best efforts to Boston. His pitching opponent, Lee Stange, was hardly a motivational force. Stange was but a spot starter and long reliever, but he outpitched Coleman in the all-important second game. Coleman could not command his new forkball and continuously fell behind in the counts. He walked three batters and grooved a pitch to Carl Yastrzemski, who was only too happy to send Coleman to the showers with his 35th home run in the first inning.

It was the home run in the second inning to light-hitting rookie Syd O'Brien that was the final straw for Williams, who took Coleman out after he had handed the Red Sox a 6–0 lead. Lee Maye's home run and three hits by Ken McMullen made the final score almost respectable, but the 9–5 loss dropped the Senators six back in the loss column to the Red Sox, and the visions of the first division, of rising above the 1967 American League champs, were burnt toast.

In the final game of the series, Casey Cox and the lower end of the batting order were able to put a bit of salve on the team's wounded pride with a 3–2 win. Cox got his 11th win of the season for five shutout innings in relief of Jim Hannan. Del Unser's pinch-hit home run in the top of the tenth inning won the game, and Frank Howard's solo home run off Jim Lonborg — his 44th — tied the score in the sixth inning to set up Unser's game winner.

Povich covered none of the games in Boston. Perhaps it was being drawn into enthusiastic support of the team, only to have his hopes dashed earlier in the summer against Detroit. Whatever his motivation, it was not until the miracle of the 1969 Mets burst onto the scene that Povich switched back to baseball. The only baseball he was writing about now was in Flushing Meadows, New York. Never in the month of September, during the stretch run of the best Senators team in decades, did Povich devote any ink to the home team.

The team took its disappointments south to Baltimore for a rare midweek double-header that would wrap up the season between the two mid–Atlantic teams, and none too soon. Baltimore was a runaway train headed toward the first AL East divisional pennant. When the two games on Tuesday were completed, Washington would own only five wins all season against Baltimore to go with thirteen defeats.

The Senators looked flat losing, 6–1, to Mike Cuellar in the first game, and Joe Coleman pitched just poorly enough to lose again in the second game by a 3–2 margin. Frank Howard's 45th home run was a rallying cry, but it fell on deaf ears. Washington's record against the Orioles was the Senators' worst head-to-head record against an American League team, although the nearly identical five-win eleven-loss record against the expansion Kansas City Royals was more embarrassing.

Despite the disappointing losses against Boston and Baltimore, there was still much going right for the Senators. Ken McMullen was hitting higher than .500 for the eight games leading up to the Orioles mini-series. The pitching — despite Coleman's inconsistent starts — was helped by the re-emergence of an effective Jim Hannan that was allowing Casey Cox and Jim Shellenback to provide an assist to the overworked bullpen.

The pennant races in early September were getting more ink than in recent years. Although Baltimore's two wins against Washington meant the Orioles needed only six games to clinch the Eastern Division championship, there was a growing sense of excitement over the pennant races shaping up in both National League divisions.

The New York Mets were the headline-grabbing story on September 10 — an off-day for the Senators. Jerry Koosman and Tom Seaver pitched the Mets past the Cubs in a double-header sweep in New York, where seats were hard to find. There were 43,000 fans for the first game and 51,000 for the second. It was in the stretch starting in the middle of September when the team would earn the title "Amazing Mets" as they won 24 games during the month and lost only seven, capturing much of the baseball excitement in New York City that once had been the sole province of the Yankees.

The Yankees were playing "Off Broadway," in relative obscurity in RFK, where they had two games against the Senators. For the Senators, the homestand would mark the beginning of its own winning streak that would stand as a landmark for Washington baseball until the game moved back to D.C. in 2005. Yet Washington was not paying attention to the exploits of its baseball nine. In the first game, against the best draw the American League had in the New York Yankees, the attendance consisted of fewer than 6,000 fans for a mid-week game.

Dick Bosman, the Washington ace, was up against Mel Stottlemyre, who seemed to always be pitching for the Yankees whenever they played the Senators. Stottlemyre was six-for-six in his prior six starts: six wins, six complete games. But it was Bosman who "flirted with baseball immortality" in the game as he carried a no-hitter into the eighth inning. Stottlemyre was gone by the sixth as Lee Maye, Mike Epstein and Ken McMullen had multi-hit games, and Frank Howard hit his 46th home run to provide the winning margin of 6–1. The first hit for the Yankees was a Jimmy Hall double with one out in the eighth. A single by Jerry Kenney scored the only run of the game for New York, and Bosman had to hang on to get the last five outs, but it was a masterful performance.

There were even fewer fans for the Wednesday night game won by Jim Hannan. Although the team managed only seven hits against Stan Bahnsen, he threw in four walks and gave up a three-run homer to Mike Epstein in the first inning. The real news was the Mets' double-header sweep against the Expos. The two victories were enough to take first place away from the faltering Cubs, and New York City was going crazy with its unlikely group of heroes.

The 1969 Mets were after all a team of mostly unknown players. The lineup was composed of blue collar pedigrees from the likes of Art Shamsky and University of Maryland alumnus Ron Swoboda. Both were making plays and headlines in very non-blue collar New York City, and the press in the Big Apple responded by making Shamsky and Swoboda into legends.

The Mets offense included Donn Clendenon, Tommy Agee, and Ken Boswell, but during the stretch run, it was the eight shutouts by the New York pitching staff that pushed them to the top and kept them there. While the Senators were playing the Yankees, the Mets pitching staff threw remarkable back-to-back-to-back complete-game shutouts by Gary Gentry, Jerry Koosman, and Don Cardwell. Pitching, pitching, and more pitching was the real story of the Amazing Mets.

The Detroit Tigers, second in the AL East to the Orioles, came to Washington for a three-game weekend series. With the pennant race largely over, Tiger manager Mayo Smith was talking about team chemistry and how much Denny McLain's shenanigans had cost the team. Friday night attendance for the game against the reigning American League champs was a paltry 9,000. The fans saw Casey Cox prevail in an exciting contest won by the Senators, 4–3. Cox got two hits to go with his 12th win in a complete game that kept the fans on edge until the end.

Leading 4–1 going into the ninth, Cox surrendered two runs and was protecting only a one-run lead. He was facing Willie Horton, who had homered against him twice before in the season. Horton's prior hit against Cox had been a grand slam — a hit particularly hard to forget. But Cox remained in the game and retired Horton on an infield pop fly and the small but appreciative crowd gave him a standing ovation as he came off the field a winner.

The second game against the Tigers might have been Ken McMullen Day as the Washington third baseman went 4-for-5 with a home run and five runs driven in. It was another exciting game watched by fewer than 10,000 fans as the Senators bats banged out twelve hits and posted another victory for Darold Knowles by a score of 11–6. Three thousand of the fans in attendance were kids, who were allowed in free as part of a promotion, making the paying crowd again fewer than 6,000. The loss by the Tigers clinched the first-ever AL East divisional championship for the Orioles.

The Senators set their own high water mark for the year. The team stood at six games over .500 with a record of 76 wins and 70 defeats. No Washington team had been in such a rarified atmosphere since the 1952 and 1953 Senators had finished in fifth place when the American League sported only eight teams. Only the 1952 Senators had managed to win more than they lost, going 78–76.

Frank Howard had established his own career mark of 46 home runs, eclipsing his prior year's high of 44. As the American League's best sluggers headed down the stretch, Howard was tied with Reggie Jackson. But Jackson was hospitalized in Oakland with a mysterious rash. Harmon Killebrew was trying to single-handedly bull the Minnesota Twins into the playoffs, and his 43 home runs were pushing Jackson and Howard for the league lead. Oakland had fallen as Jackson's bat had cooled and Minnesota was pulling away, making the AL West pennant race of little more interest than the AL East. The home run race was the only intrigue left in the American League.

Howard was still accomplishing what he cared about most, the struggle to hit .300. With more than three weeks to go in the season, he was at .307, good for the seventh-best average in the American League. On the home run front, Howard demurred, "It would be no disgrace to finish behind Jackson and Killebrew." Bob Short failed to take up the cheering for his slugger, reiterating his earlier claims that he would trade Howard and Epstein for Reggie Jackson. Ted Williams' impressions of Jackson may have been part of the logic behind Short's assessment. Short was a sucker for loud statistics and loud marketing, and Williams was saying, "I really thought he (Jackson) would hit 60. He was off to such a good start and he may never get another chance."

Howard admitted that he thought he could reach 50 home runs, a mark few major league hitters had attained and one that clearly had allure for the big man. "I am going to have to get back in a groove to do it," Howard said, though he had hit six long balls during a twelve-game stretch. "I haven't been swinging good since those two days off," he added, referring to the two-day layoff on September 3 and 4.

Howard knew his chances were improved by having Epstein and McMullen batting behind him in the lineup. Epstein's late surge and McMullen's hot bat were giving pitchers fewer chances to pitch around Howard, though Hondo was willing to take a walk in 1969. He was on a pace to walk more than 100 times, almost doubling his prior career high.

It was Mike Epstein who continued with the hot bat in the Sunday afternoon game at RFK Stadium against Detroit. He hit a grand slam, and the four runs gave Washington a late 4–2 lead against Mickey Lolich, who struck out ten over nine innings. The lead did not hold for long as Darold Knowles gave up two runs in the top of the ninth and the Tigers won an extra-inning affair by a 7–4 margin.

There was a good crowd of 12,000 fans for the Tiger game, but more were probably at home watching the Redskins. New Washington coach Vince Lombardi lost the last exhibition game to the Eagles on four interceptions thrown by Sonny Jurgensen, but hope was still running high that Lombardi could work Ted Williams' magic for the Skins.

The Senators' field of play shifted as the divisional champs, the Baltimore Orioles, came to town for the last time. Jim Palmer and Dick Bosman were locked in as tight a race for the ERA crown as Howard, Killebrew, and Jackson were for the home run title. Palmer had a slight lead with a 2.13 ERA, Bosman trailing at 2.20.

The first game of the Baltimore series pitted the two men against one another head-to-head. On that Monday in September, Bosman clearly had the better stuff. Palmer walked four batters and managed only two strikeouts. With the score tied, 2–2, in the bottom of the ninth in a closely contested game, Palmer gave up the winning run on a single by Eddie Brinkman, who was still hitting at a lusty .273 clip. Bosman looked great, but Ted Williams pulled him for a pinch-hitter in the top of the ninth that set up the winning score. While the win went to Bob Humphreys, who was having an excellent year out of the bullpen, Williams' move gave Bosman a one-run edge for the ERA race.

The last game of the year against the Orioles provided another pitchers duel. A Tuesday night crowd of 8,000 saw Dave McNally beat the rejuvenated Jim Hannan by a 1–0 score. There were almost as many walks in the game as hits as veteran umpire Ed Runge's crew called the new strike zone with zeal. Hannan gave up six walks and McNally four. McNally, stubborn in pursuit of his 19th victory and determined to log his second straight 20-win season, drove in the only run of the game with a double in the sixth inning.

The Orioles were a particular devilment to the Senators in 1969. Between the Kansas City Royals and the Orioles, every winning streak, every chance the team had to build momentum had run into one of those two teams, and they had always been able to burst the bubble. But the last two weeks of September would feature three games against the Red Sox and five against Cleveland. Washington had been successful against Boston and the Indians. The season would end with the Senators playing the Red Sox in RFK for a three-game series. It was one last chance to wrestle third place away from Boston and show the uninterested fans in Washington that a new sheriff was indeed in residence in Washington, and his name was not Vince Lombardi.

17

Catching a Second Wind

Gil Hodges' New York Mets were like a Triple Crown winner coming down the stretch, each stride putting greater distance between the certain winner and the pack. Jerry Koosman and Tom Seaver were establishing reputations that would last for decades as they won every game they started and often in impressive fashion. Seaver won his 20th game early in September against the Phillies. It was a complete-game five-hitter in which he gave up only a run. The game was part of a remarkable stretch of games by Seaver, in which he won five more decisions, two of them shutouts. He allowed only five runs over the stretch of six complete-game wins that moved his season record to 25 wins and 7 defeats for the 1969 campaign.

Only a brief losing streak against the Pirates suggested the Mets might falter, and Koosman and Seaver went out and won the next two games to allay any doubts. Bob Short should have seen hope in the two Met aces, neither of whom had been expensive signings. Koosman had come gratis as a recommendation from an usher at Shea Stadium. Management in New York insisted that the Mets had more talented pitchers waiting in the minors. Young pitchers with great futures like Nolan Ryan were learning their craft as they shuttled between the big club and the minors.

The pennant races were over in both leagues except in the NL West, where four teams were slugging it out for what some still believed would be an easy win over the "Miracle Mets" in the playoffs. California's golden teams, the Dodgers and Giants, were tied for the lead with the Braves, and the young Cincinnati Reds team was only a game off the lead. It was the kind of race the baseball brain trust had hoped for during the winter months before the '69 season. In a rare baseball column, Shirley Povich handicapped the field, giving the nod to Atlanta.

The Senators traveled up the northeast coast to New York City to begin their drive for the finish line. They had two games against the Yankees, who still trailed in fifth place in the AL East. Once again Washington could not close the deal. Casey Cox pitched well in the opener, but the rain-shortened contest went to New York, 2–1. The second game was another start for Cisco Carlos, who needed early relief again and lost, 4–3, despite Mike Epstein's 28th home run.

The road trip continued with two games in Cleveland and three in Detroit before returning to the nation's capital. Bosman pitched another great game, lasting into the tenth inning and allowing only two runs. The outing lowered his ERA and kept him on the heels of Jim Palmer for the ERA title. But again he could not get the win, as it took twelve innings for the Senators to eke out a victory against the lowly Indians, 5–3. The three low-scoring contests against the teams below Washington in the standings exposed a new problem. It was the hole in the middle of the Senators lineup and its name was Frank Howard.

Howard's remarks about not swinging well after the two-day layoff at the beginning of the month had been taken as self-effacing at the time, but now looked prescient. Since hitting his 46th homer against Lonborg in Boston on the seventh of September, Howard had collected only a pair of singles. His batting average had fallen to .301. When he went 0-for-4 against Cleveland in the second game — a 4–3 loss on the 20th of September — his average slipped below .300.

For the first time in the 1969 season, Hondo resembled the everyday player for the Dodgers in 1964 who could not fight off long slumps and ended up hitting only .226 for the year. The memories of that season and the stormy relationship with Walter Alston were what made hitting .300 such a meaningful goal for the Gentle Giant.

As bad as Howard was for those two weeks in September, Mike Epstein and Ken McMullen were just as good. Epstein had three late-inning clutch hits that had tied games to give them chances to win. He was hitting .400 over a stretch of games dating back into August, during which Ted Williams had increasingly eased the platoon and allowed Epstein to hit against left-handed pitching. Scouts from other American League teams were noticing. Epstein attributed it to "catching a second wind."

Back home at RFK, as the first pitch was thrown for the second game in Cleveland, Sonny Jurgensen and Vince Lombardi were teeing it up for the season opener against the New Orleans Saints. The Redskins found someone they could beat and posted a 10–0 win. Professional football had expanded to New Orleans, which could only boast a Triple-A baseball team. Harmon Killebrew belted two home runs in Bloomington, Minnesota, to pull even with the slumping Frank Howard in the race for slugging honors in the AL. The next day he hit his 47th as the Twins clinched the AL West divisional championship, while the Senators were off.

Many in the media were surprised that the Twins had been able to rise above the clubhouse acrimony and the bad press that pugnacious manager Billy Martin generated with such ease. But the team had a veteran pitching staff with stars like Jim Kaat and Jim Perry. The Twins also had Killebrew, who was staking a claim as the best slugger in the league. Reggie Jackson and Howard would be chasing *him* in the last weeks of the season.

Regardless the trigger, whether it was the pressure of Harmon Killebrew breathing down his neck, the rest, or just the realization that the fun would be over in a few short days, Howard's trip to Detroit became a magic elixir. Against Denny McLain in the first game of the double-header, Howard had a double, a homer, and a walk in four trips to the plate. The homer was Howard's 47th, and he was even with Killebrew. He also surpassed a historic benchmark in Washington baseball annals. His hits gave him more total bases in a single season than any other Senator for a full season.

Ken McMullen was still pulling the offensive weight hitting behind Howard, as he had two hits and three driven in. Bernie Allen added a two-run homer and Jim Hannan got the win. Ken McMullen continued to provide the offense in the second game, when he added his 18th home run. It was Del Unser's two-run triple in the eighth that was the difference, and Dennis Higgins finally got his 10th victory to join a host of relievers who recorded double-digit wins in the year the bullpen specialists made their mark.

The get-away game saw only four thousand fans at Tiger Stadium for a mid-week contest, but it mattered little to Dick Bosman, who quietly pitched another gem and finally got the win, this one his 13th, by a score of 7–2. McMullen had his third multi-hit game in a row, going 3-for-4 with his nineteenth home run. Frank Howard went cold again with an 0-for-5 night. His average was slipping further south of the .300 mark.

The sweep against the Tigers had huge importance for the team. It raised the Senators record to 81 wins and 75 losses. There were only six games remaining on the schedule, all of them at RFK and all against teams the Senators had been able to handle throughout the season — the Indians and Red Sox. The 81 victories meant Washington would not finish with a losing record. None of the expansion Senators since taking the field in 1961 had managed to finish over .500. No Washington team since the 1945 Senators, playing at a time when many major league players were still completing military duty, could contemplate so lofty a finish. If the Senators were playing for nothing but pride as the season neared its conclusion, there was a long streak of wounded pride to avenge by besting the mark of the '52 team.

Sportswriters were extolling the rise of the Mets, who had begun play in 1962, a year after the birth of Washington's expansion Senators. They noted the rise of the Senators, but the ascent of the Mets left Washington in the dust, just another newly competitive expansion team streaking toward the finish. Winning the series in Detroit could be written off as beating a team that was troubled. For the defending champion Tigers, 1969 had been a disappointment, a year they had lost focus when pitching star Denny McLain had spun further and further out of control. If Detroit was ripe, then Cleveland was more so. The Indians had never been in contention and could only be counting the days until they could head home for the winter.

Joe Coleman pitched the first game of the homestand against the dispirited Indians and had his first good outing in a month. It was several weeks too late, but with slightly fewer than 7,000 fans in the stadium for a Friday night game, Coleman returned to the form he had in the heat of the summer. He went the distance and allowed only a single run — unearned after a rare error by Ken McMullen. Lee Maye provided the only fireworks with a grand slam homer in the fifth inning. It was all Coleman needed to earn his 11th win. Frank Howard was hitless again in four trips to the plate.

With the team now assured of a winning season, the Senators and their fans began to look up in the standings again. Boston had won five in a row and was making it difficult to gain ground. But their latest win had come against the Tigers, and it pulled the Red Sox even with Detroit for second place. The Senators were four back with five games to play. The odds were tough ones, but it had been so long and there was nothing to lose.

The next day in front of a Saturday afternoon crowd of only 10,000 fans, Ted Williams put Barry Moore back into the rotation to start the game. He responded with a short but effective outing that gave him his first win in more than two months. He went five innings, giving up only a single run and walking no one, which no doubt pleased Williams. Bob Humphreys pitched a perfect eighth and ninth inning for the save. Frank Howard had two hits, but it was Eddie Brinkman's two-run triple that accounted for all three runs in a tight 3–2 victory.

George Minot, the *Washington Post* beat writer who covered the Senators, opined in the morning edition that the only thing that could stop Washington now was the end of the season. It was certain that Cleveland posed no threat, unless you were the Redskins. On Sunday the Redskins played the Browns in Cleveland, where they had less luck than the Senators. But it was the Redskins' loss that was the sports headline, even after the Senators extended their winning streak to six games with a 7–6 extra-inning win over the Indians.

With the Redskins game on television, there were only 8,000 fans in attendance on Sunday afternoon for an exciting contest that had plenty of offense as the two teams combined for 23 hits. Del Unser was the engine of the Senators' attack as he went 3-for-5. His 10th-inning home run was a walk-off affair that allowed for noisy celebrations by the fans and team. Darold Knowles pitched almost four innings of perfect relief to put down the Indians, who had rallied off Jim Hannan in the fifth inning to score five times.

The win kept the team's statistical chance for a third-place finish alive as the Red Sox lost another game to the Tigers. There were still the three games left with the Red Sox at RFK to end the season. A sweep of those games would move Washington into third place and give Ted Williams something very sweet to remember during the off-season. Casey Cox took the mound for the Senators against Sonny Siebert in the first game, and the numbers were on Ted's side. Cox was the better pitcher on paper, but the Red Sox batting order was among the best.

In the first three innings Cox could not get Rico Petrocelli and Tony Conigliaro out. The Red Sox collected eight hits off Cox over that stretch, good for five runs and a 5–2 lead. Frank Howard's 48th home run in the sixth inning made the score 6–5 and got Williams moving the pieces on the chess board. He went to his bench numerous times in the last two innings. He watched raptly intent from the top of the dugout steps late in the first game, searching for an answer that would not come. It was not a game when he had the Midas touch.

He got an important run-scoring hit from Ed Stroud as a pinch-hitter in the seventh inning, but Brant Alyea could not deliver in the ninth. The pitchers did not help, either. Ted brought in Bob Humphreys, the fourth pitcher, for the eighth inning, and he kept Boston off the board. But in the ninth, Williams left Humphreys in, and he gave up two runs and the Red Sox won by an 8–5 margin. The loss ended the Senators' chances of a first-division finish.

The final two games of the season left only hopes for individual records of significance to players who would point to their performance in the off-season when talking salary with owner Bob Short. Frank Howard wanted 50 homers, but was two short with two games to play. The player who would hit two home runs in the final two games was not the Gentle Giant, but the observant Jew, Mike Epstein. Epstein had sat for two games during the religious holidays in September, but had been hot ever since, as though the prayers or the brisket had given him extra strength.

In the Tuesday game, Epstein's 29th home run gave Dick Bosman all the help he needed as he won his 14th game of the season in a 7–2 win. The two runs over seven innings pushed his ERA to 2.19, but Jim Palmer's had mushroomed to 2.34 with his team cruising to the finish line on auto-pilot.

Bosman took the prize for the lowest ERA in the American League. It was an award well deserved.

The next night when Joe Coleman took the mound, 17,000 fans visited the stadium to say "goodbye" and "thank you" to a team that had given them more than any other in more than two decades. When Ted Williams took the lineup cards to the umpires before the start of the game, the crowd stood and cheered the surprising season in which he had engineered a miracle no less impressive than the Mets. Williams appeared oblivious to the noisy fans, but one of the umpires said to him, "Ted, that's for you." Williams did what he seldom did for fans or anyone else — he doffed his cap like he had finally done in Boston in April.

Joe Coleman gave them something to remember, something to instill hope during the long off-season as he mowed down the powerful Red Sox lineup for nine innings. Other than Dick Bosman's almost no-hitter, it may have been the best pitched game of the year as he allowed only two hits over nine innings. One of them was Carl Yastrzemski's 40th home run of the season. Coleman's final game gave him 12 wins for the year. The big three in the Washington rotation turned out to be Bosman, Coleman and Casey Cox (11 wins). Of the big four that the *Washington Post* had touted in the spring, only Coleman and Hannan had finished the season with the team.

Mike Epstein's 30th homer drove in three runs and provided the winning margin after Boston got another unearned run when Brant Alyea — never known for his fielding — committed two errors. The final margin was 3–2, and the Senators' final record for the year stood at an amazing 86 wins and 76 losses, ten games over .500 and a hare's whisker — one game — behind the Red Sox for third place. At the end of the game the 17,000 fans stood to cheer the team one last time. Discounting the World War II years when Clark Griffith was able to cobble together two winning seasons on the cheap, no Senators team since Joe Cronin had bid Washington goodbye from such a lofty plateau of success.

For a team with the long tenure of the Washington Senators, reaching back to the beginnings of the American League in 1901, it was an unmatched record of futility. Only the Philadelphia Athletics had a longer losing streak, and they had been relocated to Kansas City after the many years of frustration.

The Chicago Cubs' long years without a championship had produced similar problems, but they had managed — starting in 1967 — to put together a winning team, and in '69 reached their highest mark in many years by finishing second to the Mets in the NL East. There was no undercurrent of skepticism about the future of the Cubs; they were at Wrigley Field to stay.

Washington wrapped up its season at RFK Stadium without any such assurances.

The last compete game of the season by Joe Coleman gave him 247 innings for the year, the most on the staff. Pitching 250 innings had once been a hallmark of a great starting pitcher, and Coleman hewed to that line of reasoning, instilled by his father. Baseball in 1969 was moving away from that era. Although Coleman would go on to throw 280 innings in each of the next four years in his career, he would blow out his arm before he was 30 years old. He would be done at age 31.

Dick Bosman was at his peak in 1969 with his 14–5 record. He would pitch 230 innings in each of the next two years, but he would falter after that and be relegated to the bullpen for the last six seasons of his career after his arm could not stand up to the demands of throwing his sinker-slider combination. Getting that old "tilt" back came at a higher and higher price, and fewer pitchers were able to pay it with each passing year. Pitchers who threw the hard slider or big curve had to put more into it to get the sharp break, and the effort to do so over the course of a season or a career began to extract a cost on the elbow and shoulder tendons that made the pitches possible.

The lowering of the mound and the shrinking of the strike zone in 1969 did not mark a sudden and dramatic change. The offense bounced back, but pitchers adjusted as well. In 1969 there were 15 pitchers who reached the 20-win mark. Pitchers were making the adjustment to the new conditions, but did not know the cost the changes would have over time. New pitches like the splitter added back the old downward movement in the strike zone, but took a toll on the pitcher's arm as well. It was not just Coleman and Bosman. The number of innings thrown by starting pitchers declined steadily through the seventies and eighties.

Great pitchers were able to defy the odds. Hall of Fame pitchers like Nolan Ryan and Steve Carlton reached the 300-inning mark in the 1970s repeatedly. Both men pitched into their 40s with few ill effects of the wear and tear that making forty starts in a season could cause. Roger Clemens threw 271 innings, but it is a record that may stand for some years to come. Pitchers increasingly had their starts limited so that the total number of innings rarely exceeds 250 in any season. It is just one reflection of the changes that baseball set in motion in 1969.

The game of baseball appeared headed into a golden age when Mantle and Maris went up against one another in the home run race of 1961. But it did not last. Professional football lent itself better to the medium of television and captured the imagination of an increasingly sedentary viewing audience. The term "Monday morning quarterback" came of age, and nothing the game of baseball could do would change that.

The changes instituted in 1969, expansion and divisional play, brought new fans out to major league ballparks. It did not show up in the American League for another few years. Shirley Povich may have been right that cities like Seattle and Kansas City were not initially as attractive, but they grew into their status as the nation and its cities grew exponentially.

Attendance started to climb and a new economics of baseball was created that depended on building new single-use ballparks for high-end fans who watched the games from glassed-in luxury boxes. Like the pitchers, the game of baseball was forced to change, but new ideas proved ultimately better for everything except throwing arms. Pitchers were brought back to earth in 1969 and have stayed closer to it ever since.

TABLE 17-1. FINAL 1969 SEASON STANDINGS, OCTOBER 2, 1969

AMERICAN LEAGUE
East Division

Team	Wins	Losses	Pct	GB
Baltimore	109	53	.673	—
Detroit	90	72	.556	19
Boston	87	75	.537	22
Washington	86	76	.531	23
New York	80	81	.497	28½
Cleveland	62	91	.385	46½

West Division

Team	Wins	Losses	Pct	GB
Minnesota	97	65	.599	—
Oakland	88	74	.543	9
California	71	91	.438	26
Kansas City	69	93	.426	28
Chicago	68	94	.420	29
Seattle	64	98	.395	33

NATIONAL LEAGUE
East Division

Team	Wins	Losses	Pct	GB
New York	100	62	.617	—
Chicago	92	70	.568	8
Pittsburgh	88	74	.543	12
St. Louis	87	75	.537	13
Philadelphia	63	99	.389	37
Montreal	52	110	.321	48

West Division

Team	Wins	Losses	Pct	GB
Atlanta	93	69	.574	—
San Francisco	90	72	.556	3
Cincinnati	89	73	.549	4
Los Angeles	85	77	.525	8
Houston	81	81	.500	12
San Diego	52	110	.321	41

Source: *Sporting News/Washington Post*

18

For Now's the Time
for Your Tears

After bringing new life to baseball in Washington, D.C., Ted Williams' star was ascendant again in the baseball galaxy. There was speculation the Boston Red Sox, who had fired manager Dick Williams late in September, would approach their greatest living player to take the reins, but Ted said he fielded no such call. After the season was over, accolades began to pour in for the changes he had wrought in the Senators' hitters.

Although Harmon Killebrew had beaten out Howard for the home run title — hitting his 49th on the next-to-last day — and though Howard had tailed off below the magic .300 level at the end of the season, the Gentle Giant finished in the top ten for the American League in batting average with a .296 mark. It tied his early career high. Howard's exemplary year and those of other players like Mike Epstein had baseball singing the praises of the Splendid Splinter all over again. Even the Orioles' pennant-winning manager Earl Weaver expressed his admiration for the baseball acumen Williams had demonstrated in his first year.

Williams was proud of players like Howard and Epstein, but he took special pride in Eddie Brinkman, and noted that though his gloveman ended up at only .266, he drove in clutch runs all season long. Brinkman would never boost his average as high again. Williams was proud enough of the entire team to leave every player a Ted Williams fishing rod and reel in their lockers on the last day.

During the World Series, Williams several times joined Bob Short, who attended every game. Williams took advantage of those meetings to share his evaluation of the players from the manager's perspective and discuss the needs of the team for the following year. Williams had very specific ideas that he outlined to Short about how the team could get better and what the trade focus should be for the off-season. He knew the team needed to build for the future. That meant trades in which Washington could land two or three young and talented players with upside in exchange for one of several veteran players who had established themselves in 1969.

The off-season began in earnest after the New York Mets finished off the Orioles in the World Series. New York's easy win against the Orioles in five games surprised everyone. Baltimore had looked so strong with Frank Robinson — who Williams said deserved the MVP — and Boog Powell in the middle of the lineup. Their pitching staff also should have stacked up well with the Mets. But the Mets' October success that followed their great September run put a huge exclamation mark at the end of one of the more exciting seasons baseball had seen in years.

The Amazing Mets left everyone in baseball sanguine about the game's future, and the 1969 season was hardly concluded before the pundits began to focus on the next. Trade rumors began to surface in the weeks following the series, and the most widely speculated commodity was Mike Epstein. Williams and most others recognized that in Frank Howard and Mike Epstein, the team had two power hitters most suited for the same position — first base. Howard was not adroit in the outfield, and while Epstein could play first with some skill, his offensive power was no match for Hondo's. It made sense to trade Mike for the kind of young talent for which Ted Williams yearned.

Epstein was expecting a trade. He was hopeful the same way Howard had been when playing in a platoon for the Los Angeles Dodgers five years earlier. Epstein wanted a new team that would give him a full-time position. Like Howard had felt in 1963, Epstein believed he had earned a full share with his performance in 1969. As a Jewish ballplayer, Epstein expected that a New York City team would be interested in him, and when asked he said, "Art Shamsky was there first, but if I should be traded to the Yankees, there's enough for both of us," referencing the large pool of Jewish baseball fans in New York City.

Williams left for a month-long hunting trip to Africa, assuming that the trade talks would be on hold until the winter meetings in December. It wasn't just Epstein, however. Williams' success had created interest in many of the better players on the team. Besides Epstein, the Mets coveted Ken McMullen and numerous teams had scouted Darold Knowles. Short responded to press reports about the trade potential of all his players by consistently noting that "the price is high."

Short announced at the beginning of December that ticket prices were going up again. There was more groaning from fans and sportswriters who pointed out that the prices were already among the highest in the majors. Short continued to feud with the D.C. Armory board over petty issues that did nothing except add to his constant clamoring in the press that he was a mistreated philanthropist who had lost over a million dollars on the team in 1969.

Bob Short never opened his books to validate his claims. Yet it was hard to believe that higher ticket prices and increased attendance could have left the team in the red. Overall the turnstiles at RFK Stadium were busier than all but six other venues in the American League. If ticket prices were higher and more people were paying them, where was the money going?

In truth, Bob Short was weighted down, not by the fans, not by the city politicians or crime. He was laboring under the debt and the heavy costs he incurred in his highly leveraged purchase of the team. Short was competing against better funded American League teams, many of them more focused on putting a winning product on the field. It seemed increasingly as if Short was just trying to keep a precarious investment afloat until he could flip it.

As the winter meetings approached, trade talk about Mike Epstein ramped up. Epstein was hearing correctly. The most intense discussions came from the Yankees, who were indeed excited about a Jewish superstar. They offered Fritz Peterson, who was a proven quality starter. He was exactly what Mike Epstein would say years later was the missing ingredient for the Senators: one more good pitcher. With Peterson, Coleman, and Bosman, Washington would finally have a legitimate big three. Hannan and Casey Cox had good enough stuff to fill out a good rotation.

There was other talk that had Epstein headed back to California. Oakland was interested and was reportedly offering Catfish Hunter straight up for Epstein, but Short wasn't interested in young talent like Hunter. He was looking for box office returns and wanted proven names, exciting players like Reggie Jackson. His mantra that he would trade Epstein and Howard for Jackson was chanted again, but if such a deal were really proffered, it was refused. And Short refused the deal for Hunter.

Epstein ultimately would be traded to Oakland and would play for the 1972 Oakland team that beat the Big Red Machine — the Cincinnati Reds — in the '72 World Series. In 1969 the ongoing rumors frustrated Epstein, who said that "the Senators don't have anyone in the front office capable of making a trade." Epstein's contention was accurate.

The Mets discussed two young pitchers, Tug McGraw and Nolan Ryan, in return for McMullen, but again Short wanted big names, not the young talent that Williams was seeking. Shelby Whitfield, the Senators' radio and television announcer, said it as succinctly as anyone, "Every time Short thought about a deal, he was thinking about what would help at the box office." Short either did not accept the idea that building a winning team would improve his gate receipts or something else was on his mind.

Catfish Hunter was a young and unproven pitcher in 1969, but would win 18 games in 1970 and 21 in 1971 while he led the Oakland pitching staff to the World Series and became a powerful fan magnet. Nolan Ryan harnessed his control problems in 1972 after being traded to the California Angels and won 20 games. Tug McGraw had broken out in 1969 and would become one of the best and most durable relief pitchers in the National League.

Epstein would have a brief though productive career, but 1969 was his best offensive year, and Williams was right to market him when his value as a young player with potential was at its zenith. Either the McMullen or Epstein trades would have put Washington baseball fortunes on the upswing. They were exactly what Williams was exhorting Short to consider. But the inaction on Short's part continued and the chances to capitalize on the '69 season slipped away one by one.

Short's inaction and bad judgment began before the end of the season when trade offers were made for Brant Alyea. Alyea was a typical flash-in-the-pan talent. In the first half of 1969, he had 10 homers but failed to hit another after the Fourth of July. He had a long swing that could hit a ball a long way, but had more holes in that swing than home runs to show for it. Additionally, Alyea came up convinced that he was the real thing and nothing Williams could tell him would persuade him otherwise.

Minnesota Twins owner Calvin Griffith thought he saw a spark in Alyea, something he liked. He offered Short a third baseman named Graig Nettles for Alyea in mid-season, but Short refused. Nettles was a minor leaguer that scouts liked a great deal, and was considered by most to have much more upside than Alyea. He would hit 26 home runs in his first full season in 1970 and almost 400 across a twenty-year career. Williams had heard the hype about Nettles and liked what he knew of him in contrast to his certainty that Alyea would flounder. Short, however, believed adamantly that Alyea was on the threshold of becoming another Frank Howard.

When Alyea failed to hit in the second half of the season, Short had to admit that Williams had been right. But the moment was gone and when they unloaded Alyea to Griffith, Washington received only two journeymen pitchers in return. One of the two, Joe Grzenda, with 15 years of mediocrity behind him, was destined to throw the last pitch at RFK Stadium by a Senators pitcher.

After turning down trades for Alyea and Epstein, Short began to avoid Williams when trade talks surfaced. He used his business manager, Joe Burke, to shield information from Williams about contact he had from other clubs. Mike Epstein's assessment of the Washington front office was an astute one. Short did not have the baseball acumen to be his own general manager. Short clearly lacked the ability to man his own front office, but his real goal was not to build a long-term winner in Washington. After turning down so many trades with long-term potential, it was obvious the real goal was short-term profitability.

Ted Williams had a scout's eye and could assess talent quickly. But he alone was not enough to force conventional baseball wisdom on a business-man like Short. Williams did not have the negotiating skills to land talent, so even had the two men worked together more effectively, they were miss-ing key elements of a successful baseball management team.

Williams' ideas about professional baseball talent were the best he was likely to get. Williams said, "Damn, I wish Short had the money to hire the scouts we need to be competitive. We need scouts in South America. The successful clubs have them there. That alone can be the difference in being a winner and a loser in the league."

Williams recommended Minnie Minoso and Camilo Pascual as Latin scouts to Short, but was told there was no money. Williams believed Short in the same way the Silent Majority believed Richard Nixon. Short con-vinced Williams that the problem with the team was the financial bind in which Washington itself placed him. The town was flawed as a place for baseball, according to Short. The assertion explained why there was no money, but it did not keep Williams from developing connections on other teams to get information about players being discussed in trades. He con-tinued to complain bitterly about an organization so bereft of reliable infor-mation on the players of other teams.

In December, after Williams returned from Africa, he accompanied Short to the winter meetings in Florida. Williams' haul from his safari was an im-pressive one to hear him tell it, but at the end of the winter meetings, Williams had bagged no big game. Instead of players like Nolan Ryan and Catfish Hunter, the Senators brought home players like George Brunet, Horacio Pina and Dave Nelson. For this treasure trove of talent, Short parted with Barry Moore, Dennis Higgins and Dave Baldwin, three of the better pitchers of 1969 and certainly the equal of the three they got.

The trades may have been reasonably balanced, but they were not what Washington needed, and did not help the club at all. Moore's second half in 1969 had been a disaster, but Higgins had been an important part of the bullpen. Replacing them were only journeymen players. None of them would have an appreciable impact in 1970, and Williams, like Mike Epstein, must have begun to understand the situation into which Short had pitched him.

The idea of upgrading the team with talented young players was not finding a receptive ear. Williams had talked confidently during the 1969 sea-son about the future, but that tone began to disappear as the off-season wore on. In the spring of 1970, Williams intervened with Short on a trade in what would prove to be the last positive impact he would have on the team.

In April of 1970, Williams learned that the California Angels had made an offer to the Senators for Ken McMullen. California was offering Rick Reichardt and Aurelio Rodriguez. Reichardt was a good outfielder with an offensive profile similar to McMullen's. Aurelio Rodriguez was a 23-year-old third baseman who had shown real potential at the minor league level and had played briefly for the Angels in 1969. He was having a good spring in 1970. The proposed trade was two-for-one and would bring back a young player, the type that Williams knew was missing from the Senators roster. It was the kind of trade Williams had urged for months.

Williams is alleged to have learned of the Angels' trade offer from Shelby Whitfield, who informed Williams that Short was against the deal and wanted to keep McMullen. Williams was upset to hear that Short was against the move and expressed his dismay directly to the owner. Seeing openly contentious rebellion from his star manager, Short relented and the trade went through. It may have been the only smart trade Short made as the Washington owner.

The high point of Williams' managing career in Washington came in the post-season, after 1969. Shortly after the World Series, the *Sporting News* named Gil Hodges Manager of the Year for the great job he had done with the Mets, and soon thereafter, Ted Williams was chosen by the Associated Press as its American League Manager of the Year. He was in Zambia on safari when the news was released, and again Ted sought to ban the press or anyone else from contacting him during his trip. But when the award was announced, the ban was lifted long enough to allow President Nixon to wire his congratulations.

Williams gloried in his first-year accomplishments as Senators manager. In his remarks shortly after receiving the award, he talked in optimistic terms about building on his record with a better season in 1970. Yet by the time spring training rolled around in 1970, there were the first signs of the change in Williams. Players reported that the level of enthusiasm and excitement so apparent in '69 had faded in 1970.

It had been a long off-season that brought none of the changes Williams had openly sought. He expressed concern to the local press about getting another year out of the Senators like they had in 1969. It was going to be much the same players, some of whom, like Frank Howard, were getting older. He saw no young players coming into the system, and he was worried about a future to which he was now committed but had little ability to change for the better.

During the spring of 1970, players reported him as preoccupied. All accounts agreed that in his second year, for whatever the reason, Williams' clubhouse presence did not have the keen sense of possibility and focus it had in 1969. In '69 Williams had been engaged, willing to try various tactics to get through to players. He had been able to manage players like Epstein, who had a reputation for being difficult, and who in 1968 sat rather than report to Baltimore after a trade. Williams had cajoled and wheedled his way into the confidence and hearts of his players and they had listened, responded, and been in awe of the baseball legend.

In 1970 the era of good feeling slowly came to an end. During that season and the one that followed in Washington, Williams was increasingly at odds with his players. Frank Howard and Dick Bosman were among the few who stayed constant in their performance and their affection. Players sensed a growing frustration in Williams, and at times he appeared sullen and defeated. The early assessment that Williams would not be able to handle the imperfections of players came to fruition. The jocular behavior in 1969 when players could not guess the pitch, or guessed it and fouled off a fat one, drew anger and dark frustration from Williams as the 1970 season wore on.

If the players made a mistake, they knew Williams would be scowling at them if they looked his way, and sometimes it got much worse as he launched into tirades against players and insulted them openly. Merrell Whittlesey reported that Williams seemed disappointed and disgusted after the beginning of the 1970 season as it became more obvious that Short was not in the process of building for the future in Washington and that Williams was just along for the ride.

Williams was largely quiet about his dealings with Short. His negative assessment of the baseball side of the relationship came from Shelby Whitfield in his book, *Kiss It Goodbye*. Whitfield was the TV and radio announcer for the Senators during the 1969 and 1970 seasons. It was his contention, as corroborated by others, that Williams was largely ignored about trades even before the McMullen deal with the California Angels. Whitfield's well-documented analysis portrayed a Bob Short whose primary motivation was to keep afloat a shaky investment during the three years the RFK Stadium lease required him to remain in Washington.

It is hard to imagine that a man as proud as Williams, a man who considered his knowledge of the game of baseball as keen as anyone's, was content to be ignored by someone with as little knowledge as Short. But Williams kept his tongue and his position within the organization.

After the spring of 1970, Short's directions became increasingly obvious. He made some of the worst trades in baseball history that can only be explained in terms of short-term profits. He acquired Denny McLain at the end of the 1970 season after the pitcher's worst year in baseball. McLain had been suspended from baseball for gambling and illegal possession of a firearm during the season. Short had to get Bowie Kuhn to make a special dispensation to allow the trade to go through since a suspended player could not be traded, according to the rules. It was as if a man bent on destruction asked Kuhn to remove the "Bridge Out" sign because he was determined to go full speed ahead anyway. Short was a man of singular purpose.

The famous Denny McLain deal became known as the one where Short traded away the entire left side of the infield. Short sent infielders Aurelio Rodriguez and Eddie Brinkman to Detroit. It was bad enough given the intense trouble McLain was in to trade Rodriguez, who was proving to be an excellent third baseman and a more than adequate replacement for Ken McMullen, who was traded to California. But Short was not satisfied and he sweetened the pot with one of his two best pitchers, adding Joe Coleman and Jim Hannan into the deal to complete the disaster.

In addition to McLain, the Senators received Don Wert, Elliott Maddox, and pitcher Norm McRae. None of them was anything more than placeholders, journeymen to fill out the roster. In Aurelio Rodriguez and Joe Coleman, Detroit received two of the mainstays of their team for years to come, years when the Tigers finished near the top of the AL East. Coleman was an excellent replacement for McLain, whose horrible 1970 season proved to be no aberration as the man spiraled toward personal oblivion and a long jail sentence.

The lop-sided trade raised questions even among the players dealt. Jim Hannan years later told Shelby Whitfield that he believed the trade included a "future consideration," specifically a favorable vote from Detroit's ownership when Short sought to move the team. In retrospect the McLain trade can be taken as the first overt sign that Short truly was committed to the move.

The trade was harbinger of more to come. Short tried to use McLain's name to sell tickets, but there was little to recommend the team to fans. The team had suffered through a horrible September in 1970 when, instead of finishing strong as they had in 1969, Washington lost 14 consecutive games and wound up 22 games below .500. Attendance dropped by a scant 80,000 for the '70 season, but the impression left in September was enough to undercut significantly season ticket sales for the next year.

When the Redskins were playing, Washington lost sight of its baseball team, and if the last thing fans remembered was a fourteen-game losing streak, then buying tickets for the following season seemed almost foolhearty. Short tried in early 1971 to create the impression of a winner the only way he knew how — with hype. He had hired Ted Williams as hype in his first move as owner. Williams was thought by almost everyone in baseball as uniquely unsuited to manage. Williams had proven them wrong, but that ignores Short's motivations. It is not certain whether Short cared if Williams could manage as long as he could draw paying patrons to the ballpark.

For Short, the fact that McLain was getting so much press was a good thing. As with Williams, Short was less concerned about McLain's ability to deliver 30 wins again than with the interest he could spark among season ticket holders who might have soured during the discouraging 1970 season. Williams knew that in McLain they were buying terrible trouble. He argued vehemently with Short about the trade, but in the end Williams appeared to lose heart. By the end of the 1970 season, Williams was a different person than the man who convinced Short in the spring to make the Aurelio Rodriguez trade.

When Short outlined the particulars of the McLain deal in October to his manager, Williams is alleged to have said, "You're giving up way too much, but if you are going to make the deal, I can't stop you." The situation repeated itself within a few short months. Williams counseled against Short's last and worst move, bringing Curt Flood back to baseball. Flood had retired at the end of the 1969 season rather than be traded to Philadelphia. Flood had sat out the entire 1970 season and was focused through much of it on his court case challenging baseball's reserve clause that would go to the Supreme Court. That court case had left Flood broken as a man and a player. Few of his friends in the game stood by him, and worse yet, he was broke. In the spring of 1971, he desperately needed the money that Short was holding out to him to return to the game.

Short saw in Flood the black superstar he had sought in Reggie Jackson. He thought Flood would bring out fans. He did not care about or focus on the player who was overweight and out of shape. It was like the word on the street about Williams. Short ignored the conventional wisdom almost every time if he saw an angle to make money. It worked with Williams, but it would not with Curt Flood and Denny McLain.

Short may have had greater gifts as a carnival man than as a baseball owner. In that respect, he was reminiscent of Calvin Griffith working for his father to arrange wrestling matches to keep old Griffith Stadium packed with paying customers. Short liked to put on a show, but the Curt Flood show did not last out the month of April in 1971. Flood was smart enough to take Short's money and run. The money sustained Flood at a difficult juncture and gave him the ability to fend off disaster. By sustaining Flood in the spring of 1971, Short ultimately helped the case that broke open the financial floodgates of free agency.

Curt Flood got off better than most. Almost everyone who came into contact with Short lost in the end, even Williams. Rebellion began to foment in Williams' clubhouse, and in 1971, Denny McLain became a lightning rod for sentiment against Williams. He and Tim Cullen, who had never thrived under Williams as others had, became ringleaders for a larger group of disgruntled players who carped and were openly contemptuous of their boss.

When Flood was forced on Williams to begin the '71 season, the scenes in the clubhouse became uglier as McLain sought to enlist Flood on his side. The problems were in some ways wider than just baseball. Players were going through their own cultural revolution. Drug use became more common among players. The buzz cut look of Frank Howard became rarer. Short hair like Bosman's almost disappeared as longer hair, beards and garish clothing became acceptable. It was not Williams' scene and he gradually withdrew.

Richard Nixon had been elected at the end of 1968 because of a general unease about the direction that the culture and the country were heading. His support for squares like Frank Howard had been appealing in the first half of the 1969 season, but after the All-Star Game, Nixon did not attend another game. The Senators' number one fan lost interest. After basking in the glow of the moon landing in 1969, Nixon became increasingly defined by one thing: the Vietnam War.

Nixon yoked the U.S war efforts to a South Vietnamese government and military that was short-sighted and corrupt. In negotiations at the end of 1969, Nixon ignored serious entreaties from Hanoi for peace and backed the uncertain claims of the South Vietnamese. American students took to the streets to protest the never-ending war in record numbers.

On the day that Tom Seaver crafted one of the best games by any pitcher in the World Series, a 10-inning win against Baltimore to put the Mets up three games to one at Shea Stadium, marches were held around the country to protest the war. The Vietnam Moratorium, as it was called, brought out hundreds of thousands in cities across the country. In San Francisco, Boston, New York and Washington, protesters took to the streets by the thousands.

Nixon countered with troop pullouts, but the death toll in the war continued unabated. In the last two weeks of the 1969 season with the Amazin' Mets at full throttle, almost 300 American troops were killed in combat action in Vietnam. Casualties would diminish over the next few years, but Nixon's reputation would not recover.

Bob Short was not distracted by wars of any kind. He was singular in his devotion to the job at hand, busy as ever with his business dealings whether in Washington or back home in Minnesota. In Washington, that business was increasingly about paving the way to move the faltering baseball team to greener pastures.

The signs had been constant. In 1969 realtors were ready to offer Teddy

Ballgame a deal in the best parts of town and Williams "got excited about the plush $80,000-$125,000 homes in the area." Short told Williams not to buy because he knew the team and Williams were only in town for the "short-term." Short counseled Mike Epstein and Del Unser similarly against buying real estate in the area.

Short signed only one-year contracts with the media, the D.C. Armory Board and everyone else. He refused to pay even a third of the cost for artificial turf at RFK after the Redskins and the D.C. Armory Board put up their shares because Short would have been unable to take it with him. He did everything possible for three years to limit his financial exposure in Washington. In the months to come, pundits and writers would look back and wonder whether Short had tried consciously to alienate fans and supporters in Washington to prove that he had no choice but to relocate the team.

It was not just the increases in ticket prices each year that alienated fans. He even quit offering free tickets to children and Vietnam veterans rehabbing at Walter Reed Army Hospital. It was all about business to Bob Short, and his business may have been tied to the move that he had envisioned from the very beginning, from the first exhibition game in Dallas in the spring of 1969.

It was not easy. The first move in 1960, when Calvin Griffith had begun the process of uprooting baseball from Washington, D.C., soil, had provided a case study as to the forces that would array against Bob Short. Congress and the other major league team owners would need to be bucked, placated, and cajoled into accepting Short's version of reality and ignoring seven decades of baseball history in the nation's capital, one that extended back to the very founding of the American League. Short had always been a good student and he went to school on Griffith's move.

Short was playing a risky game. Raising ticket prices might help balance the books, but it also helped to make the city look less able to support baseball because fewer fans were willing to pay more to see a bad team on the field. That much made easy financial sense. Yet hiring Ted Williams only increased interest and ticket sales, so Short yelled all season long about how the fans were not attending in sufficient numbers to make a profit, even in 1969. American League officials and owners heard only that attendance was failing, when in fact attendance in Washington was not out of line with what other AL teams were seeing at the time.

Even when he traded away the best players and the team on the field included misfits such as Flood and scoundrels like Denny McLain, attendance did not drop precipitously. Yet Short's wailing only grew louder about how his targets were not met. Short continued to assert that he could not make money unless there was enough support in Washington for baseball, but he did nothing to create a winning team. Even in 1970, 825,000 persons paid the second-highest ticket prices in the American League to see a losing baseball team at RFK Stadium. It was hard to prove that he was bereft of opportunity in Washington after so many paid so much to see so little that year.

Whatever Short's original intentions may have been, relocating the Senators a short decade after the first move was certainly a difficult proposition and one that required focus and determination. In some ways, the move was made more difficult by the many commitments to fans and to the Congress made as Calvin Griffith left for Minnesota. In other ways, Griffith had surfaced the argument that the city was no good for baseball and made it ready for Short to use again.

In 1960 Congress had put considerable pressure on baseball to disallow the first move out of Washington. Congress in the form of powerful Senators like William Proxmire had openly and aggressively threatened baseball's treasured anti-trust exemption, but a deal had been worked out. Working out another deal to pacify Congress was a tall order. Short could not count on baseball putting another expansion team in Washington. He had to prove that the city did not deserve a major league baseball team at all. The long succession of losing seasons provided the greatest weight to the argument, and in that sense, 1969 was Bob Short's worst.

The most compelling evidence that Short sought the team in 1968 only to move it was the lease on the stadium. When he bought the team, he had a lease that ran until the end of 1971. He was in town not a day longer, and when viewed through that prism, it is not difficult to see that much of what Bob Short was about from the very beginning was about scuttling the team, readying it for the move.

Did Short know he was giving up too much for McLain, dooming the team to a desperate and losing season? Did he refuse to hire a general manager so that he had control over the personnel decisions that would be necessary to pull the plug on the team? Was he making trades purposely to weaken the team, knowing that a losing team would never play well enough to generate the increased attendance he was demanding? Was he generating rancor in the fan community with ticket increases, squabbling with the Armory Board and just about everyone else to create negative publicity that he could portray to the other owners as proof that Washington, D.C., was unfit for baseball, that owning a baseball team in the nation's capital was a fool's errand?

In 1971, after the debacles of the off-season trade for McLain and with everyone's least favorite player, Curt Flood, in tow, attendance finally dropped more noticeably. By the end of the '71 season, only 655,000 fans had come to RFK, just 100,000 more than in 1968, the year of the riots. By the end of the '71 season, many of the players from the 1969 team were gone. Frank Howard and Del Unser stood alone in the lineup like survivors from an ugly battle after the lines have been overrun by the enemy. Dick Bosman, Casey Cox, and Frank Shellenback were the lonely survivors on the pitching staff.

Darold Knowles and Mike Epstein had been the last to go, traded in the early months of the '71 season. When the last season began its stretch run, the only question about the Senators was whether they would lose 100 games — not the kind of question to lure fans to the ballpark.

After the 1971 season began in earnest, Short made his most serious and most overt noises about getting out of town. All of the dire predictions about not making money, about crime and the lack of support for his team, crashed together in Short's carefully managed intersection when he announced his only available avenue was to sell the team.

After months of bad publicity coming out of Washington, the baseball owners convened to hear Short's complaints and assess the chances to sell the franchise. Short asserted to the ownership that conditions were so bad, he was losing so much money, there was no option but to sell the team. The other owners were concerned whether he could find a bona fide buyer and gathered in Detroit in June of 1971 to discuss the chaos into which the Washington Senators were swirling.

Bob Short presented his case. At the meeting Short admitted for the first time that he had been talking to interested parties from Dallas, Toronto, and New Orleans about moving the team. He portrayed Washington as a town that lacked the civic infrastructure to support baseball, a city council that was arbitrary, local media that failed to provide necessary support for the team, and a general failure on the part of everyone in Washington to help Short prosper economically. It was a one-sided presentation. There was no rebuttal, no counsel to represent the D.C. fan base.

The meeting reached its conclusion with the owners group officially urging "the president of the American League ... to consider the urgent Washington matter ... report the results of each study and make recommendations to the league." Joe Cronin was the president of the American League and was tasked with finding the facts and reporting them back to the owners.

Bowie Kuhn was Cronin's boss and he joined with the American League president in seeking a solution. There was a sense of urgency brought on by the months of bad publicity Bob Short had created. Both Kuhn and Cronin had ties to Washington, D.C., baseball and the soft spot Kuhn had for the Senators led him to look seriously for ownership that would keep the team in D.C. They sought out major corporate interests that might find it attractive to have a showpiece in the nation's capital, only a mile or so from the Capitol itself. They were powerful advocates, but there was just as loud a group arrayed against them.

Short had always been friends with Calvin Griffith. Before Short bough the team, the two men had known each other in Minnesota, and in the early press conferences Short had cited Griffith as his friend and connection to the game of baseball. Griffith's animus for the city of Washington — or his need to justify the decision to leave it — never abated, and from his new home in Minnesota he began to cast aspersions anew at the city. He loudly declared Washington as unfit for baseball.

Anyone who had a microphone could get Griffith to talk about the sorry predicament in which his friend Bob Short found himself. With the debate raging in the late summer of 1971, he let everyone know his willingness to support Short when the issue of moving the team was put to a vote before the owners.

As Kuhn and Cronin fanned out looking for buyers, Bob Short was in a precarious position. He had to appear willing to sell the team. He told the press and anyone who would listen that the asking price was $12.4 million. His price included the $9.4 million he had paid originally and the $3 million in losses over the prior years. Shirley Povich, who had soured on the entire enterprise, Ted Williams, Bob Short and the rest of it, said of the $12 million asking price, "Short's demand has been equated with the curious logic of a man who paid $9,000 for an automobile, mishandled and maltreated it, paid $3,000 in repairs, and says, 'Now I've got a car that's worth $12,000.'"

Povich was being kind. Short had spent two of his three years trying to convince anyone who would listen that Washington was not a fit town for baseball, yet he was asking a price for the franchise that would have ranked well above the average franchise value at the time. Economists estimated that the value of the average franchise in 1970 was slightly more than $10 million, and in 1971 the country was in the grip of a recession that did little to increase the value of Short's team. The fabled Yankees franchise, one of the most profitable in the history of the game, was sold in 1973 for only $10 million.

The estimated average value of $10 million was in line with what Short paid originally. However, given the litany of Short's assertions that there was no future for a team in D.C., asking for more than three million above the original price was a curious exercise in logic. Many in Washington came to doubt Short's interest in the $12.4 million sale price. The belief grew that Short was looking at a bigger pot of gold waiting for him at the end of a rainbow in the western skies above Dallas, Texas.

Short's enterprise in Washington had been hamstrung by the heavy borrowing he had needed to pay the initial price for the Senators. Because the loans were poorly collateralized, the interest rate was considerably above prime. Short by all objective indicators seemed strapped for capital. He was using the very attractive tax write-offs that the team provided, but was behind on other obligations.

For the cash-starved Short, the city fathers of Dallas were exactly what Minneapolis had represented to Calvin Griffith. It was almost an identical deal. Dallas was offering to Short a $7.5 million advance on broadcasting rights in Texas as soon as the move was finalized. Jerome Holtzman in the *Sporting News* questioned the wisdom of Short's move in an article titled, "A $7.5 million Bonanza for Short?" The bonanza was enough money to pay off the debts from his highly leveraged original purchase of the Senators.

The money would give him the funds to operate the team in Texas while he built up the value of the assets there prior to selling. It was the exact same business plan he had used with the then-Minneapolis Lakers before they became the Los Angeles Lakers.

The dire nature of Short's cash flow problems came to the fore when it surfaced that he was seriously in arrears on his rent to the D.C. Armory Board. The news surfaced in the critical summer of 1971. Short had been in arrears for more than a year, but when the D.C. Armory Board heard the news that the baseball owners were meeting to discuss the relocation of the team, and given Short's aggressive scheming to leave town, they became worried about the $160,000 that Short owed them.

When pressed by D.C. officials, Short refused to pay and used the letters from the board as further evidence to Bowie Kuhn that Washington, D.C., was a town not fit for baseball — curious logic in retrospect, but it seemed to work. The D.C. Armory Board threatened to turn off the lights at the stadium if Short did not pay. Short fired back that he would seek immediate permission from the ownership group to move to Dallas in mid-season.

President Nixon, the Senators' number one fan, said that the prospect of not having baseball in Washington was "heartbreaking." Short, suddenly a Democrat again, said that Nixon had no more way to hold him in Washington than Cronin or Kuhn. Kuhn, meanwhile, had little luck in finding potential owners. Bob Hope, Bill Veeck, and Hank Greenberg talked briefly about the idea but demurred. Other buyers made overtures to Short, including a local one that received considerable press and provided a real source of hope.

The president of Washington's large regional supermarket chain, Giant Foods, was a man named Joseph Danzansky. He made an initial offer estimated at $8.4 million for the team. Danzansky made an initial blunder.

Believing the owners were eager to find a buyer, he asked the other owners to leverage his purchase. The owners were not impressed and the figure fell far short of Short's asking figure.

Holtzman of the *Sporting News* questioned Short's real commitment to selling the team. "But wasn't it a hollow effort?" asked Holtzman. Then he posed a more critical question of the baseball ownership group. "Should the owners have left the decisions about potential buyers to Short himself?" Was Bob Short a disinterested party or did he have motivation to ignore legitimate buyers because his economic interest was served by the move, not by staying in D.C.?

In his article, Holtzman concluded that Short had never been interested in selling and that Kuhn should have intervened to work directly with suitors seeking to buy the team. Kuhn should have worked to determine a realistic estimate of its value and a fair asking price. Oddly enough, it was exactly the advice that was heeded by the baseball commissioner's office three decades later when the financial interests of ownership were better served by such an intervention.

In September of 1971, the baseball owners scheduled a final meeting to decide the matter for the 20th of the month. They would weigh the conclusions from Cronin and Kuhn's reports and resolve the situation before the end of the season. They examined Danzansky's proposal prior to the meeting. Danzansky's opening proposal was quite similar to Short's deal to buy the team. Danzansky was putting little of his own money into the purchase, an estimated $50,000. His proposal called on the collective baseball ownership to secure his loans for the vast proportion of the cost of the team. Danzansky seemed to believe the baseball brain trust was concerned enough about baseball in Washington to throw itself under a train. He was wrong.

Preceding the meeting, the D.C. Armory Board tried desperately to appease Short, offering him free rent if the team drew one million in attendance the next year. He could control concessions. In 1969, when Short may have briefly toyed with the idea of staying in D.C., he believed that controlling the concessions might allow him to make real money on the team. Those prospects had faded in the first year, but it was an important part of the picture of obstruction that Short painted about the city.

Then the favorite of every Washington baseball drama lurched onto the stage. The Washington City Council filed suit against the D.C. Armory Board and Short for the back rent on the stadium, which was technically the property of the D.C. taxpayers. The city was paying interest on loans it had obtained to finance the stadium in 1961. Those original construction bonds were backed by revenue from the stadium, and Short was reneging on paying his portion of it. The lawsuit effectively complicated the sale of the team since it meant that the suit would have to be resolved as part of the sale.

It was a last straw and it made almost certain the decision of the owners when they met. In the last few days prior to the meeting, Danzansky sought out new partners and brought more money to the table. He informed the owners that he could marshal $10 million for purchase of the team, of which $3.5 million was investor cash. That money would have given the team a badly needed infusion of $1 million in working capital over and above the purchase price. The additional funds would be used to operate, hire scouts, and bolster the minor league operations. It was the kind of operation that Ted Williams had assumed going in, the kind of deal under which Washington might have been able to field a competitive team in the long term.

Instead, Short's representatives said that Danzansky's deal would "be an encumbrance to the team." The only encumbrance the deal posed was to Short getting out of town, making off with the Dallas money and making ready there to sell the team for the profit that he had been seeking all along.

Ted Williams got involved in the discussion very late. Williams believed the situation was grim because he had heard for so long from Short that baseball in D.C. was part of a dismal local political situation that undercut the financial supports for the team. The local press, the fans, and everyone else except Bob Short were to blame. He told Williams that D.C. was too close to Baltimore, which everyone could see was a great baseball town in stark contrast to the one in which Williams and Short found themselves. Williams was buying everything that Short was selling.

Before the final ownership meeting on the 20th, Bob Short engaged in a wild and final round of politicking. He had Ted Williams call Tom Yawkey, who thought it important to keep baseball in D.C. Williams portrayed the situation as hopeless. Williams might have been describing his own plight as the manager of a team in open rebellion. He knew the town had great fans. He had tipped his hat to them after the great run at the end of the '69 season, but so much had happened since then and none of it had a positive effect on Williams' desire to stick with the Senators venture at RFK. Besides, he still had a ten percent stake in Short's baseball enterprise, and the boss was saying the better value was Dallas.

The ownership meeting was held in Boston. It began early and lasted all day. The first vote was eight votes in favor of the move and two against. The Orioles and the White Sox voted against the move and Oakland and California abstained. A three-fourths majority was needed to ratify the deal. It was one vote short of the nine needed. The meetings dragged on and a last-minute reprieve almost surfaced from the most unlikely of places. Charlie Finley, who had moved the Athletics to Oakland after shenanigans very similar to Short's, was attempting to find a corporate owner and had the ear of a corporate sponsor.

That deal fell through. The airlines executive who initially was receptive to the idea said he could not make the decision in the time allowed. Finley gave up. Then late in the day, Gene Autry, owner of the California Angels, called in his vote in favor of Short from his hospital bed. So a new vote was held and the team's departure was approved by a 10–2 margin, this time with no abstentions.

The Danzansky group and Bowie Kuhn were shell-shocked. Danzansky thought his last-minute investment group had presented enough commitment to sway the owners, but it did not fly. The owners had listened too long to Short's allegations that the offer was problematic. Kuhn had the power to veto the move using his controversial "best interest of baseball" clause. He discussed it with his legal counsel, but in the end, the men who had been there with Bob Short to throw out the first pitch on Opening Day in 1969 — Ted Williams, Richard Nixon, and Bowie Kuhn — all hung their heads, held onto their jobs, and allowed the Senators to be moved for so many pieces of silver.

After the meeting's results were announced, Senator William Spong, a Democrat from northern Virginia, said it best, "Mismanagement should not be rewarded. Short got the club with the purpose of trafficking with it. He did the same thing with the Lakers. Short was a man who knew little about sports and did a very poor job. The owners possess and savor immunities and privileges. In recent years, the game has taken on the aura of big business first and the interest of the fans second."

Why did so few see it as clearly as Senator Spong? Decades of losing fueled a deep cynicism about baseball in Washington, D.C. Reason and intellect might suggest, however, that Washington was a perfect city for baseball. In 1970 the U.S. Census forecast sharp growth for the Washington metropolitan area, the eighth largest in the country. It was the nation's capital, where 2.7 million persons lived in 1968. The area was growing faster than any other in the country with the exception of suburban Los Angeles.

Dallas, now in line to become the next home for the Senators, was only 16th in size, and though it was growing exponentially, Washington's population and growth rate were double that of the Dallas-Fort Worth metro region. What Washington did not have was Texas oil money or any other kind that could support a wealthy patron who would invest in baseball.

A lawyer, Edward Bennett Williams, had stepped forward to buy the Redskins when George Marshall died in the late summer of 1969. The Redskins were the favorite son of Washington sports, but baseball, by contrast, was like an orphaned child. Clark Griffith had been the father of baseball in

Washington, but after his death there had been no real heir. Calvin Griffith, James Lemon, and Bob Short had one common trait — they lacked the financial resources to support the team, and two were only in it to exploit the team's economic value.

From the moment the expansion Senators were first created in 1961, the enduring problem had been finding ownership with deep enough pockets to even field the team, let alone invest the necessary money in farm teams, scouts, and staff that would craft a new winning tradition. Those most cynical about baseball in Washington were the investment class. Baseball as a sport was loved in Washington, but it was perceived as bad business. Sustaining attendance over the long season, over the long, hot summers in D.C, was difficult, and without a winning team, it was impossible. Football season always rolled around with the baseball team in the cellar, and the fans were happy enough to turn the page, to flip to whatever channel would hold the attention spans the experts were saying grew shorter all the time.

Yet for all of the data, all the long history of baseball, the *Damn Yankees*, Walter Johnson, Sam Rice and other Hall of Fame players, the cynicism had been fed too much, too long, like the fires burning down 14th Street on those April nights in 1968. There was no salve that could be found to soothe it.

On most nights there were not 10,000 persons who would come to RFK to watch baseball in the final month of the season. There was University of Maryland football, the Redskins, and even Congress meeting to pass another budget that seemed to offer more magic, more excitement. It was the fans who ultimately came to believe the hype. It was the fans that let the team leave town, but even they would not go down without a fight.

In the '60s and early '70s, there was no injustice too small to spark a riot. The anti-war generation was angry about the moral poverty of their forbears who bequeathed them carpet bombings of innocent civilians in the name of an enigmatic national interest. Dogs were set upon civil rights protestors. Indignity was not a rare commodity at the time and Washington, D.C.'s, baseball fans — the die-hards who breathed in the same game the players did — were outraged by what had transpired in Boston; outraged that their team and their game were being stolen from them without any champion rising from the back streets.

Barry Svrluga interviewed one of those ardent fans, Alan Alper, for his book on the 2005 Washington Nationals. Alper provided a poignant insight into what baseball means to fans, especially young ones. "This was my sense of belonging," Alper said. "This was my sense of identity, being a Senators fan, having a baseball team." Alper had been there for the All-Star Game in 1969, had camped out seeking the autographs of the players as they came and went after the game and landed signatures of Reggie Jackson and Frank Howard. He had stood in the pouring rain waiting for his father to pick him up the night the game was rained out, and came back for the game the next day. Alper said of the move, "They took my identity away from me that night."

The night Alper referred to was the last game of the season, the last game in the long life of the Washington Senators baseball team. The game was against the same Yankee team that had so little life in 1969. They were ahead of the Senators now, but still in the bottom half of the league. The game meant little to anyone except the roughly 18,000 fans, many of whom had jumped the turnstiles rather than pay another cent to Bob Short. Yankee pitcher Mike Kekich grooved a pitch to Frank Howard, who hit his last home run at RFK. Howard was thrilled to give one last moment to the fans and waved to them after he circled the bases.

Howard said of the moment, "This isn't exactly a pleasure. I've been playing for the Senators for seven years and I think of this city as my home, no matter how bad we were. Nobody's going to buy a horseshit product, and that's what we've been the last two years." There was raw anger in the assessment, and that rancor was rampant in the stadium that night. Banners and signs threatening Bob Short's well-being and questioning his lineage were carried by Alan Alper and many others in attendance. There was little reason for restraint, and the crowd was drinking beer and getting louder and uglier with each inning.

Home plate umpire John Odom sensed the mood of the crowd and told a batter in the bottom of the eighth inning, "I'm getting ready to get the hell out of here." When the Senators took the field in the top of the ninth, ahead 7–5, the ugly mood of the crowd was electric and all of the players were hoping to escape whatever scene ensued unscathed. They did, but RFK Stadium was not as lucky. There were two outs, and Joe Grzenda of the awful Bob Short trades was on the mound when the crowd jumped the low walls adjacent to the infield and rushed the field in large numbers. They ripped anything they could get their hands on from the field of play, from the stadium, taking anything that could provide a bitter souvenir of seventy-one years of baseball history.

Bob Short's era had started in the shadow of the 1968 riots after the assassination of Dr. Martin Luther King, Jr. Those riots had scarred the city and in some small part the baseball team that carried a piece of its pride, a piece of its heart. So it was fitting that the Bob Short era ended in an angry riot.

All the seeds of hope that Ted Williams had sown in 1969 shriveled and died on the vine during the two years of horse manure, as Frank Howard is alleged to have described them. Bob Short had waltzed the fans into believing that winning baseball was possible in Washington, D.C. He had introduced them to baseball greatness in Ted Williams, had made Frank Howard their finest champion and Dick Bosman yet another. He had shown them a last winning season of emotional uplift, but in the end when the dance was over, he had his way with Washington baseball and the fans who had given their hearts to it. He left them and their game in shame with the obscene legacy that Washington, D.C., was just a sleepy southern town, not fit for major league baseball.

Epilogue

After the team moved to Texas, it was as if a curse followed them. The team did not draw well in the early going. Blackie Sherrod, a Dallas sportswriter, said of the move at the time, "Even if our people are enthused, which they don't seem to be, it's too damned hot to go to a ball park." Ted Williams could not light a fire under the fans or the team. The inaugural Texas Rangers finished the 1972 season accomplishing what the Senators had been unable to do in '71—lose 100 games. Williams quit at the end of the season, saying, "Managing was a great experience, one I'm glad to have had." Neither Bob Short nor anyone else was sorry to see him return to fishing.

Short had soured on Williams after the move. It may have been that Williams had served his purpose, had kept the Senators economically viable long enough for Short's game to play out. Or, he may have been just another owner choosing to fire the manager rather than the entire team at the end of 1972. Short offered Williams no face-saving move to the front office, and Williams was left with nothing other than his ten percent ownership and the opportunity to work with the Rangers as a hitting instructor in spring training.

Ted Williams was replaced in Texas by Whitey Herzog and later by Billy Martin. Martin, the black knight of managing in 1969 who called Williams out in their first series that year and then was runner-up for rookie manager of the year, went on to become one of the best skippers in the history of the game, using his fists, videotape and whatever he could find to craft winning teams.

In 1972, Short tried to dispel the bad press he received in the months following his departure from Washington. After the facts from the ownership meeting were made public, writers began to examine Short's claims. Writers like Pete Axthelm at *Sports Illustrated* and others at the *Sporting News* began to question the facts Short had presented to the owners. In response he opened his financial records to detail the losses he claimed to have suffered during his years of operating the Senators in D.C. Two economists from the Brookings Institution, Roger Noll and Benjamin Orker, examined the claims and concluded the losses were "paper deficits" that were conjured up for public consumption to provide a rationale for moving the team. It was too late. In 1974, Bob Short completed the deal he began late in 1968 by selling the Texas Rangers to local ownership.

He had milked the tax advantages available from short-term depreciation of the purchase price for the full five years and he hardly waited a day thereafter to sell. The sale price was reported at $13 million by Short, but pundits at the time called the figure unlikely. It was never confirmed. Short returned to Minnesota, where he tried one last time to gain elected office. He lost his race for the U.S. Senate in 1978 and died in 1982.

Short was kind enough after the move to Texas to extend to the Washington Senators fans one last chance at retribution. During the '73 season, the Rangers played an away game in Baltimore, and the local press got wind that Short would be in attendance, playing up the fact widely enough that old Washington fans, still nursing their pride, read about the event. Several hundred Senators fans made the trip to Baltimore's old Memorial Stadium and made their presence known to Short throughout the game.

Fans bulled their way into the area where Short was sitting long enough to present him sarcastically with a Bob Short effigy, but the climax came when one of the fans made it through the cordon of protection around the owner and poured a cup of beer on him. As she was led from the stadium, she is alleged to have expressed her satisfaction about pouring beer on the head of the bum who stole baseball from Washington, and no doubt won the hearts of many Senators fans that day.

Frank Howard and Dick Bosman went with the team to Texas. Bosman was the Opening Day pitcher in 1972 and 1973 before being traded to Cleveland. Although he remained an effective starter until 1972, '69 was his best year. Frank Howard did not fare as well. Although he came back to have another great year in 1970 with 44 homers, he turned thirty-five in 1971, which was his last season as a middle-of-the-lineup slugger. He played in Texas, then was mercifully traded to Detroit for one last season, away from the unbearable heat.

Richard Nixon fared least well of all. Like Bob Short, he could package a deal and he continued to sell the voting public on his vision of cultural stability and peace in Vietnam. But after a landslide win in the 1972 elections, he was brought up on charges of impeachment for an intricate web of deceit he conceived to support spying on his political adversaries. Before Congress acted, he resigned as one of the most disgraced figures ever to hold the office of president.

The game of baseball fared extremely well. In an article that appeared as a postmortem for the 1969 season, Pete Axthelm pronounced the experiments begun by the rules committee a success. "Powerful pitchers overwhelmed an endless parade of faceless .200 hitters while fans stifled yawns and turned to football and other more exciting diversions," Axthelm wrote of the conditions affecting the game in 1968, which he described not as the national pastime, but as the "Great National Bore."

Axthelm concluded after the 1969 season that the "game has come a long way — celebrating its 100th birthday by taking in a bright youthful look." But Axthelm believed the one thing that had brought back some of the "magic" was the pennant run and subsequent victory of the New York Mets. The Amazin' Mets had captured the heart of the nation in a way that Richard Nixon had failed to do. Axthelm quoted a Lou Harris Poll of baseball fans nationwide that found 54 percent believed baseball had made a comeback, though it continued to rank second to football in popularity.

Washington baseball fans fared best of all, though it took them the longest to reach their goal. Baseball was rumored to return to the nation's capital numerous times. It was in competition for an expansion team, but Denver, Arizona, Tampa, and Miami received teams as the rumors persisted that Washington was not a good town for baseball, that it was too close to Baltimore.

Finally, in 2005, Commissioner Bud Selig gave permission for the faltering Montreal Expos to move to Washington. Montreal saw its English-speaking population flee and wealth drain away during the decades in which citizens worried that the Quebecois Movement would splinter the province away from the nation of Canada. The Expos were crippled by the loss of wealth and fans and were bought by the combined ownership of Major League Baseball, Inc. The consortia of owners retained title to the team until the middle of 2006, when Ted Lerner and his family of Washington area real estate developers bought the team for a cool $450 million. Bob Short's grave must have erupted on the day of the sale.

The Lerners are among a small minority of truly local entrepreneurs ever to own the team. Clark Griffith was from Missouri who moved to Washington as a retired player and managed the team for a decade before buying it. The early owners after 1901 resembled those that served in 1961 as trustees of the expansion Senators. None of those individuals sought out ownership of a baseball team so much as they had it thrust upon them by politicians and baseball officials looking for a way to get the game in the nation's capital.

Bob Short was neither local nor did he have the financial capacity to invest in the team. He was rightly called a carpetbagger owner. None of the

lot of them, not the original owners after 1901, not the Griffiths, James
Lemon, nor Bob Short, ever had the money to manage the team properly.
The only exception was Clark Griffith, who scraped and borrowed to put
together the winning teams of the 1920s, but those debts were his ultimate
undoing when the Great Depression hit.

Ted Lerner worked at the old Griffith Stadium in the late 1930s when
he was a boy. He knows the traditions of Washington baseball from the bottom up, and he has been waiting as long as anyone for a winner. The Lerners brought in Stan Kasten to help it make the deal stronger. Although
Kasten's roots are in Atlanta, he knows how to build a sports franchise. He
worked with Ted Turner to build the Atlanta Braves, and served as both general manager and president of the NBA Atlanta Hawks.

As president of the team, Kasten adds a layer of management Bob Short
never could have afforded. He announced early in his tenure an aversion to
building a team of "personalities," of expensive free agents who might provide a temporary boost to attendance. Instead he embarked on the path that
Ted Williams had advocated throughout the 1969 season. Build a team of
young, talented players with a farm system, scouts, and teachers who can
take raw talent and mold it into a winning tradition.

In 1969, Ted Williams illustrated the impacts of good instruction on
talented baseball players. Williams may have suffered from personality flaws
that undid his ability to teach the game, but he knew the importance of
teaching. He had many great and gifted teachers who had helped a poor kid
from San Diego make it to the big leagues, and he knew it. The lessons of
1969, the seeds that could have sprouted once many years ago have finally
found fertile soil in the twenty-first century. There will be winning baseball
in Washington again.

Late in the summer of 2007 when I was doing research for this book
at the Library of Congress, I came out of the library to cross Independence
Avenue, heading away from the Capitol and toward the Capitol South Metro
Station. The sun was bright, and when I got to the Independence Avenue
intersection, I looked across to pick up the "Walk" signal. In the background
behind the signal light, I could see the upper decks of the new Washington
Nationals stadium rising to the south down First Street, less than a mile
from the Capitol.

The metal framing of the light standards glittered in the bright, early
afternoon sunlight above the upper decks. As I looked southward, I thought
about how the lights of the new stadium would look at night, how they
would illuminate the whole of the night sky that could be seen from the Capitol grounds, the National Mall and its surrounds, how the cheers of the
crowds might sound in the distance. I thought of the thousands of fans

making joyous noises there, happily oblivious to the essential business our nation transacted so few blocks away.

It was then that I realized the essential truth of what Bob Addie, the *Washington Post* sports columnist from the late sixties, wrote. "This is sacred territory to baseball," he said, in his July 5 column in 1971, defending the city against the desires of Bob Short to move the team. Just as baseball has a unique place in the nation's history, Washington as the nation's capital has a unique place in baseball's history. The history of the game and the history of the nation wrap their troubles around one another unconsciously.

I thought of how easily Richard Nixon had betrayed the nation and how he had failed baseball in Washington, how Bob Short had conspired to pry the sport from its cherished home here in Washington. And I thought how good those lights would look shining forth in the spring of 2008.

The lights gleaming from the banks of the Anacostia River represent a turnaround, a reversal of fortune for both the game and this city. The successful reestablishment of baseball in Washington has washed back against talk that cities should give up their major league teams. In 1969, baseball was expanding, looking for ways to restore the appeal and excitement of the game. At the beginning of the twenty-first century, baseball seemed to be giving up on that struggle. Owners in concert with Commissioner Bud Selig were looking for ways to contract the game, saying that there were too many teams, not enough fans.

The commissioner forgot that baseball is the national pastime; gave up seeking to restore baseball to its rightful place at the heart of American sport and culture. Bowie Kuhn began those efforts in 1969 and they should be a lesson to the current leadership of the game. Without looking for ways to bring excitement back to the game, without expanding the fan base, the game cannot thrive, and the economics will never make sense if the lights are purposely turned off on millions of fans much the way they were in Washington in 1971.

The game should always seek ways to bring the magic closer to fans. Experiencing an evening beneath the stars watching the best talent in what some of us still consider the national pastime is a singular passion for many Americans to this day. The success of bringing baseball back to Washington is just part of a rebirth of the game well beyond Washington. The lights of Washington baseball will hopefully shine on a new tradition of winning seasons, but also hopefully on a new rebirth for the game. Now that the game has returned, beginning in the spring of 2008, and those lights are on officially down on South Capital Street, keep 'em on, and let 'em shine, let 'em shine, let 'em shine.

Appendix A. Career Statistics
for Selected Senators Players

Frank Howard Born: 8/8/36 Columbus, Ohio

Year	Team	AB	R	H	2b/3b	HR	RBI	BB	SO	AVG
1958	Dodgers	8	3	7	1	1	2	1	11	.241
1959	Dodgers	9	2	3	0	1	6	2	9	.143
1960	Dodgers	448	54	120	17	23	77	32	108	.268
1961	Dodgers	267	36	79	12	15	45	21	50	.253
1962	Dodgers	493	80	146	31	31	119	39	108	.296
1963	Dodgers	417	58	114	17	28	64	33	116	.273
1964	Dodgers	433	60	98	15	24	69	51	113	.226
1965	Senators	516	53	149	28	21	84	55	112	.289
1966	Senators	493	52	137	23	18	71	53	104	.278
1967	Senators	519	71	133	22	36	89	60	155	.256
1968	Senators	598	79	164	31	44	106	54	141	.274
1969	Senators	592	111	175	19	48	111	102	96	.296
1970	Senators	566	90	160	16	44	126	132	125	.283
1971	Senators	549	60	153	27	26	83	77	121	.279
1972	Rangers/Tigers	320	29	78	10	10	38	46	63	.244
1973	Tigers	227	26	56	10	12	29	24	28	.256
Career	16 Seasons	1895	864	1774	280	382	1119	782	1460	.273

Mike Epstein Born: 4/4/43 Bronx, New York

Year	Team	AB	R	H	2b/3b	HR	RBI	BB	SO	AVG
1966	Orioles	11	1	2	1	0	3	1	3	.182
1967	Orioles/Senators	297	32	67	11	9	29	41	79	.226
1968	Senators	385	40	90	10	13	33	48	91	.234

Year	Team	AB	R	H	2b/3b	HR	RBI	BB	SO	AVG
1969	Senators	403	73	112	19	30	85	85	99	.278
1970	Senators	430	55	110	18	20	56	73	117	.256
1971	Senators/A's	414	49	98	15	19	60	74	102	.237
1972	A's	455	63	123	20	26	70	68	68	.270
1973	Rangers/Angels	397	39	83	13	9	38	48	73	.209
1974	Angels	62	10	10	2	4	6	10	13	.161
Career	9 Seasons	2854	362	695	109	130	380	448	645	.244

Ken McMullen   Born: 6/1/42   Oxnard, California

Year	Team	AB	R	H	2b/3b	HR	RBI	BB	SO	AVG
1962	Dodgers	11	0	3	0	0	0	0	0	.273
1963	Dodgers	253	16	55	9	5	28	20	46	.236
1964	Dodgers	67	3	14	0	1	2	3	7	.209
1965	Senators	555	75	146	24	18	54	47	90	.263
1966	Senators	524	48	122	23	13	54	44	89	.233
1967	Senators	563	73	138	24	16	67	46	84	.245
1968	Senators	557	66	138	13	20	62	63	66	.248
1969	Senators	562	83	153	27	19	87	70	103	.272
1970	Senators/Angels	481	55	110	14	14	61	59	81	.229
1971	Angels	593	63	127	21	21	68	53	74	.250
1972	Angels	472	36	127	19	9	34	48	59	.269
1973	Dodgers	85	6	21	5	5	18	6	13	.247
1974	Dodgers	60	5	15	1	3	12	2	12	.250
1975	Dodgers	46	4	11	2	2	14	7	12	.239
1976	A's	186	20	41	8	5	23	22	33	.220
1977	Brewers	136	15	31	8	5	19	15	33	.228
Career	16 Seasons	5131	568	1273	198	156	606	510	815	.248

Eddie Brinkman   Born: 12/8/41   Cincinnati, Ohio

Year	Team	AB	R	H	2b/3b	HR	RBI	BB	SO	AVG
1961	Senators	11	0	1	0	0	0	1	1	.091
1962	Senators	133	8	22	8	0	4	11	28	.165
1963	Senators	514	44	117	23	7	45	31	86	.228
1964	Senators	447	54	100	23	8	34	26	99	.224
1965	Senators	444	35	82	15	5	35	38	82	.185
1966	Senators	582	42	133	27	7	48	29	105	.229
1967	Senators	320	21	60	11	1	18	24	58	.188

Year	Team	AB	R	H	2b/3b	HR	RBI	BB	SO	AVG
1968	Senators	193	12	36	3	0	6	19	31	.187
1969	Senators	576	71	153	23	2	43	50	41	.266
1970	Senators	625	63	164	19	1	40	60	41	.262
1971	Tigers	527	40	120	20	1	37	44	54	.228
1972	Tigers	516	42	105	20	6	49	38	51	.203
1973	Tigers	515	55	122	20	7	40	34	79	.237
1974	Tigers	502	55	111	18	14	54	29	71	.221
1975	Cardinals	75	6	18	4	1	6	7	10	.240
1976	Rangers/Yankees	65	2	11	5	0	2	3	7	.169
Career	16 Seasons	6045	550	1355	239	60	461	444	845	.224

Del Unser   Born: 12/9/44   Decatur, Illinois

Year	Team	AB	R	H	2b/3b	HR	RBI	BB	SO	AVG
1968	Senators	635	66	146	20	1	30	46	66	.230
1969	Senators	581	69	166	27	7	57	58	54	.286
1970	Senators	322	37	83	6	5	30	30	29	.258
1971	Senators	581	63	148	25	9	41	59	68	.255
1972	Indians	383	29	91	12	1	17	28	46	.238
1973	Phillies	440	64	127	24	11	52	47	55	.289
1974	Phillies	454	72	120	23	11	61	50	62	.264
1975	Mets	531	65	156	20	10	53	37	76	.294
1976	Mets/Expos	496	57	113	23	12	40	29	84	.228
1977	Expos	289	33	79	15	12	40	33	41	.273
1978	Expos	179	16	35	5	2	15	24	29	.196
1979	Phillies	141	26	42	8	6	29	14	33	.298
1980	Phillies	110	15	29	10	0	10	10	21	.264
1981	Phillies	51	5	9	3	0	6	13	9	.153
1982	Phillies	14	0	0	0	0	0	3	2	.000
Career	15 Seasons	5215	617	1344	121	87	481	481	675	.258

Dick Bosman   Born: 2/17/44   Kenosha, Wisconsin

Year	Team	Wins	Losses	G	Inn	H	BB	SO	ERA
1966	Senators	2	6	13	39	60	12	20	7.62
1967	Senators	3	1	7	51	38	10	25	1.76
1968	Senators	2	9	46	139	139	35	63	3.69
1969	Senators	14	5	31	193	156	39	99	2.19
1970	Senators	16	12	36	231	212	71	134	3.00

Year	Team	Wins	Losses	G	Inn	H	BB	SO	ERA
1971	Senators	12	16	35	237	245	71	113	3.72
1972	Rangers	8	10	29	173	183	48	105	3.64
1973	Rangers/Indians	3	13	29	137	172	46	55	5.65
1974	Indians/A's	11	6	28	152	145	32	53	3.61
1975	A's	4	2	27	112	118	19	34	4.10
Career	10 Seasons	82	85	306	1591	1594	412	757	3.67

Joe Coleman   Born: 2/3/47   Boston, Massachusetts

Year	Team	Wins	Losses	G	Inn	H	BB	SO	ERA
1965	Senators	2	0	2	18	9	8	7	1.50
1966	Senators	1	0	1	9	6	2	4	2.00
1967	Senators	8	9	28	134	154	47	77	4.63
1968	Senators	12	16	33	223	212	51	139	3.27
1969	Senators	12	13	40	248	222	100	182	3.27
1970	Senators	8	12	39	219	190	89	152	3.58
1971	Tigers	20	9	39	286	241	96	236	3.15
1972	Tigers	19	14	40	280	216	110	222	2.80
1973	Tigers	23	15	40	288	283	93	202	3.53
1974	Tigers	14	12	41	286	272	158	177	4.31
1975	Tigers	10	18	31	201	234	85	125	5.55
1976	Tigers/Cubs	4	13	51	146	152	69	104	4.31
1977	A's	4	4	43	128	114	49	55	2.95
1978	A's/Blue Jays	5	0	41	81	79	35	32	3.78
1979	Giants/Pirates	0	0	15	25	32	11	14	5.04
Career	15 Seasons	142	135	484	2572	2416	1003	1728	3.69

Darold Knowles   Born: 12/9/41   Brunswick, Missouri

Year	Team	Wins	Losses	Saves	G	Inn	H	BB	SO	ERA
1965	Orioles	0	1	0	5	15	14	10	12	9.00
1966	Phillies	6	5	13	69	100	98	46	88	3.06
1967	Senators	6	8	14	61	113	91	52	85	2.71
1968	Senators	1	1	4	32	41	38	12	37	2.20
1969	Senators	9	2	13	53	84	73	31	59	2.25
1970	Senators	2	14	27	71	119	100	58	71	2.04
1971	Senators/A's	7	4	9	55	68	57	22	56	3.57
1972	A's	5	1	11	54	66	49	37	36	1.36
1973	A's	6	8	9	52	99	87	49	46	3.09

Year	Team	Wins	Losses	Saves	G	Inn	H	BB	SO	ERA
1974	A's	3	3	3	45	53	61	35	18	4.25
1975	Cubs	6	9	15	58	88	107	63	66	5.83
1976	Cubs	5	7	9	58	72	61	22	39	2.86
1977	Rangers	5	2	4	42	50	50	23	14	3.24
1978	Expos	3	3	6	60	72	63	30	34	2.38
1979	Cardinals	2	5	6	48	49	54	17	22	4.04
1980	Cardinals	0	1	0	2	2	3	0	1	9.00
Career	16 Seasons	66	74	143	765	1091	1006	480	681	3.12

Appendix B. Washington Senators Schedule and Results, 1969

Game Date	Opponent	Score	W–L	Record
04-07-1969	New York Yankees	4–8	L	0–1
04-09-1969	New York Yankees	6–4	W	1–1
04-10-1969	New York Yankees	9–6	W	2–1
04-11-1969	at Baltimore Orioles	4–0	W	3–1
04-12-1969	at Baltimore Orioles	0–9	L	3–2
04-13-1969	at Baltimore Orioles	0–2	L	3–3
04-13-1969	at Baltimore Orioles	0–9	L	3–4
04-15-1969	at New York Yankees	2–8	L	3–5
04-17-1969	at New York Yankees	3–7	L	3–6
04-17-1969	at New York Yankees	5–2	W	4–6
04-18-1969	Baltimore Orioles	0–6	L	4–7
04-19-1969	Baltimore Orioles	7–5	W	5–7
04-20-1969	Baltimore Orioles	1–2	L	5–8
04-20-1969	Baltimore Orioles	5–2	W	6–8
04-21-1969	Detroit Tigers	0–2	L	6–9
04-22-1969	Detroit Tigers	2–4	L	6–10
04-23-1969	at Boston Red Sox	9–3	W	7–10
04-25-1969	at Cleveland Indians	10–3	W	8–10
04-26-1969	at Cleveland Indians	8–1	W	9–10
04-27-1969	at Cleveland Indians	6–5	W	10–10
04-28-1969	at Detroit Tigers	6–1	W	11–10
04-29-1969	at Detroit Tigers	4–5	L	11–11
04-30-1969	Boston Red Sox	1–0	W	12–11
05-01-1969	Boston Red Sox	7–6	W	13–11
05-02-1969	Cleveland Indians	5–0	W	14–11
05-03-1969	Cleveland Indians	6–1	W	15–11

Game Date	Opponent	Score	W–L	Record
05-04-1969	Cleveland Indians	4–3	W	16–11
05-06-1969	at Oakland Athletics	1–4	L	16–12
05-07-1969	at Oakland Athletics	4–5	L	16–13
05-09-1969	at Seattle Pilots	0–2	L	16–14
05-10-1969	at Seattle Pilots	13–16	L	16–15
05-11-1969	at Seattle Pilots	5–6	L	16–16
05-12-1969	at California Angels	2–3	L	16–17
05-13-1969	at California Angels	2–1	W	17–17
05-14-1969	at California Angels	0–1	L	17–18
05-16-1969	at Chicago White Sox	6–7	L	17–19
05-17-1969	at Chicago White Sox	0–6	L	17–20
05-18-1969	at Chicago White Sox	3–2	W	18–20
05-18-1969	at Chicago White Sox	3–2	W	19–20
05-20-1969	Seattle Pilots	6–5	W	20–20
05-21-1969	Seattle Pilots	2–6	L	20–21
05-22-1969	Seattle Pilots	6–7	L	20–22
05-23-1969	Kansas City Royals	3–4	L	20–23
05-24-1969	Kansas City Royals	4–5	L	20–24
05-25-1969	Kansas City Royals	2–3	L	20–25
05-26-1969	Minnesota Twins	1–7	L	20–26
05-27-1969	Minnesota Twins	5–1	W	21–26
05-28-1969	Minnesota Twins	4–3	W	22–26
05-30-1969	Chicago White Sox	5–4	W	23–26
05-30-1969	Chicago White Sox	5–8	L	23–27
05-31-1969	Chicago White Sox	7–5	W	24–27
06-01-1969	Chicago White Sox	9–2	W	25–27
06-02-1969	at Kansas City Royals	7–6	W	26–27
06-03-1969	at Kansas City Royals	3–5	L	26–28
06-04-1969	at Kansas City Royals	3–1	W	27–28
06-06-1969	at Minnesota Twins	1–0	W	28–28
06-07-1969	at Minnesota Twins	1–10	L	28–29
06-08-1969	at Minnesota Twins	7–5	W	29–29
06-10-1969	Oakland Athletics	4–6	L	29–30
06-11-1969	Oakland Athletics	4–6	L	29–31
06-12-1969	Oakland Athletics	4–1	W	30–31
06-13-1969	California Angels	6–2	W	31–31
06-14-1969	California Angels	2–3	L	31–32
06-17-1969	Baltimore Orioles	1–5	L	31–33
06-18-1969	Baltimore Orioles	1–3	L	31–34
06-19-1969	Baltimore Orioles	0–2	L	31–35

Game Date	Opponent	Score	W–L	Record
06-20-1969	at Detroit Tigers	7–2	W	32–35
06-21-1969	at Detroit Tigers	5–9	L	32–36
06-22-1969	at Detroit Tigers	9–4	W	33–36
06-22-1969	at Detroit Tigers	9–5	W	34–36
06-23-1969	at Baltimore Orioles	3–5	L	34–37
06-24-1969	at Baltimore Orioles	3–6	L	34–38
06-25-1969	at Baltimore Orioles	11–8	W	35–38
06-27-1969	Boston Red Sox	2–4	L	35–39
06-28-1969	Boston Red Sox	4–3	W	36–39
06-29-1969	Boston Red Sox	5–4	W	37–39
06-29-1969	Boston Red Sox	11–4	W	38–39
07-01-1969	at Cleveland Indians	4–1	W	39–39
07-01-1969	at Cleveland Indians	7–5	W	40–39
07-02-1969	at Cleveland Indians	5–1	W	41–39
07-03-1969	at Cleveland Indians	2–7	L	41–40
07-04-1969	at Boston Red Sox	5–1	W	42–40
07-04-1969	at Boston Red Sox	4–7	L	42–41
07-05-1969	at Boston Red Sox	6–2	W	43–41
07-05-1969	at Boston Red Sox	4–11	L	43–42
07-06-1969	at Boston Red Sox	5–0	W	44–42
07-07-1969	Cleveland Indians	7–2	W	45–42
07-08-1969	Cleveland Indians	5–6	L	45–43
07-09-1969	Cleveland Indians	3–0	W	46–43
07-11-1969	New York Yankees	3–4	L	46–44
07-12-1969	New York Yankees	1–3	L	46–45
07-13-1969	New York Yankees	5–4	W	47–45
07-13-1969	New York Yankees	10–1	W	48–45
07-14-1969	Detroit Tigers	3–0	W	49–45
07-15-1969	Detroit Tigers	7–3	W	50–45
07-16-1969	Detroit Tigers	0–3	L	50–46
07-17-1969	Detroit Tigers	3–4	L	50–47
07-18-1969	at New York Yankees	0–5	L	50–48
07-19-1969	at New York Yankees	0–9	L	50–49
07-19-1969	at New York Yankees	4–0	W	51–49
07-20-1969	at New York Yankees	2–3	L	51–50
07-24-1969	at Oakland Athletics	1–2	L	51–51
07-25-1969	at Oakland Athletics	3–4	L	51–52
07-26-1969	at Oakland Athletics	3–1	W	52–52
07-27-1969	at Oakland Athletics	2–7	L	52–53
07-29-1969	at Seattle Pilots	4–2	W	53–53

Game Date	Opponent	Score	W–L	Record
07-30-1969	at Seattle Pilots	3–4	L	53–54
07-31-1969	at Seattle Pilots	7–6	W	54–54
08-01-1969	at California Angels	5–3	W	55–54
08-02-1969	at California Angels	8–7	W	56–54
08-03-1969	at California Angels	2–3	L	56–55
08-05-1969	at Chicago White Sox	4–11	L	56–56
08-06-1969	at Chicago White Sox	4–3	W	57–56
08-08-1969	Seattle Pilots	10–3	W	58–56
08-09-1969	Seattle Pilots	6–8	L	58–57
08-10-1969	Seattle Pilots	7–5	W	59–57
08-11-1969	Kansas City Royals	2–1	W	60–57
08-12-1969	Kansas City Royals	3–6	L	60–58
08-13-1969	Kansas City Royals	3–7	L	60–59
08-15-1969	Minnesota Twins	0–2	L	60–60
08-16-1969	Minnesota Twins	6–5	W	61–60
08-17-1969	Minnesota Twins	3–4	L	61–61
08-19-1969	Chicago White Sox	3–1	W	62–61
08-20-1969	Chicago White Sox	4–1	W	63–61
08-22-1969	at Kansas City Royals	2–3	L	63–62
08-23-1969	at Kansas City Royals	4–2	W	64–62
08-24-1969	at Kansas City Royals	10–3	W	65–62
08-25-1969	at Minnesota Twins	7–3	W	66–62
08-26-1969	at Minnesota Twins	4–6	L	66–63
08-27-1969	at Minnesota Twins	2–4	L	66–64
08-29-1969	Oakland Athletics	0–5	L	66–65
08-30-1969	Oakland Athletics	11–3	W	67–65
08-31-1969	Oakland Athletics	8–3	W	68–65
09-01-1969	California Angels	4–0	W	69–65
09-01-1969	California Angels	7–8	L	69–66
09-02-1969	California Angels	2–0	W	70–66
09-02-1969	California Angels	3–2	W	71–66
09-05-1969	at Boston Red Sox	8–9	L	71–67
09-06-1969	at Boston Red Sox	5–9	L	71–68
09-07-1969	at Boston Red Sox	3–2	W	72–68
09-09-1969	at Baltimore Orioles	1–6	L	72–69
09-09-1969	at Baltimore Orioles	2–3	L	72–70
09-10-1969	New York Yankees	6–1	W	73–70
09-11-1969	New York Yankees	7–3	W	74–70
09-12-1969	Detroit Tigers	4–3	W	75–70
09-13-1969	Detroit Tigers	11–6	W	76–70

Game Date	Opponent	Score	W–L	Record
09-14-1969	Detroit Tigers	4–7	L	76–71
09-15-1969	Baltimore Orioles	3–2	W	77–71
09-16-1969	Baltimore Orioles	0–1	L	77–72
09-17-1969	at New York Yankees	1–2	L	77–73
09-18-1969	at New York Yankees	3–4	L	77–74
09-20-1969	at Cleveland Indians	5–3	W	78–74
09-21-1969	at Cleveland Indians	3–4	L	78–75
09-24-1969	at Detroit Tigers	8–4	W	79–75
09-24-1969	at Detroit Tigers	7–4	W	80–75
09-25-1969	at Detroit Tigers	7–2	W	81–75
09-26-1969	Cleveland Indians	4–1	W	82–75
09-27-1969	Cleveland Indians	3–2	W	83–75
09-28-1969	Cleveland Indians	7–6	W	84–75
09-29-1969	Boston Red Sox	5–8	L	84–76
09-30-1969	Boston Red Sox	7–2	W	85–76
10-01-1969	Boston Red Sox	3–2	W	86–76

Chapter Notes

Chapter 1

p. 8 "I don't like to predict violence..." Martin Luther King at Washington Cathedral, *Washington Post*, April 1, 1968, p. 1.

p. 9 "Now you want us on the front of the bus..." Fred Valentine interview, February 26, 2007.

p. 10 "[J]ust a sleepy little southern town," Karl Vick of the *Washington Post* attributes the quote to Chalmers Roberts of the Post and others in his Sunday, April 20, 1997, article, "In FDR Years, Sleepy Southern Town Work Up," in the *Washington Post*.

p. 10 "I shall not seek, and..." Lyndon Johnson quote. *The Washington Post*, April 1, 1968, p. 1.

p. 10 "Nineteen sixty-eight was a year..." Tom Wicker on Nixon. Tom Wicker, *One of Us*, p. 287.

p. 11 Population growth in D.C., U.S. Bureau of the Census, Statistical Abstract, 1889, p. 223.

p. 12 Joe Cronin's sale to Boston, Al Hershberg, *From Sandlots to League President*, p. 16.

p. 12 Clark Griffith's financial losses, Andrew Zimbalist, *Baseball and Billions*, p. 511. Zimbalist cites as his source for Depression era baseball profits and earnings the following report: U.S. Congress. House of Representatives. Committee on the Judiciary. Subcommittee on Monopolies and Commercial Law. Organized Baseball, Hearings (1951). 82nd Congress, 1st Session. Washington, D.C.; USGPO, 1952.

p. 13 The Grays at Griffith Stadium, Brad Snyder, *Beyond the Shadow of the Senators*, p. 233.

p. 13 Old Griffith Stadium, Lawrence S. Ritter, *Lost Ballparks*, p. 82–83.

p. 14 "[G]etting to be all colored," Snyder, *Beyond the Shadow of the Senators*, p. 288.

p. 14 "You only have 15,000 blacks..." Ibid. p. 289.

p. 15 Washington fan view of the Twins in '65, John Briar telephone interview, July 15, 2007.

Chapter 2

p. 17 "[B]aseball was dull and lacking," Jerome Holtzman, *Official Baseball Guide for 1969*, p. 198.

p. 17 "[E]ven the competition between pitcher and batter," Red Barber, "Can Baseball Be Saved," *Reader's Digest*, April 1969, p. 155.

p. 17 "There used to be quite a few ballparks..." Holtzman, p. 199.

p. 18 The changes were not bold enough. Barber, *Can Baseball Be Saved?*, p. 156.

p. 18 "[T]he most divisive time of battle..." Myra McPherson, *Long Time Passing*, p. 5.

p. 18 Sale of team announced. Shirley Povich, "This Morning," *Washington Post*, December 4, 1968.

p. 18 "[G]ot took." John Underwood, "Teaching Them Ted's Way," *Sports Illustrated*, March 19, 1969, p. 23.

p. 18 "[L]ong period of years," Povich, *Washington Post*, December 4, 1968.

p. 19 "His purchase of the team was highly leveraged..." Dan Daniels interview, July 14, 2007.

p. 19 Whitfield's claims on Short's purchase investment were tempered later to include $2 million in equity put up to secure the loans. Shelby Whitfield, *Kiss It Goodbye*, p. 42.

p. 21 "Wait'll you see Jimmy Foxx hit," Leigh Montville, *Ted Williams*, p. 44. Quoted differently by Mike Seidel, *Ted Williams: A Baseball Life*, p. 31.

p. 21 Claims about Williams' eyesight, Montville, *Ted Williams*, p. 105–106.

p. 22 "Managing is essentially a loser's job. They are..." Ted Williams, *My Turn at Bat*, p. 267.

p. 22 "Manage twenty-five men, heck, he can't..." Whitfield, p. 42.

p. 22 "I think that's where my strength lies, they'll..." Povich, "This Morning," *Washington Post*, February 25, 1969.

p. 22 "I would play for nothing..." Williams, *My Turn at Bat*, p. 163.

p. 23 "You're going to inherit the worst team..." Whitfield, p. 44.

p. 23 Williams' financial incentives. John Underwood, "The Newest Senator in Town," *Sports Illustrated*, February 24, 1969, p. 20.

p. 24 "I've been sitting around doing very little..." Whitfield, p. 44.

p. 24 "He is a self-made man." Ibid., p. 21.

p. 24 "Ted Williams can talk about the scientific theories of hitting..." John Steadman, *Sporting News*, March 1, 1969, p. 5.

p. 25 "He gives off sparks. If you stand..." Joe Falls, *Sporting News*, March 8, 1969, p. 2.

Chapter 3

p. 26 "It is 410 to center and..." George Minot, "All Eyes on Williams As Nats Open Camp," *Washington Post*, February 25, 1969.

p. 26 "It was like a hero come to life." Jim Hannan interview, April 25, 2007.

p. 27 "He was such an icon of the game." Frank Howard interview, June 15, 2007.

p. 27 "Even when he was talking to the press..." Ibid.

p. 27 "He told us from the beginning..." Hannan.interview.

pp. 27–28 Camacho's relationship with Ted Williams augmented by Bill Nowlin's interview with Camacho for *Ted Williams: Pursuit of Perfection*.

p. 28 "Epstein has the tools..." Merrill Whittlesey, "Ted Tutors Promising Pupil Epstein," *Sporting News*, March 22, 1969, p. 23.

p. 29 Williams' rules of hitting. Mike Epstein interview, June 15, 2007.

p. 29 "Repetition is the most important part..." Howard interview.

p. 29 "Taken more batting practice." John Underwood, "Teaching Them Ted's Way," *Sports Illustrated*, March 19, 1969, p. 23.

p. 29 "How can a guy hit 44..." Frederick Frommer, *The Washington Nationals 1859 to Today*, p. 141.

p. 29 "[F]rom the bill of my cap," Ibid., p. 142.

p. 29 "Heck, if you see one you can handle..." Howard interview.

p. 30 "What he helped me with most..." Frommer, p. 140.

p. 30 "His advice and admonitions..." Underwood, p. 24.

p. 30 "In the first seven innings I always..." Montville, p. 275.

p. 31 "What's the next pitch..." and typical interchange with players, Mike Epstein interview, June 15, 2007.

p. 32 "You know, football players aren't really athletes." Epstein interview.

p. 33 "Come on, bush, get a good pitch..." Epstein interview.

Chapter 4

p. 35 "The kids are trying. They are really working hard." John Underwood, "Teaching Them Ted's Way," *Sports Illustrated*, March 19, 1969, p. 23.

p. 38 "I don't think too many people realize..." James Enright, "Ted Will Need Patience — DiMag," *Sporting News*, March 15, 1969, p. 4.

p. 39 "[L]owering the net in tennis." William Leggett, "From Mountain to Molehill," *Sports Illustrated*, May 24, 1969, p. 21

p. 39 "5½ percent difference in hitting." Mark Mulvoy, "Here Come the Hitters," *Sports Illustrated*, May 12, 1969, p. 20. This analysis also attributed to Mike Marshall as a young pitcher by Jim Bouton in *Ball Four*.

p. 40 "It is going to take a lot..." William Leggett, "From Mountain to Molehill," *Sports Illustrated*, May 24, 1969, p. 21.

p. 40 "Tilt." Word used by Epstein to describe the downward break of the ball through the strike zone, Epstein interview.

p. 40 "[M]ore spin, better leverage," Hannan interview.

p. 41 Views of Mickey Lolich and Garylord Perry, Leggett, p. 21.

p. 41 "[B]ut the old curves broke sharper," Hannan interview.

p. 41 Musial's assessment of Dodgers pitching mounds. Leggett, p. 23.

p. 46 "[H]aving trouble forcing my arm and body down..." Leggett, p. 23.

p. 47 "Huck Finn, aw shucks" Bob Addie, *Washington Post*, April 4, 1969.

p. 47 "I just listened..." Leigh Montville, *Ted Williams*, p. 276.

Chapter 5

p. 50 "I'm not committed to keeping the team in Washington..." Shelby Whitfield, *Kiss It Goodbye*, p. 19.

pp. 51–52 *Washington Senators 1969 Program* cover.

p. 52 Nixon's early sports history. Roger Morris, *Richard Milhouse Nixon*, p. 118.

p. 52 [W]ho viewed the scene of the sixties..." Tom Wicker, *One of Us*, p. 290.

p. 52 "[C]ried out for the return..." Ibid. p. 291–292.

p. 54 "GI war toll highest in ten months," David Hoffman, *Washington Post*, March 7, 1969, p. 4.

p. 59 "There are signs..." Shirley Povich, "This Morning," *Washington Post*, April 10, 1969.

Chapter 6

p. 64 "Now the home team doesn't..." Shirley Povich, "This Morning," April 15, 1969.
p. 65 "It was the closest thing..." Jim Hannan interview.

Chapter 7

p. 67 "Ted Williams made me a successful pitcher..." Dick Bosman interview.
p. 67 "Those basic elements of pitching haven't changed..." Bosman interview.
p. 69 "Ted and I had a relationship..." Interview with Bosman from Frederic J. Frommer, *The Washington Nationals*, 144.
p. 73 "I'll give you the whole story..." George Minot, *Washington Post*, May 2, 1969.
p. 73 "[B]ecause he's gonna hit 40..." Ibid.
p. 73 Ted Williams in Comiskey Park. Mike Epstein interview.
p. 75 "Baseball fans don't notice each..." Melvin Durslag, *Sporting News*, May 31, 1969, p 2.
p. 75 "How do we make our..." Ibid.
p. 75 "How can I complain? Ted took..." Ibid.
p. 77 "We're dead." George Minor, "Senators' Sour Play Termed 'Crime' by Angered Williams," *Washington Post*, May 24, 1969.

Chapter 8

p. 78 "Williams was not my kind..." Shirley Povich "This Morning," June 1, 1969.
p. 79 Martin and Williams confrontation in the press. Arno Goethel, "Battling Billy Said It, But He Didn't Mean It," *Sporting News*, June 14, 1969, p. 22.
p. 79 "[P]layers like me used to..." Tom Seppy, "Billy Martin Dilutes Criticism of Williams," *Washington Post*, May 28, 1969.
p. 79 The *Washington Post* articles contend that Billy Martin brought video to Ted Williams' attention, but Bill Nowlin contends that it was actually Dick Williams who first used the technology and probably introduced it to Williams.
p. 79 The use of video by Billy Martin and Ted Williams in 1969 discussed. Associated Press, "Martin Adds TV Replay to Aid Twins," *Washington Post*, May 27, 1969.
p. 80 "Of all the changes..." Buzz Bissinger, *Three Nights in August*, p. 36.
p. 80 "I burst into laughter..." Jim Hannan interview.
p. 82 "[N]ot acting out, or bursting out..." Shirley Povich, This Morning," *Washington Post*, May 27, 1969.
p. 82 "[W]ere not really a bad team." Ibid.
p. 83 "He was the greatest hitter..." Tom Seppy.
p. 83 "[O]nly Senator who hasn't said..." George Minot, "Pascual Demoted to Relief," *Washington Post*, June 2, 1969.
p. 84 "[C]reated controversy from coast to coast..." Merrell Whittlesey, *Sporting News*, "Ted, Nixon Run Neck-and-Neck in Publicity Glare," May 31, 1969, p. 7.
p. 84 "Williams is probably the worst..." Ibid.
p. 84 "Well, it's better than..." Ibid.
p. 85 "Ted Williams' First Fifty-Six days," Shirley Povich, "This Morning," *Washington Post*, June 2, 1969.
p. 85 "Dammit, I know I can..." Ibid.
p. 85 "[T]ook and undisciplined hitter..." Frederick Fromer, *Washington Nationals, 1859 to Today*," p. 142.

Chapter 9

p. 86 "[S]wing hard and hope." Merrell Whittlesey, "Senator Alyea Earns Huzzahs for Assault on Left-Wingers," *Sporting News*, May 31, 1969, p. 22.

p. 87 Senators All-Time Team. Merrell Whittlesey adapted from, "Big Train Greatest Ever on Nat All-Time Club," *Sporting News*, June 14, 1969, p. 22.

p. 91 "Although I always root for the home team..." Merrell Whittlesey, "Nixon Displays Grasp of Game, But Nats Blow Duke," *Sporting News*, June 28, 1969, p. 9.

p. 92 "[T]he Communists are more serious..." Carroll Kilpatrick, "U.S. to Withdraw 25,000 Troops," *Washington Post*, June 9, 1969.

Chapter 10

p. 96 "Ted Williams has helped me..." Merrell Whittlesey, "Casey Cox Making Capital of Three C's," *Sporting News*, June 28, p. 9.

p. 98 This synopsis of Lee Maye's recording career is based on an August 23, 1969, article at the time of the trade in the *Sporting News*, "Platter or Plate, Lee Maye of Nats Cuts a Groovy Tune," by Merrell Whittlesey. Bill Nowlin points out that Maye sang more frequently with his own group, The Crowns, and was not a member of the original Platters as Whittlesey contended in the article.

p. 98 "I am no expert." Merrell Whittlesey, "Short Planned Whopper, But Flopped as a Swapper," *Sporting News*, July 5, 1969, p. 22.

Chapter 11

p. 101 Short's take on attendance. Bob Addie, "Short's Views," *Washington Post*, June 19, 1969.

p. 101 "Ted Williams wants me to..." George Minot, "Short Is No Expert, but He Has the Answers," *Washington Post*," June 22, 1969.

p. 102 "If I had stayed with last year's..." Ibid.

p. 102 "I'm no fool..." Ibid.

p. 102 "We didn't deserve to win." George Minot, "Senators Win on Gift Run in 9th," *Washington Post*, June 29, 1969.

p. 106 "[B]rought the city joyously alive..." Shirley Povich, "This Morning," *Washington Post*, July 3, 1969.

p. 106 "the self assurance of old war-dog..." Ibid.

p. 106 "My coorve ball," Shirley Povich, "This Morning," *Washington Post*, July 8, 1969.

p. 107 "[F]inest fielding pitcher of his time," Ibid.

p. 108 "We were just one more good pitcher..." Mike Epstein interview.

p. 109 "This was the best game..." Paul Attner, "Just Ask French: Senators Terrific in All Departments," *Washington Post*, July 8, 1969.

p. 109 "It was only my second major league RBI..." Ibid.

Chapter 12

p. 112 "[L]anding of a man on the moon," John Kennedy speech excerpted on National Aeronautics and Space Administration, NASA History Office web site.

p. 114 "Now they are coming..." William Gildea, "Stadium Infected By Natsomania," *Washington Post*, July 16, 1969.

p. 114 "[T]otal commitment to the game," Shirley Povich "This Morning," *Washington Post*, July 17, 1969.

pp. 117–118 "They're heads up and hustling..." Merrell Whittlesey, "Senators Get Ted's Message ... They're Patsies for Nobody," *Sporting News*, July 19, 1969, p. 12.

p. 120 "The Eagle has landed," Thomas O'Toole, "The Eagle Has Landed," *Washington Post*, July 21, 1969.

p. 120 "For one priceless moment..." Dan Oberdorfer, "Nixon Telephones the Moon," *Washington Post*, July 21, 1969.

Chapter 13

p. 122 Quality of play affected by racial composition of the two leagues. David Halberstam, *October 1964*, p. 55.

p. 123 "Most astute observers believed now..." Ibid., p. 5.

p. 123 George Weiss' racist attitudes are asserted by Halberstam, *October 1964*, p. 54.

p. 124 "Of the last 22, the AL has won only six." Shirley Povich, "This Morning," *Washington Post*, June 21, 1969.

p. 125 The story of the Cardinals at spring training in 1961. Halberstam, p.56.

p. 127 "I would like you to say hello to Mr. Grant. I want you to..." Hannan interview.

p. 130 "He is not ill..." Kenneth Denlinger, "Baseball's Great Men, Moments are Honored," *Washington Post*, July 3, 1969.

p. 131 Williams' All-Star Game experiences. Merrell Whittlesey, "41 Clout ... Ted's Top All-Star Thrill," *Sporting News*, July 26, 1969, p. 7.

p. 131 "I enjoyed the challenge of..." Ibid.

p. 133 "100 Years of Rainfall," Bob Addie, *Washington Post*, July 23, 1969.

p. 134 "The money really isn't that important..." Kenneth Denlinger, "Ushers, Fans Share Difficulty Rearranging Schedule for Game," *Washington Post*, July 22, 1969.

p. 135 "Howard's was the daddy of them all," Shirley Povich, "This Morning," *Washington Post*, July 24, 1969.

p. 135 "I just watched the game, kept score, and called the bullpen." Kenneth Denlinger, "Smith Apologizes to Agnew After His AL Stars Drubbed," *Washington Post*, July 24, 1969.

Chapter 14

p. 144 "I hear you can walk on water." Leigh Montville, *Ted Williams, Biography of An American Hero*, p. 277.

p. 145 Joe Mooney's heroics with the field at RFK Stadium. Merrell Whittlesey, "Joe Mooney: The Nats' Miracle Man," *Sporting News*, September 6, 1969, p. 17.

Chapter 15

p. 147 "[H]alf a million strong," Joni Mitchell, "Woodstock."

p. 148 "[T]rigger-happy frontier marshall," Bob Addie, "Summer of Discontent," *Washington Post*, August 13, 1969.

p. 148 "He hit me in the chest and..." Ibid.

p. 149 "McMullen makes great plays..." George Minot, "McMullen Says Luck Aids Key Double Play," *Washington Post*, August 17, 1969.

p. 152 "I think every city in the major leagues..." Merrell Whittlesey, "No Wonder Nats Climb ... Their Slab Staff is Super," *Sporting News*, September, 20, 1969.

p. 153 "[S]tole the lush California territory..." Shirley Povich, "This Morning," *Washington Post*, September 11, 1969.

p. 157 "I am proud of how..." Bob Addie, "Williams Already Planning for Return Next Season," *Washington Post*, August 29, 1969.

Chapter 16

p. 160 "Please continue to celebrate my birthday..." Bob Addie, "Senators Deck A's With 4 Homers," *Washington Post*, August 31, 1969.

p. 163 "Do you remember what I said..." Cy Kritzer, "Glory Days Come Alive, Ted Visits McCarthy," *Sporting News*, September 13, 1969, p. 5.

p. 163 "We did get along..." Ibid.

p. 164 "How can you miss with a man like McCarth..." Ibid.

p. 164 What made Bosman better in 1969. Merrell Whttlesey, "Boz' Blazer Singes Nat Rivals' Bats," *Sporting News*, August 9, 1969, p. 10.

p. 169 "It would be no disgrace..." George Minot, "Howard Charging Towards 50 Mark," *Washington Post*, September 14, 1969.

p. 169 "I really thought he..." Ibid.

p. 169 "I am going to have to get back in a groove," Ibid.

p. 169 "I haven't been swinging good..." Ibid.

Chapter 17

p. 172 Mike Esptein catches his second wind. George Minot, "Epstein Just Now Gets Second Wind," *Washington Post*, September 21, 1969.

p. 176 "Ted, that's for you." Leigh Montville, *Ted Williams, The Biography of an American Hero*, p. 277.

Chapter 18

p. 180 Williams left a rod and reel in each locker. Leigh Montville, p.277.

p. 181 "Art Shamsky was there first..." Merrell Whittlesey, "Epstein Arrives as Nat Hitter, But He May Go in Deal," *Sporting News*, October 11, 1969, p.14.

p. 181 "[T]he price is high," Merrell Whittlesey, "Player Safari Fails, Ted Heads for Africa," *Sporting News*, November 1, 1969.

p. 182 "[T]he Senators don't have anyone in the front office..." Whitfield, *Kiss It Goodbye*, p. 180.

p. 182 "Every time Short thought about a deal..." Ibid., p. 175.

p. 184 "Damn, I wish Short had the money..." Ibid., p. 225.

p. 187 Whitfield and Hannan on the McLain trade. Whitfield, p. 167.

p. 188 "You're giving up way too much..." Whitfield, p. 188.

p. 188 Curt Flood and Bob Short dealings. Brad Snyder, *A Well-Paid Slave*, pp. 197–232.

p. 189 "[G]ot excited about the plush $80,000-$125,000 homes..." Whitfield, p. 217.

p. 192 "[T]he president of the American League..." Whitfield, p. 234.

p. 193 "Short's demand has been equated with..." Shirley Povich, "This Morning," *Washington Post.*

p. 193 Economic analysis of franchise worth. Michael J. Haupert, "The Economic Value of Baseball," p. 3.

p. 194 Analysis of Short's economic motives. Jerome Holtzman, "A $7.5 Million Bonanza for Short?" *Sporting News,* October 9, 1971, p. 9.

p. 194 "[H]eartbreaking." Nixon on the sale. Merrell Whittlesey, "Washington Sad, Shocked, and Bitter," *Sporting News,* October 9, 1971, p. 8.

p. 195 "But wasn't it a hollow effort?" Holtzman, p. 9.

p. 195 "Should the owners have left..." Ibid.

p. 196 "[B]e an encumbrance to the team," Whittlesey, p. 8.

p. 196 Ted Williams' involvement on behalf of Short. Whittlesey, p. 236.

p. 197 "Mismanagement should not be rewarded..." Whitfield, p. 243.

p. 197 Population analysis of the two cities drawn on data from the Statistical Abstract of the United States, 91st Edition, U.S. Census Bureau, p. 18–19.

p. 198 "This was my sense of belonging. This was my sense of identity," Barry Svrluga, *National Pastime,* p. 35.

p. 199 "They took my identity away from me that night." Ibid.

p. 199 "This isn't exactly a pleasure. I've been..." Ibid. p. 36.

p. 199 "I'm getting ready to get..." Ibid., p. 38.

Epilogue

p. 201 Blackie Sherrod's quote. Shelby Whitfield, *Kiss it Goodbye,* p. 249.

p. 201 "Managing was a great experience..." Ibid., p. 257.

p. 202 "[P]aper deficits," Ibid., p. 13.

p. 202 Short's claim of '69–'71 losses. Ibid., p. 13–14.

p. 203 "Powerful pitchers overwhelmed..." Pete Axthelm, "A Whole New Ballgame," *Newsweek,* December 20, 1969, p. 105.

p. 203 "Great National Bore," Ibid.

p. 203 "[G]ame has come a long way..." Ibid.

Bibliography

Articles

Addie, Bob. "Addie's Atoms." *Sporting News*, July 26, 1969: 14.

_____. "$6000,000 for New Carpet." *Sporting News*, September 6, 1969: 4.

Axthelm, Pete. "A Whole New Ballgame." *Newsweek*, October 20, 1969: 104–105.

Barber, Red. "Can Baseball Be Saved?" *Readers Digest*, April 1969: 155.

Durslag, Melvin. "Ted and I Are Flaky." *Sporting News*, May 31, 1969: 2.

Enright, James. "Ted Will Need Patience." *Sporting News*, March 15, 1969: 4.

Holtzman, Jerome. "A $7.5 Million Bonanza for Short." *Sporting News*, October 9, 1971: 12–16.

Kritzer, Cy. "Glory Days Come Alive, Ted Visits McCarthy." *Sporting News*, September 13, 1969: 5.

Leggett, William. "From Mountain to Molehill." *Sports Illustrated*, May 24, 1969: 22–23.

Mulvoy, Mark. "Here Come the Hitters." *Sports Illustrated*, May 12, 1969: 20–21.

Munzel, Edgar. "White Sox Big 3 Locate Trouble — It's Smaller Strike Zone." *Sporting News*, July 5, 1969: 12.

Spink, C.C. Johnson. "Lowering Mound Great Idea." *Sporting News*, January 13, 1969: 14.

_____. "Nixon's the One." *Sporting News*, August 9, 1969: 14.

_____. "How to Succeed in Baseball." *Sporting News*, October 9, 1971: 17.

Steadman, John. "Why the Big Swing?" *Sporting News*, March 1, 1969: 14.

_____. "Ex-Stars Flop as Managers? Ted Breaks Pattern." *Sporting News*, October 18, 1969: 17.

Underwood, John. "The Newest Senator in Town." *Sports Illustrated*, February 24, 1969: 20–21.

Underwood, John. "Teaching Them Ted's Way." *Sports Illustrated*, March 19, 1969: 18–23.

Whittlesey, Merrell. "Ted Will Manage in Marse Joe's Pattern." *Sporting News*, March 8, 1969: 27.

_____. "Ted Tutors Promising Pupil Epstein." *Sporting News*, March 15, 1969: 23.

_____. "Close Harmony is Keynote of Ted's Debut." *Sporting News*, March 15, 1969: 15.

_____. "Ted Lays Down Law on Capitol Hill." *Sporting News*, March 29 1969: 24.

_____. "Ted Sees Hefty Clout Climb by Ed and Ken." *Sporting News*, April 5, 1969: 17.

_____. "Ted and His Senators Are the Toast of the Town." *Sporting News*, April 26, 1969: 27.

_____. "Boston Fans Go Wild at Ted's Second Coming." *Sporting News*, May 10, 1969: 7.

_____. "Ted's Tips Load Brinkman's Bat With Explosive Charge." *Sporting News*, May 24, 1969: 10.

_____. "Ted, Nixon Run Neck-and-Neck in Publicity Glare." *Sporting News*, May 31, 1969: 7.

_____. "Johnson 'Greatest Ever' On Nat All-Time Club." *Sporting News*, June 14, 1969: 22.

_____. "Air Force Vet Knowles Flying High in Nats Pen." *Sporting News*, June 21, 1969: 23.

_____. "What a Capital Setting for Milestone Star Game." *Sporting News*, June 26, 1969: 7.

_____. "41 Clout ... Ted's Top All-Star Thrill." *Sporting News*, June 26, 1969: 7.

_____. "Nixon Displays Grasp of Game, But Nats Blow Duke." *Sporting News*, June 28, 1969: 9

_____. "Casey Cox Making Capital of Three C's." *Sporting News*, June 28, 1969: 9.

_____. "Short Planned Whopper But Flopped as Swapper." *Sporting News*, July 5, 1969: 22.

_____. "Spunk and Quick Wit Help French Hold Nat Mitt Job." *Sporting News*, July 12, 1969: 19.

_____. "Senators Get Ted's Message ... They're Patsies for Nobody." *Sporting News*, July 19, 1969: 12.

_____. "What a Capital Setting for Milestone Game." *Sporting News*, July 26, 1969: 26.

_____. "Coleman Jabs Nat Foes With Sharp Fork Ball." *Sporting News*, August 2, 1969: 8.

_____. "Where Action is, You'll Find Short." *Sporting News*, August 2, 1969: 8.

_____. "Ted Sees Hefty Clout Climb by Ed and Ken." *Sporting News*, August 5, 1969: 17.

_____. "Boz' Blazer Singes Nat Rivals' Bats." *Sporting News*, August 9, 1969: 10.

_____. "Pesky Expansion Clubs Prick Senators' Balloon." *Sporting News*, August 30, 1969.

_____. "Joe Mooney: The Nats' Miracle Man." *Sporting News*, September 6, 1969: 17.

_____. "No Wonder Nats Climb ... Their Slab Staff is Super." *Sporting News*, September 20, 1969: 10.

_____. "Impossible Dream? Ted's Nats Boast a Carload of '69 Pluses." *Sporting News*, October 4, 1969: 13.

_____. "Epstein Arrives as Nat Hitter, But He May Go in Deal." *Sporting News*, October 11, 1969: 14.

_____. "Ted a Success Where Other Ex-Stars Failed." *Sporting News*, October 18, 1969: 14.

_____. "Player Safari Fails, Ted Heads for Africa." *Sporting News*, November 8, 1969: 41.

_____. "Form Chart Takes Licking From Quick Climbing Nats." Sporting News, November 8, 1969: 41.

_____. "Ted Strikes Out in Bid to Swing Nat Trades." *Sporting News*, 20 December 20, 1969: 39.

_____. "Washington Sad, Shocked, and Bitter." *Sporting News*, October 9, 1971: 23.

Books

Bissinger, Buzz. *Three Nights in August*. New York: Houghton Mifflin, 2005.

Deveaux, Tom. *The Washington Senators, 1901–1971*. Jefferson, NC: McFarland, 2001.

Frommer, Frederick J. *The Washington Nationals, 1859 to Today*. Lanham, MD: Taylor Trade Publishing, 2006.

Halberstam, David. *October 1964*. New York: Villard Books, 1994.

Hirshberg, Al. *From Sandlots to League President: The Story of Joe Cronin*. New York: Julian Messner, 1962.

Hirshberg, Al. *Frank Howard; The Gentle Giant*. New York: G.P. Putnam's Sons, 1973.

Hoopes, Roy, *What a Manager Does*. New York: John Day Company, 1970.

McPherson, Myra. *Long Time Passing: Vietnam and the Haunted Generation*. Garden City, NY: Doubleday, 1984.

Montville, Leigh. *Ted Williams: The Biography of an American Hero*. New York: Doubleday, 2004.

Morris, Roger. *Richard Milhouse Nixon: The Rise of an American Politician*. New York: Holt, 1990.

Prime, Jim, and Bill Nowlin. *Ted Williams: The Pursuit of Perfection*. Champaign, IL: Sports Publishing, 2002.

Ritter, Lawrence S. *Lost Ballparks: A Celebration of Baseball's Legendary Fields*. New York: Viking, 1992.

Roewe, Chris, and Paul Mac Farlane, eds. *Official Baseball Guide for 1969*. St. Louis: The Sporting News, 1969.

Seidel, Michael. *Ted Williams, A Baseball Life*, Chicago: Contemporary Books, 1991.

Snyder, Brad. *Beyond the Shadow of the Senators: The Untold Story of the Homestead Grays and the Integration of Baseball*. New York: McGraw-Hill, 2003.

_____. *A Well Paid Slave: Curt Flood's Fight for Free Agency in Professional Sports*. New York: Penguin, 2006.

Svrluga, Barry. *National Pastime*. New York: Doubleday, 2006.

Whitfield, Shelby. *Kiss It Goodbye*. New York: Abelard-Schuman, 1973.

Wicker, Tom. *One of Us: Richard Nixon and the American Dream*. New York: Random House, 1991.

Williams, Ted, with John Underwood. *My Turn at Bat*. New York: Simon & Schuster, 1969.

Zimbalist, Andrew W. *Baseball and Billions*. New York: Basic Books, 1992.

Interviews

Alper, Alan. 2007. Interview by Ted Leavengood. Tape recording. June 28.

Bosman, Dick. 2007. Telephone interview by Ted Leavengood. Tape recording. July 27. Tampa, Florida.

Briar, John. 2007. Telephone interview by Ted Leavengood. Tape recording. July 15. Springfield, Virginia.

Daniels, Dan. 2007. Interview by Ted Leavengood. Tape recording. July 14. Washington, D.C.

Epstein, Mike. 2007. Telephone interview by Ted Leavengood. Tape recording. June 15. Denver, Colorado.

Hannan, Jim. 2007. Interview by Ted Leavengood. Tape recording. April 25. Washington, D.C. Telephone interview by Ted Leavengood. Tape recording. July 6.

Howard, Frank. 2007. Telephone interview by Ted Leavengood. Tape recording. June 15. Loudon County, Virginia.

Nowlin, Bill. 2008. Email interview by Ted Leavengood. April 16. Boston, Massachusetts.

Valentine, Fred. 2007. Interview by Ted Leavengood. Tape recording. March 16. Bethesda, Maryland.

Newspapers

Washington Post, December 12, 1968-October 30, 1972.
Washington Star, December 10, 1968-October 16, 1969.

Public Documents

U.S. Bureau of the Census, Eighth Census of the United States, Population-Washington, D.C., 1860.

U.S. Bureau of the Census, Ninth Census of the United States, Population-Washington, D.C., 1870.

U.S. Bureau of the Census, Tenth Census of the United States, Population-Washington, D.C., 1880.

U.S. Bureau of the Census, Statistical Abstract of the Fifteenth Census, Population — Washington, D.C., 1930, Population 200 Largest Cities 1930.

U.S. Bureau of the Census, Statistical Abstract of the United States, 91st edition.

Index